Companion Planting for Beginners

The Complete Guide to Companion Planting Strategies
for an Organic, Bountiful, and Healthy Vegetable Garden

Max Barnes

© COPYRIGHT 2023 MAX BARNES - ALL RIGHTS RESERVED.

The content contained within this book may not be reproduced, duplicated or transmitted without direct written permission from the author or the publisher.

Under no circumstances will any blame or legal responsibility be held against the publisher, or author, for any damages, reparation, or monetary loss due to the information contained within this book. Either directly or indirectly.

Legal Notice:

This book is copyright protected. This book is only for personal use. You cannot amend, distribute, sell, use, quote or paraphrase any part, or the content within this book, without the consent of the author or publisher.

Disclaimer Notice:

Please note the information contained within this document is for educational and entertainment purposes only. All effort has been executed to present accurate, up to date, and reliable, complete information. No warranties of any kind are declared or implied. Readers acknowledge that the author is not engaging in the rendering of legal, financial, medical or professional advice. The content within this book has been derived from various sources. Please consult a licensed professional before attempting any techniques outlined in this book.

By reading this document, the reader agrees that under no circumstances is the author responsible for any losses, direct or indirect, which are incurred as a result of the use of the information contained within this document, including, but not limited to, — errors, omissions, or inaccuracies.

Your Free Gift

I'd like to offer you a gift as a way of saying thank you for purchasing this book. It's the eBook called 5 Easy Ways to Preserve Your Harvest. Sooner or later, you'll reach a point where you're able to grow more vegetables and fruits than you can eat, so I've created this book to help you preserve your harvest so that you could enjoy it later. You can get your free eBook by scanning the QR code below with your phone camera and joining our community. Alternatively, please send me an email to **maxbarnesbooks@gmail.com** and I will send you the free eBook.

SPECIAL BONUS!
Want this book for *free*?

Get FREE unlimited access to it and all of my new books by joining our community!

Scan with your phone camera to join!

Garden Planner, Journal and Log Book

Keeping a journal to keep track of your garden and plants can help you determine what worked well and what didn't so that you can repeat your successes and avoid mistakes in the future. To help you plan your garden as well as keep all the important information about your garden and plants in one convenient place in an organized manner, I've created a garden planner, journal, and log book. Please scan the QR code below to find out more. Alternatively, please send me an email to **maxbarnesbooks@gmail.com** and I will send you the link to the journal.

Scan with your phone camera to find out more

Contents

Introduction 8
    What This Book Will Cover 8
    Why I'm Writing This Book 9

Chapter 1: Companion Planting and Organic Gardening Basics 11
    What is Companion Planting? 11
    Benefits of Companion Planting 12
    Principles of Companion Planting 13
    Organic Gardening and Companion Planting 14
    Why Grow Organically? 16

Chapter 2: Planning Your Garden 19
    Choosing the Perfect Location for Your Garden. 19
    Evaluating Sun Requirements and Exposure 22
    Determining When to Plant Your Garden 24
    Gardening Tools 28

Chapter 3: Companion Plants 32
    What Plants Should and Should Not Be Planted Together 32

Chapter 4: Soil—Creating the Perfect Growing Medium 47
    Soil Structure and Texture 47
    Using the No-Dig Method 50
    Rejuvenating Hard or Compacted Soil 52
    Using Cover Crops to Improve Soil Quality 53

    How to Make Compost and Use It 55
    Using Organic Fertilizers 56

Chapter 5: Starting Your Companion Garden 60
    Starting an In-Ground Garden 60
    Starting a Raised Bed Garden 61
    Starting a Container Garden 64
    Selecting and Starting Seeds 67
    Growing and Transplanting Seedlings 71
    Propagating Plants from Cuttings 74

Chapter 6: Maintaining Your Garden 78
    Watering In-Ground Gardens 78
    Watering Raised Beds 80
    Watering Containers 81
    Garden Maintenance and Care 82

Chapter 7: Pest Control and Dealing with Diseases 91
    Common Garden Pests 91
    Organic Pest Control Methods 99
    Companion Plants for Pest Control 103
    Using Trap Crops to Control Pests 105
    Using Polyculture to Create Diversity 106
    Dealing With Diseases 106
    Disease Prevention 115

Companion Plants for Disease Management 116

Using Crop Rotation to Prevent Pests and Diseases
....116

Chapter 8: Weed Control 119

Organic Weed Control Methods 119

Using Mulch to Control Weeds 120

Using Companion Planting for Weed Control 122

Chapter 9: Attracting Beneficial Insects
....124

Beneficial Insects in the Garden 124

Attracting Beneficial Insects to Your Garden 125

Companion Plants for Attracting Beneficial Insects
....126

Other Useful Creatures 128

Chapter 10: Attracting Pollinators 131

What Are Pollinators? 131

Attracting Pollinators to Your Garden 131

Attracting Specific Pollinators 132

Companion Plants for Attracting Pollinators 134

Providing Homes and Habitats for Pollinators .. 135

Chapter 11: Time to Harvest the Bounty
....138

When and How to Harvest Your Vegetables 138

Storing Your Harvest 142

Chapter 12: Plant Profiles 147

Vegetables 147

Fruits 162

Herbs 167

Flowers 172

Conclusion 176

Resources 178

Index 184

Introduction

You may be wondering what is so wonderful about companion planting? When you do companion planting, you are mimicking nature and natural ecosystems. This means you will grow plants more efficiently, and there is a wealth of benefits for your vegetable garden. Companion planting will help you maximize your growing space, keep the soil nice and moist, and also prevent soil erosion. It will help reduce the number of weeds you get and will also help control pests and prevent diseases. It will also help attract beneficial insects and pollinators to your garden, which will make your garden more fruitful and productive. Companion planting also helps support plant diversity and fulfill specific needs of your plants. It seems incredible to believe that you can reap all these benefits simply by planting the right plants together. But it's true, and this book will help you learn how to do it with ease and effectively.

Many people want to grow their own food in the garden, but they're often unsure about where to start. Beginners can feel overwhelmed when they think about vegetable gardening and assume it's too complicated because they either don't have the knowledge about gardening or they mistrust the information they find online because it has conflicting information and doesn't look like it's from a reputable, quality source. This book will teach beginners to gardening everything they need to know about starting their own garden and growing vegetables organically and efficiently using the companion planting method.

What This Book Will Cover

Chapter 1 will help you understand what companion planting is and the benefits of it. It will also discuss organic gardening and why people should grow food organically.

Chapter 2 will help you plan your garden, including everything from choosing the perfect location to evaluating sun exposure and making decisions about when to plant your garden.

Chapter 3 is all about companion plants—which plants you should plant together, and which plants should not be planted together and why.

Chapter 4 will help you create the perfect growing medium for your garden. It will look at everything from soil structure and texture to using the no-dig method, rejuvenating compacted soil, using cover crops, making compost and using it to improve your soil quality, and using organic fertilizers.

Chapter 5 will look at starting your garden, whether you choose an in-ground, a raised bed, or a container garden. It will discuss everything regarding starting seeds and transplanting seedlings.

Chapter 6 will cover everything you need to know about maintaining your garden, looking at watering and garden maintenance and care.

Chapter 7 will cover pest control and dealing with diseases using organic options as well as disease prevention and how companion planting can help repel pests and prevent diseases.

Chapter 8 will give you knowledge about controlling weeds organically, using mulch to control weeds, and which plants you can put together as companions for weed management.

Chapter 9 will explain how you can attract beneficial insects to your garden and which companion plants you should plant to achieve this. You will also learn about attracting other helpful creatures, such as birds, bats, and frogs, who will help your garden thrive and get rid of any unwanted pests that may damage your crops.

Chapter 10 will cover attracting pollinators to your garden, such as bees, moths, beetles, butterflies, and others, and which plants attract which pollinators. There is also information about how you can provide homes for pollinators.

Chapter 11 will let you know the best time to harvest your vegetables, fruits, and herbs and provide information on how to store them.

Chapter 12 contains plant profiles that provide detailed information on how to grow various vegetables, fruits, herbs, and flowers. This is intended as a useful reference resource for you to refer back to when required.

Why I'm Writing This Book

My name is Max. I grew up on a farm as a child, and helping my grandmother Anna with her garden is one of my earliest childhood memories. My grandmother was very much ahead of her time and was very innovative. She experimented with different gardening methods, and I learned from this and continued to do this myself all throughout my adult life. I grow the majority of plants we eat on my property using different methods, including companion planting. Companion planting helps me live a sustainable lifestyle and get the best from my crops not only by keeping them healthy and thriving but also by making the very most of the available space.

When I'm in my garden, it always brings back fond childhood memories of helping my grandmother on her farm. I learned so much about gardening in general, and companion planting in particular, from my grandmother. Throughout my adult life and up until this day, I have continued to keep my knowledge up-to-date, and I keep experimenting with different gardening methods so that I am able to grow a variety of plants all year round—lovely, delicious organic vegetables, fruits, and herbs that make our mealtimes a delight!

I am enthusiastic about gardening, and companion planting in particular, because it has so many incredible benefits. I want to show people that companion planting is not difficult, and that the benefits of doing it far outweigh the time, money, and effort invested. It will get you better, healthier crops, and it will help you live a healthier and more sustainable lifestyle, plus it's much better for the environment too.

I've learned a lot from my grandmother. I've kept a garden all my life, and it's been key to the sustainable lifestyle we live. I want to share my knowledge on how to live more sustainably with others who have an interest in it. Over the years, I've learned a lot: what not to do and pitfalls to avoid and things that are good to do that can help reap great benefits. I'd like to help people avoid the mistakes I've made and get there a little quicker using the useful tips, tricks, and techniques I've come across during all the years I've been keeping a garden. I've had a lot of help with companion planting from my grandmother as well as my friends and colleagues from whom I've learned over the years, and I'd like to give back and share some of that knowledge.

This book is a guide to organic vegetable gardening using the companion planting technique. It is not a guide to anything else outside the realm of companion planting and vegetable gardening.

Without further ado, let's jump into Chapter 1 and learn all about what companion planting is to get you started on your journey to the most efficient way of planting vegetables.

Chapter 1: Companion Planting and Organic Gardening Basics

Have you ever seen a gardener grow different vegetables together and wondered why they were doing it? You may have seen lovely orange and yellow marigolds growing between rows of vegetables. Or perhaps you may have seen basil growing among tomatoes. These are all examples of companion planting.

So, this chapter will look at what companion planting is and the many great benefits of it. It will also cover the principles of companion planting. Finally, it will look at organic gardening and companion planting and some arguments for why you should grow organically.

What is Companion Planting?

Companion planting is when you grow plants together for the benefit of one or both of those plants. When some plants are grown together, they can help enhance each other's growth and protect each other from pests and diseases. This is something that you can do with not only vegetables but also herbs and flowers. It is a great thing to do if you want to make the most of your garden space and live in a sustainable way.

Your whole garden is a place of biodiversity. There is a wide range of plants, animals, bacteria, and fungi that live in it, which are connected. Plants interact with one another, and they have beneficial relationships. Some plants will attract insects and pollinators that are beneficial for your garden. Others will repel pests and fend off animals that can eat or damage your crops. Did you know that raccoons dislike the smell of cucumbers?

If we just plant one crop, this isn't always the healthiest thing to do, and it won't always give you a great yield either. Plants can work in harmony with one another. A key example is planting corn and lettuce together. Lettuce plants help the soil by improving nutrients, and tall corn provides shade for lettuce which doesn't like the heat from the sun. Corn is also good around crops that want need support, like beans.

You can also plant herbs that help repel pests and attract pollinators. If you allow some of your herbs to reach the flowering stage, these will attract lots of beneficial insects (this will be covered in much more detail in Chapter 9).

Another thing you can do is have flowers as companion plants. These will not only look beautiful and inject color into your garden, but they will also ensure your vegetables are not eaten by pests, and they will attract beneficial insects to your garden, especially if you plant flowers that are nectar rich. Nasturtiums planted among your vegetables will attract pests away from your vegetables. Marigolds will help repel pests and attract lots of different beneficial insects (who will eat pests) and pollinators. Flowers like comfrey, ageratum, and zinnia will attract lots of bees and other pollinators. Some of your vegetables will have flowers, such as tomatoes, squash, and beans, so any pollinators to your garden will help the growth of these.

There are three key P's connected to companion planting, and these are pest control, productivity, and pollination.

Benefits of Companion Planting

Companion planting has a lot of great benefits, including:

- **Better growth for your plants.** Plants can help each other by giving support, shelter, root space, improving the taste, making plants more productive, and creating a more biodiverse environment.
- **Fewer pests.** This is because some plants repel pests, insects, and bugs. Many insects are put off by the smell of garlic, for example. Others don't like the smell of rosemary or wormwood. Some plants taste bitter or are toxic to pests, like tansy or pyrethrum daisies. Plants can not only repel pests by their smell, but they can also mask the smell of vegetable crops nearby.
- **Plants providing nutrients for the roots of others.** Legumes, like peas, beans, and others, will enrich the soil with nitrogen. Burdock with its long roots brings up nutrients from deep in the soil, making the topsoil better for plants with shallow roots.
- **Keeping the soil nutrient rich.** Because plants absorb certain nutrients depending on their type and needs, this may alter the soil makeup, making it ideal for other types of plants to thrive in. Companion planting is about placing plants that are happy to "share" the soil rather than be in competition for the nutrients in it. If you only planted one crop, each of the plants would be in competition with one another for nutrients. Planting different crops means they'll each need different nutrients.
- **Plants providing shade for other plants that dislike too much sun.** Corn is often used to provide shade for other plants that dislike too much sun, like lettuce. You can grow some plants under the canopy of taller trees. If you are using raised beds and don't have shade, you can use taller plants to create some shade.
- **Tall plants providing support for climbing plants.** Plants like corn could function as a support for cucumbers, peas, and pole beans. You can place plants that have vines, such as peas or beans, under a tall plant, like corn, and they can grow up taller plants. The taller plants act as a "living vine". Other plants that can be used in this way include fruit and nut trees, Jerusalem artichokes, sorghum, and amaranth. Beans wrapping their vines around corn also helps provide some support for corn and can prevent breakages when the weather is windy.
- **A way to make use of more space in your garden.** If you have crops that grow quickly, like lettuce, you can plant these in between slower growing crops. There are also some plants that you can place anywhere you have a space, like radishes and green onions, and you can harvest them when they're ready. Growing several crops in the same space at the same time is called polyculture. Using a polyculture system uses less space. If you are growing beans, a polyculture system would use 2.47 acres of land, whereas if you did this using a monoculture system (growing a single crop in a given area), it would use 3.6 acres. Because some plants have long roots, and other plants have shorter roots, planting them together works. An

example of this would be planting asparagus (which have roots that go deep) and strawberries (which have shallow roots) because you can grow them together using the same amount of space that you'd need to grow one. The same applies to growing root crops, like onions, beets, or carrots, and leafy greens together.

- **A way to attract beneficial insects and pollinators to your garden.** A key example of this is borage—bees (who are pollinators) and little wasps (which eat pests) are attracted to it. Some gardeners include a few patches of clover, buckwheat, and vetch to break up their other plants and encourage beneficial insects to the garden.

- **Preventing weeds.** If you have plants with leaves that sprawl over the ground, like pumpkins or potatoes, this will help prevent weeds from growing. If you grow kale and beans together, this has been shown to prevent redroot pigweed from growing. Anything that can help you spend more time tending to your crops and less time weeding has got to be a good thing, I believe. Growing sweet alyssum between vegetable crops is a nice way to give ground cover and prevent weeds. It looks beautiful too, and pollinators love it.

- **Having a more diverse range of vegetables.** This will help make your meals more diverse and exciting and will make it easier to live a sustainable lifestyle.

- **Preventing soil erosion.** Rather than having patches of bare soil with nothing in it, companion planting allows you to fill your soil and grow more plants. Having plants in the soil helps keep it moist and shaded by the plants' leaves, so the sun isn't scorching it and drying the soil. The US in particular has had a history of droughts and dust bowls, so preventing soil erosion is a really good thing.

- **Preventing diseases.** Because companion planting breaks up the plants rather than having a clump of one group of plants all together, this can mean that it slows down the spread of diseases.

- **Easier to harvest.** When plants are right next to each other and go so well in meals too, like basil and tomatoes, it makes it really easy to pick what you want from your garden for your meals.

Principles of Companion Planting

1. Companion Plants to Repel Pests or Act as Trap Crops

Having flowers like marigolds and nasturtiums will help repel pests, such as aphids, caterpillars, and moths, from your vegetable crops. Nasturtiums can also be used as trap crops because they will attract pests, like aphids and squash bugs, away from your vegetables.

2. Companion Plants to Attract Pollinators and Beneficial Insects

Having flowers in between your vegetables will attract pollinators, such as bees, butterflies, moths, and wasps. Plants like borage, calendula, alyssum, thyme, and lavender are good for attracting pollinators. You can also attract beneficial insects that are predators of pests, such as ladybugs, lacewings, hover flies, and more. They need plants that contain nectar and plants that give them somewhere to live over winter. Fennels and marguerites attract ladybugs and lacewings, who will eat pests, like aphids and mites.

It is important to remember that you're not trying to have a bug-free garden, and this wouldn't be a good thing! You are simply trying to prevent bad bugs from attacking your vegetable crops and attract more of the good bugs to your garden.

3. Crop Rotation

One key principle of companion planting is that you should rotate your crops each year and not just keep the same crops in the same place in the garden year after year. Rotating crops will reduce the risk of pests and diseases and will prevent nutrient imbalance in the soil, as certain plants require certain nutrients from soil to grow and thrive. It also helps create biodiversity and a better ecosystem so that if pests or weather conditions should take out a plant, it won't ruin your whole crop.

4. More Productivity

Placing companion plants alongside each other helps make good use of space, and plants can be beneficial to one another in many different ways. Chapter 3 of this book goes into specific details about which plants you should plant together, and which ones you should avoid planting near each other.

If you're growing cucumbers up a trellis, you could place lettuce in the shade of this. Beans and peas can enrich the soil with nitrogen to help other plants grow. Some plants can improve each other's growth and flavor, for example, basil and tomatoes or garlic and cabbage. Garlic also helps protect other plants from diseases because it has anti-fungal properties.

Companion planting can also help maximize your growing space. For example, if you're growing melons or winter squash, you could plant lettuce or radishes in between these. The lettuce and radishes will grow quickly before the vines of melons or squash need more space. When you combine this with plants that help repel pests and plants that attract pollinators, you'll get more productive yields for your vegetable crops as a result.

5. Height of Plants

Some plants don't like to be in the heat of the sun, so you can use tall plants to create shade for them. Corn is a very tall plant, so if you were to companion plant spinach or Swiss chard with it, they will happily grow in the shade of corn. Bush beans also accompany corn well as a companion plant because they like the dappled shade from corn, and their roots go to a different level than corn's roots, so there is no competition between the plants for water or nutrients. You can also use tall, sturdy plants to protect smaller plants from the wind or sun.

6. Protecting Plants from Animals

Some plants that have prickly vines, like pumpkins and squash, can be used to stop animals, like raccoons and deer, from getting to other crops.

Organic Gardening and Companion Planting

Commercial non-organic farms have a lot of monocrops—whole fields with just one type of plant. This is because it's easy to water, care for, and harvest the crop. But the downside to this is that because the crops are identical, bugs or insects that like to eat the crops are going to be really attracted to them because they have whole fields to munch through. So, farmers use chemicals for pest control so that they don't lose their crops. If fields were planted, for example, with tomatoes and lettuce as companion plants instead of just tomatoes, the tomatoes would provide shade for the lettuce, which doesn't like too much sunlight, and the lettuce would repel some of the pests attracted to the tomatoes.

Organic gardening means that you are not using synthetic pesticides and fertilizers. It is about creating a healthy environment for the whole garden. Organic gardening is about using natural products to grow plants in your garden, and organic gardening replenishes the natural resources as it uses them.

It means creating an ecosystem that is sustainable and creates good microbes in the soil and brings in beneficial insects into the garden. Organic gardening always views the system as starting with the soil. It is about using natural sources to fertilize and deal with pests. It includes adding organic matter (compost) into the soil, which helps the soil to keep moisture in and provides nutrients, which in turn will lead to healthy plants. In Chapter 4 of this book, we'll explore how you can make compost and use it to improve your soil and how to use organic fertilizers in much more detail. Adding organic fertilizers will increase the nutrients in the soil to help feed your plants. Legumes (plants like peas, alfalfa, lentils, peanuts, soybeans, clover, and beans) are particularly good nitrogen fixers—they can take nitrogen from the air and turn it into a fertilizer that plants can use.

When people garden organically, it will work to reduce damage from pests by attracting predators of pests, such as ladybugs, lacewings, spiders, birds, toads, lizards, and bats. A good organic garden seeks to minimize exploiting or wasting resources and is about replenishing everything that is used by the garden. "Feed the soil, not the plant" is the holy mantra of organic gardening. It's about trying to make the best of soil, water, and aiming to minimize damage as well as replenishing, nourishing, and sustaining. To some extent, when you do companion planting and organic gardening, you are emulating nature because nature doesn't plant things in rigid rows and patches.

Companion planting is a perfect opportunity to use less chemicals in the garden and be more environmentally friendly. An organic garden doesn't need synthetic pesticides and fertilizers. Companion plants become natural pesticides, so this approach is much better to use around children and pets than chemicals. Lots of plants naturally repel pests. Marigolds, nasturtiums, onions, garlic, and herbs, like basil, rosemary, and mint, repel a variety of different pests, including aphids, cabbage worms, Colorado potato beetles, and many others. Some plants also help protect other plants from diseases. For example, African marigolds release a natural chemical from their roots that repels nematodes. Horseradish improves potato plants' disease resistance. Companion planting can also naturally help improve nutrients in the soil. Legumes, such as beans, are fantastic plants to bring more nitrogen into the soil.

Another approach with companion planting in an organic garden is to use plants that act as a "trap" in one part of the garden to attract insects away from your vegetable crop in other parts of the garden. Nasturtiums are a great plant to draw insects away from your vegetables. They will attract aphids, moths, slugs, and caterpillars away from other plants. If you have calendula in the garden, this will attract stink bugs, and you can just remove the head of the calendula and get rid of the insects before they eat your crops. Nettles will attract aphids to them and also ladybugs who eat aphids. Land cress is a great trap for moths, butterflies, and caterpillars. Alfalfa has been used as a trap for cotton, snap beans as a trap for soybeans, early potatoes as a trap for later potatoes, and sunflowers and yellow rocket as a trap for brassicas.

There are plants you can put in your garden that will help improve the soil. Comfrey is excellent to bring up minerals from deeper soil layers because it has really long roots that can extend for up to 10 feet (3 m). Yarrow leaves are great for speeding up decomposition. Chamomile is great to heal sick plants near it, and foxglove helps plants grow faster near it.

I view organic gardening and companion planting as a never-ending circle of life, where I work hard to enrich the soil so that it gives me healthy plants that keep me and my family healthy. With the help of companion planting, soil gets different nutrients, and I also rotate crops to help with that. It also helps keep the soil moist. When I companion plant things like herbs under the cover of fast-growing buckwheat, the delicate herbs are protected by the buckwheat's shade until they became established. I then cut back the buckwheat and use this on the ground as mulch, which helps prevent weeds and composts into the soil providing nutrients. It's a continuous process. All of this will be covered later in the book. We'll look at which plants can be planted together and how to improve your soil using compost.

Why Grow Organically?

The main reason to grow organically is that it's better for the environment. By caring for your soil and land, you can lead a more sustainable lifestyle because the soil will produce good vegetables for you and your family for decades to come. Caring for the soil reduces soil erosion and will help prevent droughts and dust bowls. There will be no water pollution from toxic chemicals that can kill fish and wildlife, and soil will not become poisoned and neither will beneficial insects and pollinators.

It's also healthier for us as consumers to eat organic food because it helps reduce the risk of diseases. Research shows that non-organic chemicals have links to things like cancer, diseases, and neurological conditions (Healthline, 2021, online). When we eat organic food, it contains more vitamins and minerals because organic food was grown in soil that has been nurtured and has developed the correct nutrients and minerals and is chemical free. Independent research has been conducted which shows that organic vegetables typically contain 27% more vitamin C, 29% more magnesium, 21% more iron, and 14% more phosphorous, so it is a significant difference (SaferBrand, 2022, online). Organic food tastes better too. While not every vegetable will be a uniform shape and size, but they will taste amazing.

When people use synthetic pesticides, these are highly toxic to pollinators and beneficial insects, and you want to encourage them to come into your garden, not kill them off. Pollinators help carry pollen, which is necessary for some plants to become fertilized and produce fruit and seeds.

It's safer for children and pets to have an organic garden rather than one that has chemicals in it. When people use pesticides, they don't just go on the soil—they spread further by air, soil, and water and cause damage to animals and people. Using chemical pesticides spoils soil and reduces trace minerals in crops grown in it. Chemical pesticides are found in food bought commercially, and no human wants to be eating chemicals! Pesticides have been linked to health issues such as cancer, neurological disorders, Parkinson's, asthma, and more. Eating organic foods helps reduce the risk of diseases.

When you grow organically, this can give you benefits for your physical and mental health. When you're outdoors doing gardening work, it can help reduce stress and improve your mood. Gardening is also a great exercise that can help you stay in shape.

It can also save you money because you won't have to purchase as many vegetables from the shops or supermarkets. Perhaps at some point, you'll be able to grow everything you need on your property. Organic gardening works to improve the soil, so you'll get a better crop from what you plant, which gives you more food to feed yourself and your family. If you purchase organic food from a supermarket, it can be quite expensive, and it costs quite a bit more than "regular" (or conventional) food. However, this means that if you're growing vegetables to sell locally or at a farmer's market, your organic produce could fetch more. You can also preserve any excess food for later. In Chapter 11, we'll look at storing your harvested food.

Organic gardening can also help reduce waste. Composting is an incredible technique to improve your soil and to reduce landfill waste. You can compost food scraps and leaves that would otherwise go to waste, and compost will help enrich your soil with nutrients, so it's a win-win situation.

I first heard about companion planting from my grandma when I was a child and I was helping her around the garden. I do specifically recall my grandma using the Three Sisters companion planting method of growing corn, pole beans, and pumpkins together. The tall corn provided a wonderful support for the beans as they grew up their vines, and the pumpkins were shaded by the corn as they grew, and their leaves helped keep the soil moist and prevent weeds. I always associate buttery charred corn, delicious green runner beans, and pumpkin pies with my grandma any time I eat them. As an adult, I continued researching the topic of companion planting further and applying it in my own garden, and I rapidly started to see the many benefits of this for the environment, my family's health, and for better, more abundant, and tastier crops. I have been using companion planting in my own garden ever since.

Key takeaways from this chapter:

1. Companion planting is a practice of growing plants together for the benefit of one or both of those plants. It can be used to repel pests, prevent diseases, maximize growing space, attract beneficial insects and pollinators, improve soil nutrients, help with shade/mulching, prevent weeds and soil erosion, and some plants can even act as trellises.

2. Organic gardening does not use synthetic pesticides, fertilizers, or chemicals. It creates healthy soil by adding organic matter to it and uses natural pesticides and fertilizers. Plants can be used to repel pests or trap them and lure them away from your vegetable crops. Some plants can also be used to improve the quality of soil.

3. Organic gardening is better for the environment because it helps prevent soil erosion and pollution. Food that has been grown organically is healthier for people. It has more vitamins and minerals and tastes better. Most importantly, it contains no chemicals. Financially, growing your own organic vegetables is a better option too.

4. When you're doing companion planting, you need to think about crop rotation, the height of vegetables, and plants that will repel pests and attract beneficial insects and pollinators. You can also use trap crops to lure pests away from your vegetables. Some plants can enhance each other's growth and flavor, and some (legumes, like beans and peas) can enrich the soil with nitrogen.

This chapter has covered what companion planting is and the great benefits of it. It's also covered what organic gardening is and how companion planting is related to it. Hopefully, this has inspired you further to start companion planting because the benefits are overwhelming, and it just seems ridiculous not to use this technique. The next chapter is all about planning your garden, choosing the perfect location for your plants, looking at what light your garden gets, and deciding when you should plant your garden.

Chapter 2: Planning Your Garden

So, now you know what companion planting and organic gardening are and their many benefits. You're probably feeling all enthused and ready to start your own garden. The next steps are to plan your garden to ensure it is a success. You may have lots of questions about how much sun your garden should get, how to find the perfect location for your garden, and when you should start planting. This chapter will help you choose the perfect location for your garden, evaluate sun requirements and exposure, determine when to plant your garden, and this will be discussed for in-ground gardens, raised bed gardens, and container gardens.

Choosing the Perfect Location for Your Garden

It's really important to find the perfect location for your garden prior to planting. This is especially important for in-ground and raised bed gardens. Container gardens can be moved around, but depending on the size of the containers, they can be quite heavy and difficult to move once filled with soil. Moving in-ground or raised bed gardens is really difficult and virtually impossible in most cases, so it's best to get the location right from the outset. In order to choose an ideal location, you need to consider the following:

Sun Exposure

The more direct sunlight per day your plants get, the better. Most plants need at least 6 hours of sunlight per day. Evaluating sun requirements and exposure will be covered in the next section of this chapter in more detail.

Water

Consider how easy it is to get water to where you plan to have your garden. Ideally, you want your vegetable garden to be near a water source because you'll need to water your plants weekly. If the weather is hot, you'll need to water your plants more often, and if you have a long way to fetch water, this makes it a more difficult task.

It's sensible to give some thought to water conservation. Consider if you could set up some water butts. Also, give thought to how to water your garden if you're ever away from home. Will a friend or a family member do this for you? You could also consider reservoirs with drip irrigation.

If you don't have access to an outside tap or water butts, then a hose is a really good addition to make watering your garden easier. If your property has a well, you could hook a hose directly to the well for watering. If you're thinking about watering your garden with a watering can, this will soon feel like a chore. Watering cans are heavy, and you'll need far more of them than you expect. This isn't meant to sound negative, but it is something to be aware of when considering where you will get water for your garden.

When watering your plants, you should try to water them at the base and avoid getting water on the leaves in order to avoid fungal diseases, which is why I would suggest avoiding sprinklers. You can opt for a drip irrigation system, though. Drip irrigation is a method for watering your garden that uses a system of pipes and valves connected to a water source, and it drips water onto the soil slowly. There are different types of drip irrigation systems, and this will be covered in more detail in Chapter 6.

Soil Quality

Soil is the very foundation of your garden, and it's important to always seek to improve and enrich it. Vegetables tend to like well-drained soil, which means that soil allows water to drain at a moderate rate and without water pooling and puddling. You need to ensure that there are no contaminants getting into your garden too. For example, sometimes sidewalks have ice melting treatments put on, and you don't want that running off into your vegetable garden.

If you have a lawn on your property, this can give you an indication of the health of your soil. If your lawn is lush and healthy, you probably have good soil. If your lawn is poor, your soil quality may need some work.

Soil shouldn't contain too much clay, probably only about 20%, and soil should have 40% sand and 40% silt. If there's too much clay in soil, it will remain too wet, and your plants' roots could rot and suffocate the plants. If it's too sandy, it will dry out too quickly, and plants will become parched. It is possible to improve the soil quality of most soils by adding organic matter. Determining your soil quality, structure, and texture and improving it will be covered in detail in Chapter 4. However, if the soil quality is really poor in your area, you could consider starting a raised bed or a container garden. Raised beds and containers are filled with special potting mixes that you can buy in garden centers, or you can make your own.

Ease of Access

If you can easily get to your garden, this will make it easier for you to water, maintain, and harvest it. It should be as convenient as possible for you. It's wonderful if you're able to see your garden from your kitchen and makes it perfect to just pop out to snip off some herbs to use in your evening meal cooking.

Fencing

Having a fence helps protect your plants from wildlife, such as deer, rabbits, and other animals.

Protection From the Elements

If possible, try to ensure that your crops aren't battered by windy weather. Crops need some shelter, and this is especially true for tall crops that could bend or snap in the wind, like corn and sunflowers.

Walls and fences can help. If they have some gaps in them, this can be even better because the wind will filter through them. Certain tall plants that grow upright and produce fruit, like tomatoes, peppers, peas, beans, and eggplants, all benefit from an area that is not too windy so that they don't snap by being blown about.

Level Ground or a Gentle Slope

The ideal location for your vegetable garden would be on level ground or ground that has a very gentle slope. Try to avoid areas that stay wet throughout the spring or ground that is at the bottom of a slope because water will run downhill when you water your garden or when it rains. If the ground is always wet, the plants will suffer, and seeds or seedlings can get washed away.

Lower parts of your garden are cooler than upper slopes. South-facing areas are warmer than north-facing ones. If the land is on a hill, the soil will be shallow, and if it's in a valley, the soil will be deeper because of erosion from above.

Analyze the Environment

There may be things in your garden that can cause different conditions, so carefully analyze structures, trees and shrubs, and hard surfaces when you're considering a location for your garden.

You could have parts of your or your neighbor's property that casts shade. I have a part of my garden that is in the shade until later in the day just because of where the fence is. You should look at trees and hedges too. Some structures, like hedges, fences, and trees, may help protect your crops from strong winds, but they may also create shade or could become snow drift areas in the winter. Areas under trees may be warmer, but they will also likely be drier because the tree canopy may catch some of the rain. If you have hard surfaces, like rooftops, you could get water runoff from these, so do think carefully about where this water is running off onto so that you don't drown your plants.

Vegetables planted in the shade aren't as productive as those in full sun and may be more susceptible to diseases and pest damage. If you live somewhere exceptionally hot, then plants may need some shade in the summer. You can use a shade cloth or plant taller plants nearby to create some shade.

You can also consider which side of your garden faces north and which side faces south with regards to planting too. You can plant smaller crops in the south and taller plants in the north. For example, you can plant cabbage in the south and sugar snap peas in the north. This way, sugar snap peas won't cast too much shade on your cabbage.

Consider Time and Effort

It's highly likely you will need to prepare your land before you can plant your garden. You'll need to remove rocks, grass, and weeds. You'll need to prepare your garden beds by adding organic matter and compost. You may need to put up a fence to keep out wildlife. If you decide to go for a raised bed garden, you'll obviously need to build raised beds. You will need to weed your garden regularly so that your plants (and not the weeds) get the nutrients they need. Gardening is enjoyable, but it's probably best to start small and grow gradually rather than have a garden that's too big for you to take care of.

Enough Space Between Plants

While companion planting is about planting plants that support one another close by, they do still need room to breathe and have air circulating because this will help prevent mold, fungi, and mildew from attacking your plants. Having good airflow will also help keep pests away.

Take Time to Check It's Safe to Dig

Check the plans of your house to see where pipes lay, or ask the local authorities. What you don't want to do is dig up a water or a gas pipe, or even worse, hit an underground electric line, which could be fatal.

Best Place for a Raised Bed Garden

You should consider the same factors when choosing a location for your raised beds as with an in-ground garden: you should consider the sunlight the area gets, wind exposure, how close it is to your home for convenience, whether there are any trees in close proximity, and how easy it will be to water it. You can also consider the aesthetics and how nice it looks, as it is meant to bring you pleasure and not be an eyesore.

Best Place for a Container Garden

When choosing a location for your container garden, the same things apply as with in-ground or raised bed gardens. You need to consider how much sunlight your plants will get, how close they are to your home, how easy it is to water them, whether they're protected from the wind, whether they have enough space, and whether there's something that might case a shade on them, such as a tree, a structure, or a fence.

You will also need to think about what you want to grow, and therefore what size containers you require, and this will to some extent dictate the space that you need. It may also be determined by where you live and whether you have a garden, a backyard, a balcony, a patio, a driveway, an apartment room, or a rooftop available. Container gardening does have an element of flexibility because you do have the option to move them around until you find the perfect location for them, provided that the containers are not too large and heavy. Also, you can easily bring containers indoors when it's cold outside or over winter.

While container gardening can be an excellent option for those limited for space, I personally believe that if you have some land available, plants grow slightly better in the ground. They have more room and can spread their roots further. You also need to water containers much more frequently when it's warm because they dry out quicker.

If you have a sunny spot in your garden, but you already have something there, like patio furniture, a BBQ, or a swing set, my advice would be to move it because you're still likely to use that equipment in another part of your garden and enjoy it just as much, but your vegetables will only grow and thrive in sunny conditions. They can't be placed just anywhere, which is why the location is so important to get right.

Evaluating Sun Requirements and Exposure

All plants require a certain number of hours of daily exposure to sunlight in order to grow and thrive. When you purchase seeds, seedlings, or plants from a nursery, their ideal sunlight requirements are almost always printed on the seed packet, tag, or label. Most vegetables require at least 6 hours of sunlight per day to grow.

If you look at a seed packet or a plant label, you'll find the following terms that describe sun requirements:

- Full sun
- Full sun to partial shade
- Partial shade (or part shade)

---

[1] Image from https://www.gardenary.com/blog/where-to-put-your-raised-beds-how-to-choose-the-ideal-location

- Dappled sun/shade
- Full shade

Full sun means that an area must receive 6–8 hours of direct sunlight on most days mostly between the hours of 10 a.m. and 4 p.m. Many plants need full sun to grow, flower, and produce fruit, but some plants can't handle the intense heat and/or dry conditions that often come with that much exposure to the sun. You can place a 2–3-inch (5–7.5 cm) layer of mulch on top of soil to help keep the soil cool and keep in moisture (this will be discussed in more detail later in the book). When you choose plants, do some research on the species to determine if there are limitations on their full sun requirement. Plants that are sensitive to heat will usually come with a caution that they require some shelter from direct sunlight in mid-afternoon in hot climates. One way around this is to place these sensitive plants where they receive most of their sunlight in the morning or very late afternoon when temperatures might be cooler. As long as the plants receive at least 6–8 hours of direct sunlight, they should grow well.

The terms "partial (or part) sun" and "partial (or part) shade" are essentially the same and are often used interchangeably. Partial sun or partial shade means that an area must get 4–6 hours of sun exposure per day, preferably in the cooler hours of the morning. There is a subtle difference between these two terms, though. Partial sun puts greater emphasis on plants receiving at least the minimum sun requirements of 4–6 hours. These plants are typically more resistant to heat and need sunlight to flower and produce fruit, just not as much as plants that need full sun. If they're not flowering or growing up to expectations, you can try moving them to a location that gets more sun. Partial shade means that plants don't tolerate heat as well as plants that need partial sun, and they may need some relief from heat, especially in the afternoon. You can place these plants where there is some shade, for example, near a tree or a fence or on the east side of a structure, which would typically be shaded in the afternoon.

Dappled sun is a rare term, but you might find it used to describe sun requirements of a few plants. Dappled sun is similar to partial shade, but it means the sunlight filters through the branches and foliage of deciduous trees. Deciduous trees shed their leaves annually. Woodland plants, such as trillium, Solomon's seal, and understory trees and shrubs, prefer dappled sun.

Full shade means that plants need 4 hours of sunlight mostly in the morning or late afternoon or a full day of dappled sunlight. Some people think that full shade means no sunlight at all, but that's not true. Very few plants, other than mushrooms, can survive without sunlight.

Direct sunlight means that sunlight is physically hitting the leaves of plants. Indirect sunlight can mean that sunlight is going through a window or through dappled leaves or is bouncing off walls to reach the plant. If somewhere is classed as shaded, it means that sunlight mostly doesn't reach the plants in this area.

Once you have considered the space you have, you then need to spend some time monitoring which areas of the space receive sun and make notes of how this changes throughout the course of a day. The best way to measure average sunlight exposure is to simply observe the area where you plan to start your garden every hour during the daylight hours over a week or two. Make notes to determine the average amount of sunlight the area receives each hour and where the shadows fall. Make notes whether it's full sun, filtered or dappled light, or full shade.

The path of the sun changes throughout the year, so it's best to measure the light in your garden during the growing season for your plants. You can make a note of how this changes over the seasons so that you're able to select the best plants for your garden.

You can also use flags or stakes to show the light and shadow in your yard. Or you could use some sheets of tracing paper and sketch the yard outline onto each page, then mark where the light and shade is every hour each time using a different sheet of tracing paper, and then you can layer the pages together to get an indication of how much light your yard receives.

If you don't personally have the time to monitor your garden each hour of the day, other options include purchasing a garden light meter, which may also measure soil moisture and pH levels too. Or you could take a picture of your garden every hour or set up a time-lapse camera that will do it for you. When you have a sun map, it's much easier to choose suitable plants for your garden by reading seed packets and seeing whether they like full sun, partial sun or shade, or full shade.

When you have determined the average amount of sunlight an area receives, you can choose plants that match the conditions your space has. If you don't have an environment that gets 6–8 hours of sunlight per day, then growing some vegetables may be tough, but you could still grow leafy greens, such as kale, spinach, Swiss chard, mustard greens, and lettuce, and also herbs, such as basil, parsley, mint, rosemary, oregano, thyme, sage, and chives. These leafy greens will give you so many good nutrients and vitamins, and herbs will really give your food a kick of flavor.

If the only space you have is completely in the shade, then you may be able to grow some medicinal plants or houseplants that enjoy the shade.

Determining When to Plant Your Garden

In the springtime, it can be tricky to determine when you should sow seeds or transplant seedlings outside because the weather can vary so much from being very cold and rainy one day to being warm and sunny the next day, and you can also still get some frost in the spring too. When you start to see signs of life in the spring, it can be easy to get too carried away and think you can plant right away, but there can still be some frosts, so you may be better off waiting a little.

Here are some tried and tested ways to know when to plant your garden:

Check The Seed/Plant Packaging

You will notice that on most seed packets it is suggested they should be sown after the last frost in your area. The last frost date refers to the average final spring frost in your area. Last frost dates are only an estimate based on historical climate data and are not set in stone. In the US, the National Weather Service tracks this data and has created charts that show the average last frost dates for various areas. You can find them by simply going online and typing in the phrase "last frost date by zip", and you'll find websites where you can check the last frost date for your specific zip code.

Check the Temperature of the Soil

Another way to determine when to plant your garden is by taking the temperature of the soil. Most seeds germinate when the soil temperature is between 60 and 85°F (15–30°C). If the soil temperature is below 50°F (10°C), most seeds won't germinate. You may find that raised beds and containers warm up earlier than the soil in your garden does.

Watch Nature for Signs

You can look around you and watch nature for signs to determine when to plant crops. This is called phenology—it's the study of periodic events in biological life cycles and how these are influenced by seasonal and interannual variations in climate. By observing the natural growth, blooming, and/or leafing out of indicator plants, you can determine when you can plant crops. Many believe this is a more accurate way to time gardening chores than simply looking at the calendar, and in my experience, it works really well.

Nature's signs are obviously different in every region, but you should still relate to some of these examples of phenology:

- You can plant lettuce, spinach, beets, peas, and other cool-season crops when lilacs show their first leaves or when daffodils begin to bloom. When lilac flowers are in full bloom, plant beans, cucumbers, and squash.
- Half-hardy vegetables, including beets, carrots, and chard, can be planted when daffodils blossom.
- When forsythia blooms, it is safe to plant peas, onion sets, and lettuce.
- Wait for apple trees to bloom before planting bush beans.
- When apple blossoms fall, plant pole beans and cucumbers.
- When swallows return, you can plant basil and tomatoes.
- Plant peppers, melons, and eggplants outside when bearded iris is in bloom.
- When peonies blossom, it is safe to plant heat-loving melons, such as cantaloupe.
- When black locust and Vanhoutte spirea bloom, plant cold tender seedlings of zinnias, marigolds, tomatoes, and peppers.
- Plant tomatoes when lilies of the valley are in full bloom.
- When catalpas and mock-oranges bloom, sow fall cabbage and broccoli seeds.
- Plant potatoes, beets, and carrots when dandelions bloom.
- Plant cucumbers and squash when lilac flowers fade.
- Blooming crocuses are your cue to plant radishes, parsnips, and spinach.
- Plant corn when oak or elm leaves are the size of a squirrel's ear, or when apple blossoms start to fall, or when dogwoods are in full bloom.
- Plant pansies, snapdragons, and other hardy annuals after aspen and chokecherry trees are leafed out.
- Perennial flowers can be planted when maple trees begin to leaf out.

- By the time lilacs are in full bloom, it will be safe to plant tender annual flowers and squashes.

Succession Planting

Succession planting is the practice of seeding crops at intervals of 7 to 21 days in order to maintain a consistent supply of produce throughout the season. It also involves planting a new crop after harvesting the first crop.

Succession planting can be done in several different ways. You can plant the same vegetables with staggered plantings. This means spacing out plantings of the same vegetable every 2–4 weeks. Many vegetables fade after producing their initial crop, so rather than planting your entire row of beans all at once, you can plant part of the row at the beginning of the season and then plant more in about 2–4 weeks. This way, a new crop will be continually coming in. As the first plants start to flag, you can replant that area with beans or use it for a different crop.

You can plant different vegetables in succession. Some crops, such as peas, have a short growing season, and the space they were using can be replanted with later season crops, like eggplants.

You can grow the same vegetables with different maturity rates. Some vegetables have different varieties with different maturity rates, including early-, mid-, and late-season varieties. Sometimes this will be mentioned on the seed packet, and sometimes you will just have to read the "days to maturity" number. Vegetables with different maturity rates include pole beans, broccoli, Brussels sprouts, cabbage, carrots, cauliflower, celeriac, celery, collard greens, corn, eggplants, kale, melons, peas, summer squash, and tomatoes.

You can also pair vegetables in the same spot. This is known as intercropping, and it will be discussed in more detail later in the book. While most companion plants provide certain benefits to one another, such as natural pest control, enriching the soil with nutrients, or providing shade or support, some are grown together because they feed from different levels of the soil and don't compete for nutrients, which allows to maximize your growing space. This is an excellent way to squeeze even more productivity from your vegetable garden.

If you live in the US, there is the USDA Plant Hardiness Zone Map, which divides the US into 13 different zones that show the best start time to plant plants. You can find it online by searching "USDA Plant Hardiness Zone Map", or you could ask a county cooperative extension in your area for a local calendar to ensure you get planting timings right.

Hardy Crops

You would tend to plant mid-season crops in early spring, while in the summer you'd plant crops that you want to harvest in the fall. It is good advice to wait until there's no risk of frost. Once the soil is no longer frozen and can be worked (typically 4 weeks before the last frost), then you can start planting your plants.

Crops that can survive cold weather are planted first—they are known as hardy. Gardeners typically use the term "hardy" to describe a plant that can survive a freeze, frost, or a cold snap. Hardy crops include asparagus, broccoli, cabbage, garlic, kale, onions, peas, radishes, rhubarb, spinach, Swiss chard, and turnips. Some of these hardy crops (peas, cabbage, broccoli, radishes, and cauliflower) can also be planted in late summer for fall harvest.

While you can plant hardy crops early, there's no point in doing so if your soil is soaking wet. And while they'll put up with a bit of cold weather, they still won't germinate until the temperature is around 55°F (13°C). If you want an early harvest, you can start seedlings indoors early and then transplant them outside. You can buy frost covers at garden centers or online to protect your plants from an unexpected frost. Or if you don't have access to these, you could use a blanket or a piece of sack.

Half-Hardy Crops

Half-hardy crops can be planted after hardy crops. "Half-hardy" is a term used to describe plants that can survive only limited or light frost—meaning just an hour or two of frost or near-freezing temperatures. Half-hardy plants must be protected from anything more than a touch of frost. Half-hardy crops include artichokes, beets, carrots, cauliflower, celery, chard, chicory, Chinese cabbage, endive, lettuce, and potatoes.

Tender Crops

Tender crops do not do well in cold weather. "Tender" is a term used to describe plants that are injured by frost or cold weather. Tender plants must be protected from temperatures near freezing. So, you should ideally wait about 3–4 weeks after the last frost to plant these because some of them need the temperature to be at least 65°F (18°C) to grow, as they are susceptible to cold.

These include beans, corn, cucumbers, melons, okra, peppers, pumpkins, squash, sweet potatoes, and tomatoes. You can start most plants indoors and transplant them outside when the weather gets better. So, you could start growing seeds indoors 8–12 weeks before your expected last frost date. This will be covered in more detail in Chapter 5 of this book.

If it's currently early spring and you want a late spring harvest, then you could choose cool-season vegetables, such as kale, lettuce, spinach, peas, radishes, and broccoli. You could plant onions and potatoes to be harvested late summer to fall. If it's mid-spring and you want a summer harvest, then you could plant tomatoes, peppers, squash, cucumbers, eggplants, and melons. You can also get perennial plants (plants that live a few years), such as strawberries and asparagus, and these can give year upon year of fantastic produce.

Be Organized Throughout the Year

Generally, there is always something you can be doing throughout the year to prepare and be organized for gardening. You can plan where you'll place your vegetables in January (remembering to rotate crops from the previous year—this will be covered in more detail in Chapter 7). You can also make a list of what seeds you want to buy.

In February, you can order your seeds, and when they arrive, look at when they need to be sowed in the garden or started indoors, and work backwards to plan for this and organize them accordingly. Ensure you have seed starting trays, seed starting mix, and all the gardening tools you require. You could start planting asparagus, artichoke, horseradish, and rhubarb if the soil is warm enough. You can also start growing seeds for broccoli, lettuce, spinach, onions, cabbage, and kale inside at that time.

In March, you can start seeds indoors for tomatoes, peppers, squash, sweet corn, eggplants, snap beans, and pumpkins. If the soil temperature is above

40°F (5°C), you could start planting kale, lettuce, spinach, and onions. At the end of the month, you might be able to plant peas, provided that the soil is not too wet.

In April, it can still be cool, so you may need frost covers just in case of cold weather. You can keep checking the soil temperature, and when it gets above 60°F (18°C), you can transplant seedlings of radishes, onions, leeks, cabbage, beets, spinach, carrots, peas, and Brussels sprouts outside.

In May, you can plant everything else for the most part (or very early June if you're worried it may still be cold, depending on where you live). Soil temperature should be above 70°F (21°C) to plant tomatoes and peppers. You can also plant melons, eggplants, sweet corn, cucumbers, potatoes, and herbs. Always follow the instructions given on seed packets. Throughout June, you should be thinning some of your seedlings. You may need to stake up plants that require support.

In July, you could plant some more beans, carrots, cucumbers, and cauliflower where there is room to give you a late harvest. If you haven't planted for a fall harvest, it's not too late to do so in August. It's also worth making a note in a garden journal of what has worked well and what hasn't so that you can remember this next year when you come to plant your garden up. I have created a garden journal that will help you keep all the important information about your garden and plants in one convenient place. If you'd like to find out more about it, please check page 5 of this book, right before the table of contents.

In September, you may need to use frost sheets and covers to protect plants like tomatoes and keep them ripening on the vine. You could prepare new garden beds or build raised beds to be ready for springtime. If you have healthy looking herbs, you could put them in planters and put them inside over winter.

In October, you can continue to plant cool-season crops, such as cabbage, kale, cauliflower, beets, Brussels sprouts, broccoli, parsnips, celery, onions, peas, spinach, turnips, chives, parsley, radishes, lettuce, and Swiss chard.

Gardening Tools

There are so many tools you can buy in your local garden center that it's hard to figure out what you actually need in the garden. In this section, I'd like to cover the essential tools you will need as a gardener. I will also suggest a few tools that might be handy to have.

To explain why you need certain tools, we'll look at the whole process, from starting your garden to harvesting the delicious produce. This book is based on the no-dig method, so we'll follow the process of building your garden according to this method. It will be covered in-depth in Chapter 4, but in short, it involves covering the ground with cardboard to kill the weeds first, then layering compost, straw, and other organic materials, and finally, creating indentations for planting vegetables.

1. Gloves

Gardening is a lovely hobby, but it can quickly turn into a hassle without the right pair of gloves. Make sure to get gloves that are durable but not too bulky, especially for working with seeds or transplanting seedlings. Ensure they fit well too, as poorly fitting gloves can cause blisters or result in accidents from slipping off. The fabric should ideally be water resistant but also breathable—this will help keep your hands cool and comfortable. Longer cuffs will help protect your wrists and forearms from scratches and keep the soil from getting in.

2. Pitchfork

You'll need to move a lot of compost to build no-dig garden beds, and a pitchfork is perfect for that. It's also great for turning your compost pile and moving loose materials.

3. Rake

Rake is used to create a level working area once you've layered your garden beds. A good rake should have a sturdy handle, and the prongs should be made out of one piece of metal. Raking is all about spreading out topsoil to create a level surface and also loosening the topsoil to prepare garden beds for planting. This helps improve drainage and prevent water logging issues, and it also allows for better water absorption in the soil.

4. Trowel

So, your bed is leveled and ready for some transplants. For this, you can use a trowel. I'd suggest getting a high-quality trowel because cheaper ones may look good at first glance, but they break or bend easily and will probably not last you one season. This will be your tool for moving small amounts of soil, transplanting your vegetables, and weeding in tight spaces where it's hard to use a hoe.

5. Hoe

Garden hoes come in many different varieties: Dutch hoe, draw hoe, heart-shaped hoe, and more. The most common is the Dutch hoe. But we mainly use a straight hoe. Stirrup or shuffle hoes are great for shallow hoeing—it's a technique for weeding, and this will be covered in more detail in Chapter 6.

A hoe is a great tool for getting rid of weeds. To use your hoe for weeding, hold it as you would hold a broom, and angle it so the blade goes just below the surface. This way, you can slice off the tops from weeds.

6. Watering Can

As mentioned previously, there are a lot of ways to water your garden, and watering it using watering cans can be a daunting task. However, it can be fine if you have a smaller garden or a container garden, and especially if you have a water butt so that you don't have to carry heavy watering cans from your house. Even though watering by hand can be quite a task, it's also a good moment to inspect your vegetables and your soil, picking out some weeds as you go.

7. Pruners/Scissors

Pruners come in really handy when it's time to harvest your crop. You don't need to get really expensive ones. Just make sure they have a comfortable grip and look like they won't fall apart after one use.

There are two main styles of pruners: bypass and anvil. In bypass pruners, blades bypass each other to make the cut. In anvil pruners, blade slams on top of a ridge. I personally prefer bypass pruners because they seem to cut cleaner, and it's important to make clean cuts with your pruners so that you don't hurt your plants. Pruners need to be kept sharp, so if a blade goes dull, sharpen or replace it because dull pruners can damage plants.

8. Spade/Shovel

Even though the no-dig method is about trying not to disturb the soil as much as you can, you might have to do some digging when dealing with bigger plants or trees that you'd like to plant in the garden. For this, you can either get a spade or a shovel. I personally prefer a spade because it's made to really get in the soil and dig it up. Some spades have bend-over tops to rest your foot on, which makes them a bit more comfortable to use. With no-dig gardening, you won't have to use it much, so your spade will probably last you a lifetime.

9. Dibber

Dibbers are used to make holes when planting seeds or transplanting seedlings. You can use a trowel for transplanting seedlings, but a dibber can come in really handy. You simply need to put some weight on it, and you'll make a nice gap for your transplants—it's really easy to pop in your plants this way.

10. Hedge Shears

Hedge shears are meant to trim hedges, but they are a great tool for trimming or cutting down plants around the garden. After the harvest, for most plants it's time to go, so you can pull them out or cut them down with shears and add them to your compost pile. I usually cut the plants down because roots will decompose and feed the soil, so hedge shears come in really handy.

11. Wheelbarrow

If you have a bigger garden, you'll need to move quite a lot of compost and mulch around, so a wheelbarrow will definitely come in handy. You'll need it only sporadically, though, so that's something to think about. Think if you could borrow one for a few days—this will help you save some money and space. If you decide to get a wheelbarrow, make sure it stays inside when not using it. That's all you need to do to keep it for many years. If your shed is small, you can also "park" it with the handles turned up against the wall.

When I was planning our garden, initially we didn't have an outdoor tap, which meant that every time I wanted to water the plants, I had to carry watering cans from my kitchen through my front room and out the patio doors to the garden.

We then had a couple of water butts set up in the garden that collect rainwater, and this made watering the garden so much easier. I could fill two watering cans simultaneously with lovely natural rainwater. There are no chemicals added to it, which may not be the case with tap water sometimes, so it's better for plants and soil. It's also better financially because rainwater is essentially free.

The location I chose to start our garden in gets a good 8–10 hours of direct sunlight a day. I had taken the time to evaluate sun exposure using a sun map prior to planting my garden, and I do this at the start of each new season just to ensure that all my plants are planted in the best place and get enough sunlight or shade, whichever they require. The garden is right outside the patio doors of our house, so it's very easy to get to. It is also fenced, so wildlife can't easily get in, though we do get hedgehogs, toads, bats, and birds.

Key takeaways from this chapter:

1. Location: When choosing the perfect location for your garden, you need to ensure the spot you pick gets at least 6–8 hours of direct sunlight. It needs to be a space that is easy to get water to. The soil needs to be approximately 20% clay, 40% sand, and 40% silt, but even if it's too sandy or clay-like, you can improve your soil by adding organic matter. The garden space needs to be convenient for

you to get to, and ideally, it needs to be fenced off. Your garden needs protection from the elements so that your plants are not battered by the wind. The ground should be level or with a gentle slope. Look at the environment around your garden to see where shade is cast. Give thought to the time and effort that gardening takes and start off with a sensibly sized garden that will not become a chore—this should be something that you get enjoyment from. Next, ensure that your plants have plenty of space to grow. Finally, ensure that it is safe to dig in your garden and you're not going to dig up any pipes or wires that could be dangerous. Raised bed and container gardens have the same requirements in terms of sunlight, ease of watering, and so on as in-ground gardens. You will need to water containers more frequently, though, because they dry out quicker.

2. Evaluate sun requirements and exposure: Most vegetables need at least 6–8 hours of direct sunlight per day, and ideally 8–10 hours. Some leafy greens like a bit more shade. You can get cold frames to help plants grow in colder areas. Check seed packets or plants' labels/instructions for their sun requirements. Create a sun map for your garden (for relevant areas of your garden that you want to plant in) and measure the full sun, filtered/part shade, and full shade. Do this over the year to see how it differs with the seasons. Ideally, this should be done for every hour throughout the day, but every 2 hours also works. If you don't want to do a sun map, you could consider getting a garden light meter or a time-lapse camera instead.

3. When to plant: Typically, you would need to wait after the last frost before planting your garden. Check the seed packets or plant tags. Check the soil temperature—it should be 60–85°F (15–30°C). Most seeds won't germinate if the soil temperature is below 50°F (10°C). You can start seeds indoors before the last frost to get a head start on the growing season and transplant the seedlings outside when they are ready. Look at nature for signs of when to plant. You can do succession planting by planting hardy crops first, such as broccoli, peas, garlic, onions, cabbage, then half-hardy crops, such as carrots, potatoes, and lettuce, and then tender crops, such as beans, corn, peppers, and tomatoes.

The next chapter will give you advice regarding which plants you should and shouldn't plant together and why.

Chapter 3: Companion Plants

You may have done gardening previously, but if you haven't heard about companion planting before, you may be wondering which plants you should be planting next to one another. You may also be worried about planting wrong plants together that could have a detrimental effect on each other. You may have seen other people's beautiful, colorful gardens with abundant, healthy produce, and you've always wanted to have a garden like this, but you just can't figure out what you should plant and where. This chapter is here to demystify this topic, and it will explain what plants you should plant together and why and also what plants shouldn't be planted together and why. The chapter ends with a list of commonly grown vegetables so that you can swiftly check the list to know which plants should and shouldn't be planted together.

When you plant out your garden, you want to avoid patches or long rows of the same vegetable and instead have this interplanted with flowers and herbs. If you have large groups of the same vegetable, it's like a beacon to pests. However, if you do companion planting, it makes it harder for pests to find your vegetables among the scent of flowers and herbs. It will look prettier and will also attract pollinators to your garden.

What Plants Should and Should Not Be Planted Together

Perhaps the best example of companion planting is planting corn, pole beans, and squash (any trailing plant from squash family, like pumpkins, zucchini, or melons) together. These three plants have been planted together for centuries. It was done by Native Americans, and this companion planting technique is known as the Three Sisters. This works well because corn is tall and helps provide support for beans as they grow. Beans take nitrogen out of the air and enrich the soil with it, which helps corn and pumpkins grow better. Squash loves the shade provided by corn, and it helps prevent weeds from growing and keep the soil cool, which means you won't have to water the plants as much.

A 2016 study examined this Three Sisters growing method and found that when the crops were grown as companion plants (interplanted), the vegetables grown this way had more protein and calories when compared to crops grown just on their own, for example, just one clump of corn, or one clump of beans, or one clump of squash (Hicks-Hamblin, 2021, online).

Another popular example of companion planting is growing basil and tomatoes together. Basil and tomatoes are excellent companions in the garden (as well as flavorwise in many recipes). This is because the smell of basil repels thrips and moths, which lay tomato hornworms. Basil also repels whiteflies from tomatoes and is said to improve the flavor of the tomatoes. So, this companion planting strategy will prevent your tomatoes from being attacked by pests. Basil will also attract bees, which will help pollinate tomato flowers, and it means you will get a better harvest. In addition, basil repels mosquitos, and that can only be a good thing, surely!

We eat different parts of different plants. For example, we eat leaves of cabbage and fruit of tomatoes, and these types of plants are very heavy feeders. Corn is one of the heaviest feeders you could grow. Whereas root vegetables, such as carrots and beets, are light feeders. Herbs are light feeders too. So, when you are companion planting, it is a good idea to mix heavy and light feeders so that not every plant is trying to feed to the same extent.

When planting vegetables together, you should consider what plant family they belong to. The term "plant family" is used to describe fairly wide groups of plants with similar characteristics. The most commonly grown vegetables belong to the following families:

- Amaryllodaceae (lily or onion family, also called alliums)
- Apiaceae or Umbelliferae (carrot family, also called umbellifers)
- Brassicaceae (brassica or cabbage family, also called brassicas)
- Cucurbitaceae (gourd or squash family, also called cucurbits)
- Fabaceae (legume or pea family, also called legumes)
- Solanaceae (nightshade family or simply nightshades)

Plants in the onion family (alliums) include onions, garlic, leeks, chives, shallots, and other species within the Allium genus. The carrot family includes carrots, celery, chervil, cilantro (coriander), cumin, dill, fennel, lovage, cow parsley, parsley, parsnips, and more. Brassicas include broccoli, Brussels sprouts, cabbage, cauliflower, collards, kale, mustard, radishes, and more. The gourd family includes zucchini, pumpkins as well as summer and winter squash, which most people would class as vegetables. But the family also includes melons, more commonly considered a fruit, as well as cucumbers, which lie somewhere in between. The legume family includes peas and beans, although lentils are also classed within the same group. And finally, the nightshade family includes tomatoes, peppers, eggplants, and potatoes.

While planting vegetables from the same family seems the logical thing to do, it's not always the best decision. Plants from the same family generally require the same growing conditions, but they also attract the same pests. This will be covered a bit later in this chapter in regards to specific vegetables.

Companion planting works when planting not only certain vegetables together but also vegetables and herbs or flowers (or both). Certain herbs and flowers make great companion plants for most vegetables, although there are exceptions to this rule (which will be covered for each individual vegetable). Herbs like basil, rosemary, chives, dill, sage, mint, tansy, and catnip can be planted with most vegetables, and they help them by repelling pests and attracting beneficial insects and pollinators. Some herbs also have additional benefits. For example, basil can help improve the flavor of tomatoes, which makes them perfect companions in the garden. Basil, however, doesn't like growing near most other herbs, especially rue and sage. One of the best companion plants you can plant near asparagus, beans, cabbage, carrots, celery, corn, lettuce, peas, peppers, potatoes, and tomatoes is tansy. Tansy has a lot of benefits. It will attract beneficial insects, such as ladybugs and wasps, and it also repels cutworms, which attack all of the aforementioned vegetables. Tansy is a perennial, which means that once you've planted it, it will grow year after year.

Flowers like marigolds, nasturtiums, and calendula are perfect companion plants for most vegetables. Marigolds have a strong scent, which can mask the scent of vegetables so that pests don't feed on them. They also attract lots of different beneficial insects and pollinators. Nasturtiums are used as sacrificial plants. They are helpful because pests, like aphids and black flies, will attack them and leave your vegetables alone. Calendula will help attract bees and hover flies and will keep whiteflies away from tomatoes.

With companion planting, sometimes it's a case of using common sense. It's not sensible to plant three root vegetables that all grow at the same time in the same space, like potatoes, carrots, and beets, for example. They all need space, and it would be too crowded for them if you plant them together. However, planting carrots and radishes together is fine because radishes grow quickly, and they can be harvested before carrots start to mature. Other combinations that work well include planting carrots, lettuce, and peas together or Brussels sprouts with onions and nasturtiums. Peas and carrots are ideal companions when you plant them in late summer for fall harvest. Both crops thrive in cool, moist conditions, tolerate a light frost, and mature in around 70 to 80 days. Brussels sprouts are great companions for onions and nasturtiums because they grow upright on their own pole, while onions form bulbs underground, and nasturtiums spread and their leaves give excellent cover, which helps keep the soil moist and prevent weeds.

However, just like there are companion plants, there are also plants that don't grow well together. There is proper terminology to describe plants that are unfriendly to one another and don't make good companions—"allelopathy"—this means that a plant may impact the growth, survival, or development of another plant. Plants sometimes do this as a survival strategy because they want all the soil space and nutrients. Some plants grow rapidly and crowd others, and they can take more nutrients and water, which means other plants nearby may not have enough. Other plants may give off toxins that poison nearby plants so that they don't grow well or even die. A key example of this is the black walnut tree—it exudes hydrojuglone, which is toxic to a lot of plants.

If plants compete with one another for space, water, access to sunlight, or because they have similar nutrient needs, then these types of plants should not be planted next to each other. Similarly, if plants may be prone to the same diseases, such as blight, for example, then they should be kept away from one another so that if one lot of plants catches it, it doesn't spread and wipe out your whole vegetable crop.

Some plants may prevent other plants from growing well—these are known as inhibitors. This is especially true for fennel, so it's best to plant this away from other plants. Another plant that does this is the black walnut tree mentioned previously, so it's best not to plant them near your vegetables. It's also a good idea not to plant dill, cilantro (coriander), or any other members of the carrot family near carrots because they will stunt the growth of carrots. Also, don't plant garlic or onions near peas because peas will have stunted growth.

Sunflowers can have a negative impact on soybeans, rice, beans, corn, tomatoes, sorghum, and mustard. Sunflowers seed hulls are toxic to many plants, and this can mean that plants near sunflowers can have stunted growth. Sunflowers are beautiful to look at, and we do have some in our garden, but they are far away from our vegetables.

Below is a list of plants that should and should not be planted together in alphabetical order:

Asparagus

If you are growing asparagus, ideal companion plants include calendula, petunias, eggplants, and tomatoes because all of them help repel asparagus beetles. Basil and parsley help attract pollinators and also repel asparagus beetles. Cilantro (coriander), comfrey, and dill are good for repelling spider mites and aphids. Members of the aster family, like marigolds and nasturtiums, are great companions for asparagus because they repel a lot of different pests.

Asparagus does not like growing near onions, garlic, and other alliums as well as carrots and potatoes. Onions, garlic, chives, and other members of the onion family (alliums), absorb a lot of nutrients and take a long time to grow, so it's best not to plant them near asparagus. Carrots and potatoes have deep roots and use the same level of soil as asparagus to feed, so they will compete for nutrients.

Beans

There are pole and bush varieties of beans. Pole beans can grow really tall, and they usually need support, such as a trellis, while bush beans grow wide, although they may also need support sometimes. Pole beans are a part of the Three Sisters planting technique, so growing them with corn and pumpkins or squash is a great idea. You can grow beans with just corn too, and it will provide support for them. Beans enrich the soil with nitrogen, which makes them a great companion plant for cucumbers and eggplants. Lettuce and kale can benefit from the shade provided by beans because they like to grow in a cool environment. Nasturtiums and marigolds will help repel aphids and bean beetles. Lovage and rosemary will repel insects. Summer savory will repel bean beetles and improve the growth and flavor of beans.

Avoid planting any plants from the onion family (alliums), beets, peppers, fennel, or sunflowers near beans. Garlic, chives, leeks, onion, shallots, and other alliums will stunt the growth of beans. Beets affect pole and bush beans differently. Beets and pole beans impede each other's growth, but bush beans get along okay with beets. While peppers and beans both benefit the soil, beans grow pretty fast and can choke out pepper plants. Sunflowers will stunt the growth of beans.

Beets (Beetroot)

If you grow beets, growing chicory, endive, garlic, or onions near them will help prevent borers or cutworms from attacking beets, and in turn beets will enrich the soil with minerals. Garlic will improve the growth and flavor of beets. Bush beans will enrich the soil with nitrogen. Cabbage and lettuce are also good companion plants for beets. While they might not improve your beets, growing them together will help maximize your growing space, as both cabbage and lettuce have shallow root systems. Aromatic herbs, such as thyme, hyssop, rosemary, mint, and catnip, are great companion plants for beets because their strong scent will help repel pests. Broccoli, cauliflower, cabbage, rutabagas, turnips, and other members of the brassica family, with the exception of field mustard (this will be discussed later) are all excellent companion plants for beets. Not only will they help your beets, but your beets can be a big help to your brassicas. Beet leaves are high in manganese and iron, and any leaves that fall will enrich the soil and give a boost to the brassicas. Growing beets, cabbage, and mint together is an excellent companion planting strategy. Beets and cabbage will benefit each other, while mint will improve the flavor of cabbage and repel pests.

Don't plant beets near pole beans, field mustard, and chard. Pole beans and beets will stunt each other's growth. Even though field mustard is in the same family as broccoli and cauliflower (brassicas), beets grown with field mustard have been found to grow quite poorly. Chard will not directly hurt your beets, but chard and beets are very similar plants. This means pests and diseases that are drawn to chard will also affect your beets.

Berry Shrubs

Berry shrubs grow well with flowering plants and herbs that help repel pests and attract pollinators and beneficial insects. You can plant blueberries with strawberries, fruit trees, clover, yarrow, basil, and other herbs, but don't plant them with tomatoes. Gooseberries can be planted with fruit trees, citrus trees, nut trees, basil, tomatoes, beans, marigolds, nasturtiums, chives, mint, and oregano. Raspberries can be planted with rue, garlic, onions, beans, peas, tansy, yarrow, clover, lavender, marigolds, nasturtiums, mint, and thyme, but avoid planting nightshades, like tomatoes, potatoes, and eggplants, near your raspberry shrubs.

Broccoli

Broccoli grows well with leafy greens, such as lettuce, Swiss chard, and spinach. Broccoli grows quite tall and will provide shade, while leafy greens occupy space close to the ground, which helps reduce weeds and cool the soil even further. Plants from the allium family, like onions, shallots, garlic, and others, grow well with broccoli. Onions can improve the flavor of broccoli. Rosemary is a great companion for broccoli because it deters broccoli pests, such as cabbage loopers and cabbage moths, with its strong smell. Herbs such as basil, mint, thyme, sage, and dill also have the same benefit as rosemary and can repel insect pests with their strong scent. Nasturtiums, geraniums, and chamomile will help repel pests. Nasturtiums can also act as living mulch.

Avoid planting broccoli with plants from the nightshade family, such as potatoes, eggplants, and peppers, because they are heavy feeders and will compete for nutrients with broccoli. The same is true for summer and winter squash, melons, strawberry, and corn. Asparagus and broccoli will stunt each other's growth. Finally, it's best to avoid planting broccoli plants near other brassicas, such as kale, cabbage, Brussels sprouts, and cauliflower, because they all will attract the same pests.

Cabbage

If you're growing cabbage, planting nasturtiums near them will help keep away pests, such as aphids. Garlic planted near cabbage will also help repel pests, and if you plant sage, mint, rosemary, or hyssop, this will keep away cabbage moths. Nasturtiums act as a sacrificial crop—cabbage white butterflies will lay their eggs on nasturtium plants, and this will keep caterpillars away from your cabbages. Wormwood will also repel cabbage moths. If you plant buckwheat near cabbage, it will attract parasitic wasps, which will eat cabbage worms. Chamomile and garlic will improve the growth and flavor of cabbage. Southernwood deters cabbage moths and improves growth and flavor. Tansy will repel cabbage worms and cutworms. Thyme helps repel cabbage worms too. Dill is also a good companion plant because dill attracts wasps, which are natural predators of cabbage worms and other pests.

Do not plant cabbage with corn, lettuce, tomatoes, strawberries, or rue. Cabbage likes a bit of shade in the afternoon, but corn can actually block too much sun, which will stunt the growth of cabbage. Although lettuce is not in the same family as cabbage, lettuce suffers from many of the same pests. If you grow them together, they can attract pests to each other. Tomatoes and cabbage will compete for nutrients, and cabbage can also stunt the growth of tomatoes. Cabbage and strawberries both have shallow roots that feed from the same level of soil, which means they will compete for nutrients. While rue repels many pests, it also attracts whiteflies, which will attack cabbage.

Carrots

If you're growing carrots, planting chives near them will make your carrots grow and taste much better. Beans will help enrich the soil with nitrogen. Chives will also keep away aphids, mites, and flies. Planting carrots and leeks together provides mutual benefits. Carrots repel leek moths, which attack leeks, and leeks repel carrot flies, which attack carrots. Onions repel carrot flies as well, and they also have similar growing requirements to carrots. Rosemary and sage will keep away carrot flies too. Nasturtiums will repel pests and attract pollinators.

Don't plant carrots near dill, cilantro (coriander), and other members of the carrot family, parsnips, potatoes, celery, or radishes. Carrots, dill, and cilantro (coriander) are members of the same family, which means they will attract the same pests. Dill and cilantro (coriander) will also stunt the growth of carrots. Both parsnips and carrots attract similar pests and are vulnerable to the same diseases. Carrots and potatoes feed from the same level of soil, so they will compete for nutrients. The same is true for celery and radishes.

Cauliflower

If you're growing cauliflower, planting dwarf zinnia flowers nearby is a good idea because they will attract predatory beneficial insects, such as ladybugs, and these will eat pests that would otherwise attack your cauliflower plants. Dwarf zinnias will also give your garden a beautiful injection of orange, pink, and yellow colors. Potatoes are a good companion plant for cauliflower too because they occupy a different level of soil than cauliflower, which means they won't compete for space or nutrients. Dill, hyssop, and sage will attract pollinators. Thyme and mint will attract pollinators too and will also repel pests. Garlic and onions can mask the smell of cauliflower and prevent pests from attacking it.

Do not plant brassicas, such as cabbage, broccoli, or Brussels sprouts, strawberries, and tomatoes with cauliflower. Cauliflower is a member of the brassica family, so planting other plants from the same family means that they will attract the same pests and diseases and planting them all together allows those pests and diseases to spread more easily from one crop to another. Additionally, members of the brassica family will compete with each other for nutrients. Strawberries and cauliflower are heavy feeders, which means they will compete for nutrients. Tomatoes are heavy feeders too, and cauliflower can also stunt the growth of tomatoes.

Celery

If you plant chives, garlic, or nasturtiums near celery will help repel aphids. Beans will help enrich the soil with nitrogen. Celery helps repel white cabbage moth, which is a problem for broccoli, so planting them together is a good idea. Celery also helps repel cabbage white butterflies, so planting it with cabbage is a good strategy too. Chives will help repel harmful insects, and they can also give celery a sweeter taste. Spinach needs the same growing conditions as celery, and they don't compete with each other for space or nutrients.

Do not grow carrots, corn, horseradish, parsley, parsnips, potatoes, and radishes with celery. Corn is a heavy feeder, and it also grows much taller than celery, so it will deprive celery of nutrients and sunlight. Parsley can attract pests that would attack celery. Carrots, parsnips, potatoes, horseradish, radishes, and other root crops will fight for the same nutrients that celery needs to thrive.

Collard Greens

If you grow catnip alongside collard greens, it will help repel aphids and cabbage loopers. Catnip may also repel mosquitoes. Dill and mint can help repel cabbage loopers and attract pollinators. Marigolds can be planted around collard greens to keep pests away.

Rosemary and thyme can help keep away pests and insects, such as cabbage moth.

Collard greens are a member of the brassica family, so don't plant other plants from this family near them, such as broccoli, Brussels sprouts, cabbage, cauliflower, kale, and kohlrabi. They will attract the same pests and diseases, causing all of the crops to be overrun, and they will also compete for the same nutrients. Collard greens should not be grown near lettuce because they will stunt its growth. Leeks compete for the same nutrients as collard greens. Pumpkins have large leaves that can cast too much shade. Strawberries attract aphids, which are also attracted to collard greens, so planting them together can lead to an uncontrollable infestation.

Corn

Corn can be planted with pole beans, cucumbers, potatoes, melons, pumpkins, squash, and peas. The Three Sisters planting method (planting corn, pole beans, and squash together) is perhaps companion planting at its best. Planting corn, pole beans, and squash together works well because corn is tall and helps provide support for beans as they grow. Beans take nitrogen out of the air and enrich the soil with it, which helps corn and pumpkins grow better. Squash loves the shade provided by corn, and it helps prevent weeds from growing and keep the soil cool, which means you won't have to water the plants as much. Planting cucumbers, dill, and corn also works really well. Dill helps attract beneficial insects, and cucumber casts a gentle shade on the soil, which helps keep the moisture in. Cucumber plants also have shallow roots, so they won't compete with corn for nutrients, and corn can act as support for cucumbers. If you plant marigolds or white geraniums nearby, these will repel Japanese beetles. If you plant pigweed nearby, it will bring up nutrients from deeper in the soil to a level where corn can access them. Planting borage and dill will help repel pests and attract pollinators.

If you grow corn, it's best not to grow tomatoes and eggplants near it because tomatoes, corn, and eggplants are attacked by the same pest—tomato fruitworm, also known as corn earworm. Tomatoes and eggplants are also heavy feeders just like corn, so they will compete for nutrients. Corn doesn't do any harm to cabbage, but cabbage loves full sun, and tall corn can cast too much shade. You can plant cabbage on the sunny side of corn, though.

Cucamelons

Cucamelons can be planted with corn, onions, radish, tomatoes, peas, beans, asparagus and dill. Corn plants can act as natural trellises for cucamelons. Onions, radishes, and dill can help repel pests, and dill will also help attract beneficial insects. Peas and beans will enrich the soil with nitrogen.

Avoid planting cucamelons close to sage or potatoes.

Cucumbers

If you're growing cucumbers, you could companion plant them with dill to protect them from aphids. Nasturtiums will protect cucumbers from pests and will improve their flavor. Because nasturtiums have vining stems, they are good to ramble with cucumbers. Nasturtiums are also good for attracting predatory insects, like spiders and ground beetles, that eat pests.

Oregano, radishes, and tansy will help repel pests. Corn and sunflowers can act as support for cucumbers. Beans and peas will enrich the soil with nitrogen. You can plant cucumbers with root crops, like carrots, beets, and onions, to maximize growing space.[2]

Dill blooming above cucumbers

Don't plant aromatic herbs such as basil, sage, and mint near cucumbers. They can affect the flavor of your cucumbers, and sage will stunt their growth. Melons and cucumbers are attacked by the same pests, so planting them together is a definite no. Potatoes are heavy feeders and will complete with cucumbers for nutrients.

Fruit Trees

The best companion plants for fruit trees are flowering plants that attract pollinators and beneficial insects, such as comfrey, lavender, marigolds, nasturtiums, hyssop, dill, rosemary, and bee balm, along with nitrogen fixers, like legumes and clover. Garlic and chives can help repel pests. Some fruit trees need cross-pollination, which means they need another fruit tree of the same type nearby, and these include apples, pears, most sweet cherries, and most Japanese plums.

---

[2] Image from https://www.gardenista.com/posts/garden-decoder-what-is-companion-planting-gardening-best-vegetable-companions/

Avoid any plants that have deep or invasive roots, like tomatoes, asparagus, pumpkins, squash, parsnips, carrots, and others, as they'll compete with fruit trees for nutrients. Apple and pear trees do not like growing near cedar (juniper) and walnut trees. Do not plant fig trees near any plants from the nightshade family. Peach, cherry, and plum trees don't like being near peppers.

Eggplants

Eggplants grow nicely with broccoli, dwarf bush beans, pole beans, peppers, potatoes, spinach, rosemary, thyme, borage, tarragon, and nasturtiums. Generally, growing plants from the same family together is not a good idea, but eggplants are an exception to this rule. They are a member of the nightshade family, and they grow well and don't compete for nutrients with other plants from the same family, such as tomatoes and peppers. Broccoli enriches the soil with nutrients that eggplants need. Borage and nasturtiums help repel pests and attract pollinators. Pole beans will enrich the soil with nitrogen. Spinach helps eggplants conserve moisture, while eggplant creates shade for spinach. Herbs with strong scent, like rosemary, oregano, and mint, can help repel pests.

Don't grow eggplants with corn and geranium. Corn attracts the same pests that feed on eggplants, such as aphids. Geraniums are vulnerable to many diseases that can spread to eggplants.

Garlic

Garlic grows well with beets because they take up nutrients from different levels of soil, which means they won't compete for nutrients. Spinach and garlic are both hardy plants and grow well together, and the same is true for carrots and garlic. Carrots also repel pests that attack garlic. Planting garlic with potatoes can help prevent potato blight, and the strong scent of garlic will repel or confuse pests that attack potatoes. You can plant a border of garlic around tomatoes to repel pests that attack tomatoes, such as spider mites and aphids.

Don't plant garlic with beans and asparagus because garlic will stunt their growth. Sage will stunt the growth of garlic. Garlic and parsley compete for the same nutrients, so avoid planting them together. Garlic can stunt the growth of strawberries, although it will keep away pests that attack them, such as spider mites and aphids. Also, don't plant garlic near onions and leeks because this can encourage onion maggots by giving them an underground feast. Disperse them throughout your garden to avoid encouraging maggots.

Leeks

Good companion plants for leeks include carrots, onions, garlic, beets, celery, tomatoes, and apple trees. I find it interesting that foods that go well together in meals often grow well together too. We grow a lot of leeks, carrots, onions, and celery together, from which we make delicious mirepoix to give an amazing start to so many different recipes. Leeks help repel carrot flies, and carrots help repel onion flies, so planting them together is a great idea. They also can improve each other's yield. Celery can help improve the taste of leeks. Tomatoes can benefit from leeks because leeks help repel many pests that attack tomatoes. Leeks can help prevent apple scab and other types of fungi that can affect apple trees.

Don't plant leeks with beans and peas because leeks can stunt their growth.

Lettuce

If you plant chives near lettuce, they will help repel aphids. Beans and peas will enrich the soil with nitrogen, and beets will add minerals to the soil. Broccoli and lettuce don't compete for nutrients, so they can be planted together to maximize growing space, and the same is true for carrots and celery. Onions will help repel pests. You can also plant tall flowers, such as nicotiana (flowering tobacco) and cleome (spider flower), near lettuce, and these tall plants will give lettuce some shade that it thrives in. Planting poached eggplants (a wildflower) near your lettuce will attract hover flies, which are natural predators to aphids. Planting basil nearby can help improve the taste and growth of your lettuce.

Don't grow lettuce next to broccoli, Brussels sprouts, cabbage, cauliflower, kale, or kohlrabi. These plants have particular root secretions that can prevent lettuce seeds from germinating. Cabbage can also stunt the growth of lettuce, so it's best not to plant them together.

Melons

While melons are technically not a squash, they both come from the same family (Cucurbitaceae or cucurbits), which makes them suitable for planting using the Three Sisters method, so growing them with pole beans and corn is a great idea. If you're growing melons, you could plant radishes nearby. Radishes will grow more quickly, and you can harvest them before melon plants spread and need more room. Marigolds, nasturtiums, alliums, such as onions, garlic, and chives, and aromatic herbs, like basil, oregano, mint, and tansy will help repel lots of different pests, and marigolds will also repel nematodes. Bush beans can enrich the soil with nitrogen. Bush beans are a better choice than pole beans because they are shorter and won't block the sunlight as much as pole beans.

You shouldn't plant melons with cucumbers because they attract cucumber beetles, which also attack melons. They can also compete for access to sunlight. Squash, pumpkins, and cucumbers are members of the same family (Cucurbitaceae or cucurbits), so they will attract the same pests, like cucumber beetles and squash bugs. Potatoes shouldn't be planted with melons because they can attract aphids.

Onions

If you're growing onions, you could plant marigolds near them to repel onion maggot flies. Chamomile and summer savory can improve the growth and flavor of onions. If you put pigweed near onions, it will bring up nutrients from lower down in the soil for onions to use. Sow thistle will help onions grow and be healthy. If you grow mint near onions, it will confuse and repel onion flies. Onions are great companions to beets, carrots, brassicas, strawberries, and tomatoes because they help protect them from pests.

Don't plant other alliums, asparagus, legumes, and sage with onions. Alliums all attract the same pests. Asparagus and onions will compete for nutrients. Onions can stunt the growth of legumes. While onions grow well with most herbs, sage in an exception to that rule. Sage can stunt the growth of onions. It also prefers different growing conditions, so it's best to grow them separately anyway.

Peas

If you're growing peas, you could plant chives nearby to help repel aphids. Planting mint nearby will improve the health and flavor of your peas. Growing alyssum nearby will attract green lacewings, which will eat aphids. If you have a fruit tree, you could grow peas up the tree instead of using a trellis, and because peas harvest early, you'll be able to collect them before the tree blooms and creates too much shade. Corn can also act as a trellis for peas. Green beans and peas require the same growing conditions, so it makes sense to grow them together. Peas and turnips have a symbiotic relationship, as peas enrich the soil with nitrogen, and turnips help repel aphids. Peas, carrots, lettuce, and spinach are cool-season crops that thrive in cool, moist conditions, so you can grow them together.

Don't grow garlic and onions near peas because they will stunt the growth of peas. The same is true for other alliums, such as shallots, leeks, chives, and scallions.

Peppers

If you're growing peppers, planting herbs such as basil, oregano, or marjoram near them will help protect them from pests. Marigolds will help repel pests and attract beneficial insects and pollinators. If you plant pigweed and ragweed near peppers, they will lure leaf miners away from your peppers. Eggplants and peppers have similar growing requirements, so you can grow them together. Garlic can help repel pests and prevent fungal diseases.

Don't plant beans, brassicas, fennel, or strawberries with peppers. While peppers and beans both benefit the soil, beans grow pretty fast and can choke out pepper plants. Brassicas are heavy feeders and will compete with peppers for nutrients. Some of them also require different growing conditions, so growing them together is not a good idea anyway. Fennel is not a good companion for most vegetables, and that includes peppers. Strawberry plants are prone to a disease called verticillium, and peppers can contribute to that disease, so it's best not to plant them together.[3]

Marigolds growing near peppers

Potatoes

Beans will enrich the soil with nitrogen, which will help potatoes grow better. If you grow cilantro (coriander) near potatoes, this will help repel pests, such as aphids, spider mites, and potato beetles. Horseradish, calendula, tansy, and catmint all repel Colorado potato beetles, but catmint can attract cats to your garden. Putting sweet alyssum near potatoes is a good idea, as it will attract predatory beneficial insects, such as wasps, and it also has a beautiful scent that will make

---

[3] Image from https://www.homesandgardens.com/advice/companion-planting

your garden smell amazing throughout the summer. Horseradish can help repel pests and increase the disease resistance of potatoes. Garlic and onions can also help repel pests. If you live in a hot, sunny climate, growing corn on the south side of your garden can help create shade for potatoes. You can plant lettuce, spinach, or radishes between potatoes to maximize your growing space. They are all shallow-rooted crops and grow pretty quickly, so you can harvest them before competition for nutrients becomes an issue.

It's not advisable to plant potatoes near any plants from the nightshade family as well as carrots, cucumbers, squash, sunflowers, raspberries, or strawberries. Potatoes are a member of the nightshade family, so it's best not to plant them with plants from the same family, such as tomatoes, eggplants, peppers, and more. Potatoes and carrots will compete for nutrients, as they both feed from the same level of soil. Cucumbers, squash, and other cucurbits can make potatoes more susceptible to blight. The same is true for raspberries. Strawberry plants are prone to a disease called verticillium, and potatoes can contribute to that disease, so it's best not to plant them together.

Pumpkins

Pumpkins are a winter squash, which makes them suitable for planting using the Three Sisters method, so growing them with pole beans and corn is a great idea. Growing buckwheat will help attract predatory beneficial insects that will eat pests. Nasturtiums, oregano, and calendula will help repel pests, and calendula will also repel nematodes. If you plant borage near pumpkins, it will help lessen the risk of harmful worms, and your pumpkins will be healthier.

Don't grow pumpkins with potatoes because harvesting potatoes will likely damage the delicate roots of pumpkins. Pumpkins will also compete for sunlight with potatoes and will overtake the potato plants. Brassicas, such as broccoli, kale, and cabbage, can stunt the growth of pumpkins. Growing other squashes or melons with pumpkins is not a great idea because they all have a sprawling growth habit and need a lot of sunlight, so they'll end up competing with each other.

Radishes

Radishes grow well with peas because they enrich the soil with nitrogen and have similar growing requirements to radishes. Growing chervil near radishes will make them taste better. Lettuce and some varieties of radishes take approximately the same amount of time to grow (about a month), so growing they together can help maximize your growing space. Radishes can benefit other vegetables, such as squash and spinach. Radishes can help repel squash borers and leaf miners, which attack squash and spinach, respectively. You can grow radishes with herbs such as rosemary, borage, dill, or mint or flowers such as marigolds or nasturtiums to help repel pests.

Don't grow radishes near hyssop because it can stunt the growth of radishes. Be cautious when growing radishes and brassicas together. Radishes can attract flea beetles, which attack brassicas.

Spinach

If you want to grow spinach, planting it near peas or beans is a good idea, as they will provide shade for spinach and will also enrich the soil with nitrogen. Herbs such as cilantro (coriander), oregano, and rosemary grown close by will help keep insects away. The same is true for alliums, such as onions, garlic, and leeks. You can plant radishes with spinach, and they will act as a trap crop for leaf miners. They won't cause any damage to radish bulbs, but it will help keep them away from spinach, which they could otherwise destroy. You can also plant spinach with other brassicas, such as broccoli, cabbage, and cauliflower, because they feed from different levels of soil and won't compete for nutrients. Planting spinach with lettuce is a good idea to maximize your growing space. You can also interplant spinach with tomatoes or peppers for the same reason.

Don't grow spinach with potatoes because potatoes are heavy feeders and will deprive your spinach of nutrients.

Squash (Summer and Winter Squash)

Beans and peas are great companion plants for squash. They will enrich the soil with nitrogen, which will help squash grow. Radishes can help repel squash bugs. You can plant herbs such as borage, dill, oregano, or mint with squash to repel pests and insects and attract pollinators. Borage can also improve the taste of squash. Planting flowers such as marigolds and nasturtiums will help repel pests and will also help attract predatory beneficial insects and pollinators.

Don't plant squash with brassicas, such as cabbage, kale, cauliflowers, and others, because they are heavy feeders and will compete for nutrients with squash. They also attract pests that also attack squash, so planting them together is a recipe for disaster. Potatoes don't grow well with squash because they are heavy feeders and will compete for nutrients with squash. The same is true for pumpkins and cucumbers.

Strawberries

White clover can help enrich the soil with nitrogen, reduce weeds, and attract pollinators, which makes it a great companion plant for strawberries. Crimson clover can help enrich the soil with nitrogen as well as attract beneficial insects and pollinators. Growing peas and beans near strawberries will help enrich the soil with nitrogen too. Spinach plants release a substance called saponin, which helps protect strawberries from fungal and bacterial infections. Lettuce can provide cover for strawberries from birds and some pests. Or you could grow alliums, such as onions, garlic, or chives, and they will repel pests and birds due to their strong smell. Herbs like borage and thyme are great companion plants for strawberries. Borage will attract pollinators and pest predators, and thyme can help improve the taste of your strawberries.

Don't plant strawberries with brassicas, kale, cauliflower, broccoli, bok choi, and cabbage because they are heavy feeders and will compete for nutrients. You also shouldn't grow strawberries with any plants from the nightshade family, like potatoes, tomatoes, or eggplants. Strawberry plants are prone to a disease called verticillium, and plants from the nightshade family can contribute to that disease, so it's best not to plant them together.

Tomatoes

Basil is a fantastic companion plant for tomatoes because it will repel pests and improve the growth and flavor of the tomatoes. Borage will repel tomato hornworms and will also improve the growth and flavor of tomatoes. Beans and peas will enrich the soil with nitrogen, which is perfect for heavy feeders like tomatoes. Carrots and tomatoes can improve each other's flavor, and carrots also attract parasitic wasps, which are natural predators to tomato hornworms and other caterpillar pests. You can plant beets, radishes, or lettuce with tomatoes to maximize your growing space. Cucumber and squash can act as living mulch because of their large leaves. They will help control weeds and will help keep the soil cool and moist. Onion, garlic, and other alliums will mask the smell of tomatoes and save them from getting attacked by pests. Sage, oregano, parsley, and thyme attract parasitic wasps, which help control tomato hornworms. Marigolds repel nematodes, tomato hornworms, whiteflies, and other pests.

Don't plant tomatoes with brassicas, like broccoli, cabbage, cauliflower, Brussels sprouts, and others, because tomatoes and brassicas are both heavy feeders and will compete for nutrients. Plants from the nightshade family, such as potatoes, eggplants, peppers, and others, are not good companion plants for tomatoes. They are all affected by the same fungal and bacterial diseases, so planting them together is a big no. Don't plant tomatoes with corn because corn attracts corn earworms, also known as tomato fruitworms, which attack both corn and tomatoes.

Zucchini

Zucchini is a summer squash, which makes it suitable for planting with corn and pole beans using the Three Sisters method. You can also plant zucchini with just beans, and they will help enrich the soil with nitrogen. Growing buckwheat nearby will help attract predatory beneficial insects Zucchini plants need pollination, so you can grow flowers, like marigolds or nasturtiums, or herbs, like borage, dill, or catnip, to help attract pollinators and also pest predators.

Don't plant zucchini with potatoes because they are heavy feeders and will compete for nutrients. The same is true for brassicas, like kale, kohlrabi, broccoli, Brussels sprouts, cauliflower, and others. Pumpkins need a lot of space to sprawl, as do zucchini, so it's best not to plant them together because they will compete for space.

When I first started out with companion planting, I planted tomatoes and basil together. This worked well because the strong smell of basil helped mask the tomatoes from pests like thrips, aphids, and spider mites. Basil also helped repel tomato hornworms and armyworms. And it did help improve the growth and flavor of tomatoes! I got a far better crop and made good use of space in the garden using this companion planting technique. Ever after that, I have tried many other companion planting combinations to really beneficial effect, and my harvest seems to get better every year.

Key takeaways from this chapter:
1. Avoid having patches of plants, monocrops, or long rows of the same vegetable. Interplant with different vegetables, flowers, and herbs instead. Use cover or sacrificial crops to make it harder for pests to find vegetables.
2. Corn, pole beans, and squash are excellent companion plants, and they're known as the Three Sisters. It works well because corn provides support for beans, beans enrich the soil with nitrogen, and squash helps prevent weeds from growing while enjoying the shade provided by corn.
3. Basil and tomatoes are excellent companions. Basil repels thrips and moths and attracts bees and

other pollinators. It also helps improve the growth and flavor of tomatoes.

4. Tansy is a highly beneficial plant because it attracts pest predators, such as ladybugs and wasps. It also repels cutworms, cabbage worms, and grows back year after year in the garden.

5. Nasturtiums are good all-rounders to have, and they are used as sacrificial crops. Aphids and black flies will attack nasturtiums and leave your vegetables alone.

6. Beans enrich the soil with nitrogen, so beans make ideal companions for squash, celery, chard, corn, peas, potatoes, cabbage, carrots, and other plants.

7. Mint is another herb that is a great deterrent to pests. It repels flea beetles that chew holes in leaves.

8. Strawberries do well when planted with white or crimson clover, peas, beans, spinach, lettuce, borage, and thyme.

9. Tomatoes grow well together with basil, beans, peas, carrots, cucumbers, squash, onions, garlic, borage, and marigolds.

10. Some plants don't like to grow near each other, and this is called allelopathy. Some plants to be cautious with include black walnut trees, fennel, and dill. Plant sunflowers away from vegetables because sunflower seed shells are toxic to many plants. Don't plant any plants from the onion family (alliums) near beans or peas. Don't plant potatoes and tomatoes together.

The next chapter will look at a crucial part of an organic garden—its soil. This is the foundation of your garden, and it's essential to get it right. You should constantly be striving to enrich and improve your soil because it will provide you with glorious organic vegetables for years to come. The next chapter will look at soil structure and texture, the no-dig method, how to rejuvenate hard or compacted soil, using cover crops to improve soil and how to grow them, how to make compost and use it, and finally, using organic fertilizers to give your plants nutrients.

Chapter 4: Soil—Creating the Perfect Growing Medium

The soil is one of the most important things in your garden. It is the medium that gives the nutrients and moisture to your vegetables, herbs, and flowers to help them grow and create delicious produce. A key mantra for organic gardeners is "feed the soil, not the plant", and organic gardening is all about replenishing the soil and leaving it in a better condition than before and taking good care of it so that it can take care of your plants and feed you and your family for generations to come.

Soil Structure and Texture

Soil structure refers to how particles of soil are grouped together into aggregates (also called peds). Soil structure is determined by the shape, size, and strength of cohesion of aggregates. The shape, size, and strength of cohesion of aggregates determine pore structure and how easily air, water, and roots can move through soil.

There are physical, chemical, and biological aspects to this. It can depend on a lot of different factors, for example, how much calcium, magnesium, and aluminum are in the soil to bind clay. If soil has frozen and thawed, this can impact the soil, as can the process of roots pushing through the soil as they grow. The humus, fungi, bacteria, decomposing organic matter, polymers, and sugars from roots all play a part too. There are things that can make the structure of soil deteriorate, and these include cultivating soil, compaction, removing vegetation, soil being overworked, and high levels of sodium in soil.

A good healthy soil structure should be crumbly (friable) and have plenty of pore space, which allows air, water, and roots to easily move through it. This allows water to drain easily while keeping some moisture to keep plants healthy—this is also known as well-drained soil.

The image below shows 6 different types of soil aggregates and how easily water typically moves through each of these types.[4]

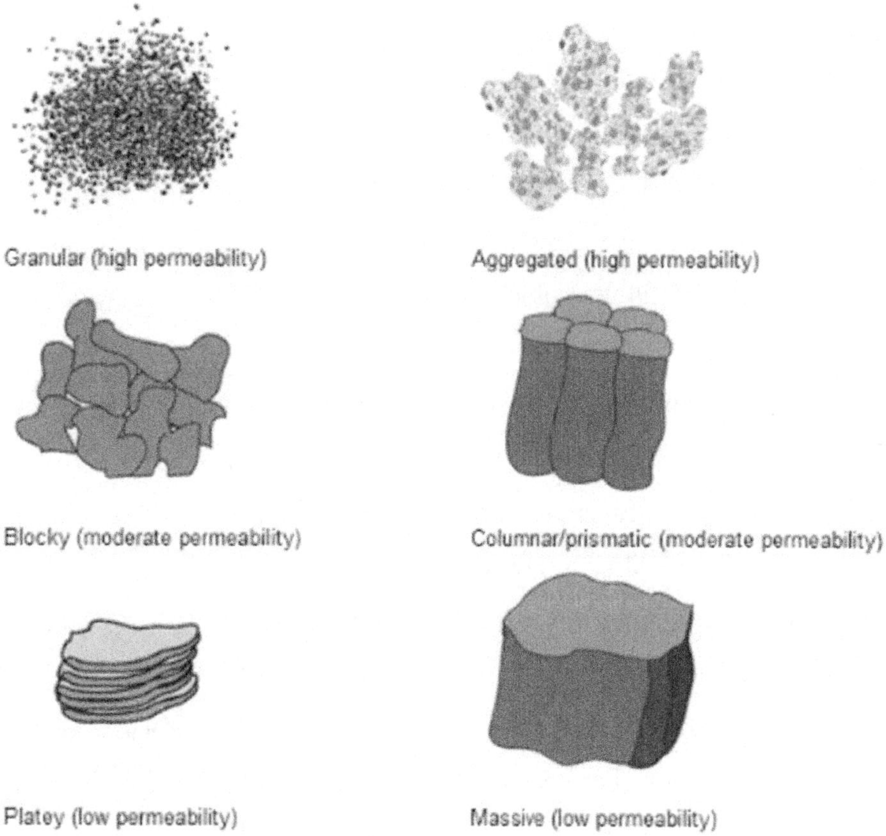

Granular (high permeability)

Aggregated (high permeability)

Blocky (moderate permeability)

Columnar/prismatic (moderate permeability)

Platey (low permeability)

Massive (low permeability)

---

[4] Image from https://www.deeproot.com/blog/blog-entries/what-is-soil-structure-and-why-is-it-important-2/

Granular structure is the most common in surface soil layers, especially those with high organic matter content. Soils with granular structure have high permeability and the most pore space of any structure.

Example of a good soil structure[5]

In soil with blocky structure, the structural units are blocklike. Blocky structures are common in subsoil but also occur in surface soils that have a high clay content. Columnar structure is often found in soils with excessive sodium. Sodium destroys the soil structure and leaves the soil effectively sealed to air and water movement. Soils with blocky or columnar structure have moderate permeability.

Platy structure has the least amount of pore space and is common in compacted soils. Some soils have no true structure, for example, single grain soils (like loose sand with little to no attraction between the grains of sand) and massive soils (large cohesive masses of clay). Soils with platy or massive structure have low permeability.

Soil texture (such as loam, sandy loam, or clay) refers to the proportion of sand, silt, and clay particles that make up the mineral fraction of the soil. For example, light soil refers to a soil high in sand relative to clay, while heavy soils are made up largely of clay.

Example of a bad soil structure[6]

Soil texture is important because it influences the amount of water the soil can hold, the rate of water movement through the soil, and how workable and fertile the soil is. For example, sand is well aerated but doesn't hold much water and is low in nutrients. Clay soils generally hold more water and are better at supplying nutrients. Most common garden plants prefer loam, which is a medium-textured soil with a balanced ratio of different particles.

How to Determine Your Soil Structure and Texture

You can dig a hole that is 1–1.5 feet (30–45 cm) deep and look at the soil by inserting a knife or a pen in 3/8-inch (1 cm) intervals. Look at root development in the soil and if there are any worms in the soil. If roots are shallow and there aren't any earthworms, then the soil structure may need to be addressed.

---

[5] Image from https://www.rolawn.co.uk/soil-structure

[6] Image from https://www.rolawn.co.uk/soil-structure

You can also take a slice of soil off the side of the hole and carefully lift it out so it stays intact. Lay the slice on its side to examine it. If the soil is crumbly—that's great. Crumbly soil is usually softer and more encouraging to root and shoot development than other types of soil structure, such as massive soils, where soil particles are all the same size, or platy soils, which break into flat platelike layers. If your soil structure is not great and you have massive or platy soil, there's no need to worry because you can improve your soil structure by adding organic matter to the soil, and this will be covered in more detail later in this chapter.

Good soil should drain well but also retain some moisture. You can evaluate this by digging a 1-foot (30 cm) pit, pouring half a gallon (1.9L) of water into it, and seeing how long it takes to drain. If it takes a few hours, that's all right, but if it is taking days, then this is much too long, and it means that your plants' roots can suffocate.

To determine your soil structure, you can use "the jar test". First, remove the top 2 inches (5 cm) of soil and all the roots. Dig a small, straight-sided hole at least 8 inches (20 cm) deep. Pointing the shovel straight down, slice off a chunk of soil about an inch (2.5 cm) thick and carefully lift it out of the hole. Remove any roots, twigs, or rocks. You can use a mesh sieve or an old colander to sift the soil. Next, fill the jar 1/3 full of the soil to be tested. Fill the jar with clean water and add a teaspoon of dishwashing or laundry detergent. Cap the jar and shake it vigorously for a few minutes. Set it on a flat surface and time for one minute. Sand particles will settle then, so mark the top of the first layer. Then wait for 2 hours, and mark the top of the next layer—this is the silt layer. Next, leave the jar for 48 hours, and then mark the top layer—this is clay. Measure the height of each layer with a ruler and the total height of all three layers. You can determine the percentage of each particle type by dividing the height of a layer by total height.

There are 12 types of soil texture depending on the proportion of sand, silt, and clay particles. Below you will find a table with soil texture types and particles proportions.

Soil Texture	Sand	Silt	Clay
Sand	85–100	0–15	0–10
Loamy sand	70–90	0–30	0–15
Sandy loam	43–80	0–50	0–20
Loam	23–52	28–50	7–27
Silt loam	0–50	50–88	0–27
Silt	0–20	88–100	0–12
Sandy clay loam	45–80	0–28	20–55
Clay loam	20–45	15–53	27–40
Silty clay loam	0–20	40–73	27–40
Sandy clay	40–65	0–20	35–45
Silty clay	0–20	40–60	40–60
Clay	0–40	0–40	40–60

Another way to determine your soil texture is to make a ribbon out of soil by squeezing it between your thumb and forefinger. First, take about 2 tablespoons of soil in one hand and add water, drop by drop, while working the soil until it reaches a sticky consistency. Then squeeze the wetted soil between your thumb and forefinger to form a flat ribbon. You can determine the texture based on the length of the ribbon that can be formed without breaking.

If it's less than 10/16 of an inch (15 mm), you have sandy soil. If it's between 10/16 of an inch (15 mm) and 1 inch (25 mm), you have sandy loam. If it's a bit over 1 inch (25 mm), you have loam or silty loam. If it's between 1 10/16 and 2 inches (40–50 mm), you have clay loam. If it's between 2 and 3 inches (50–75 mm), you have clay, and if it's more than 3 inches (75 mm), you have heavy clay.

Most common garden plants prefer loam, which is a medium-textured soil with a balance of different particles (approximately 40% sand, 40% silt, and 20% clay). Soil texture is considered to be a stable property. Changing soil texture is technically possible, but it involves a lot of effort and money and is not worth it in most cases. However, you can improve your soil structure and texture by adding organic matter to it.

You can get soil tests done where you check the pH level of your soil to see if it is acidic or alkaline. You can purchase pH testing kits online or at your local garden center. The instructions are easy to follow, and you will likely have to mix a sample of your soil with water and other ingredients and then dip a test strip in the solution. If the pH level is outside of the range, you may need to adjust it by using amendments.

The pH scale ranges from 0 to 14. The lower end of the scale is acidic, and the higher end is alkaline. The middle point—7.0—is neutral. Most plants prefer to grow in soil with a pH level between 6.0 and 7.5. Few plants, such as blueberries, need acidic soil with a pH level between 4 and 5.5.

You can use sulfur or aluminum sulfate to lower the pH level of your soil (make it more acidic). You can also use peat moss or fresh pine needles to make your soil more acidic, but these are usually not as effective and don't work as quickly as sulfur or aluminum sulfate. To increase the pH level of your soil (make it less acidic), you can add finely ground agricultural limestone. The amounts of sulfur, aluminum sulfate, or lime should be carefully measured before adding, so I would suggest checking with your local garden center—they should be able to help you with that.

If you're growing in containers or raised beds, you don't have to worry as much about the soil in the gardening area because you can fill the containers or raised beds with special potting mixes sold at garden centers, or you can make your own potting mixes to fill raised beds and containers with. This will be covered in detail in the next chapter.

Using the No-Dig Method

No-dig gardening is about trying not to disturb the soil at all or keep the disturbance to a minimum and leaving things like organic matter on the surface of the soil. The organic matter feeds the soil (which is what happens in nature) and helps with drainage and aeration. In nature, leaves fall off trees onto the ground, and bacteria and fungi attack them and turn them into natural compost. Then creatures like earthworms and beetles carry the decomposed material deeper into the soil where plants' roots can use the nutrients.

The no-dig gardening method is suited to all types of soil, even heavy clay. The soil stays healthy because it's not disturbed, and you get healthier, stronger plants. You don't use a fork or a spade to loosen or dig the soil, so you don't disturb the microorganisms, the fungi, and the worms in it. Your soil will retain more moisture, and you'll get fewer weeds. You will also end up using less fertilizers and pesticides. Plus, you won't get backache or blisters on your hands from needing to dig the soil.

With no-dig gardening, you simply enrich your soil by adding compost as well as nitrogen- and carbon-rich materials to it. These layers break down to create a fantastic growing environment for your plants. The no-dig method is an organic gardening approach that emulates nature, and it can be used in gardens of any size. The first year that you do no-dig may be the most demanding because you may need to prepare your garden beds, which includes removing rocks, grass, and weeds and adding compost and organic matter, but I promise it does get easier ever after and is definitely worth it in the long run.

The no-dig gardening method is good for the environment because digging soil can be damaging to its structure too. When you leave it alone and simply add compost, organic matter, and mulch, this improves the soil and its structure. It cuts down on the weeding you need to do, as you can simply place layers of mulch over weeds, which blocks out the sunlight and stops weeds from growing.

How to Start a No-Dig Garden Bed

Charles Dowding was the person who first started the no-dig method, and he suggests initially starting out with a small area of 4 by 8 feet (1.2 by 2.4 m). He states that you can get just as good a harvest from this area as a larger area, and he uses a space like this to do succession planting all year long. He suggests that you choose a space for your no-dig garden beds away from tall trees and hedges because they take moisture from the soil and create shade, and shady areas also host slugs. In Dowding's vast experience, he has found that using the no-dig method results in much better harvests than when you cultivate your soil. You can start a no-dig bed by layering compostable materials like a lasagna.

Here's how you start a no-dig bed:

1. Prepare the Area and Cover It in Light-Blocking Material

To start a no-dig bed, you need to remove rocks and weeds first. Remove the rocks and cut the weeds at the ground level and add them to your compost pile. Then use cardboard or newspapers to block out the sunlight so that weeds can't continue to grow. Make sure to overlap sheets of cardboard or newspaper so that no light gets through. If you're using newspapers, lay down a thick layer with 6–10 sheets. Water the cardboard or newspapers—this will help them conform to the ground better and will keep them from being blown away by wind.

2. Add Layers

After this, you can add an optional thin 1-inch (2.5 cm) layer of kitchen scraps, consisting of fruit and vegetable peels or waste, tea bags, coffee grounds, eggshells, and so on. Then you need to add a 2-inch (5 cm) layer of compost or manure, then a 3–4-inch (7.5–10 cm) layer of straw, then another 2-inch (5 cm) layer of compost or manure, and then a final 3–4-inch (7.5–10 cm) layer of straw. It's sensible to water each layer well before adding the next layer. Your bed will compact as you water it. Aim to have it at least 6 inches (15 cm) tall after watering. You can continue layering it and have it taller than that if you'd like. Here are the layers of a no-dig garden bed in order:

1) Light-blocking material, like cardboard or newspapers
2) Kitchen scraps and food waste
3) Compost, manure, or a mix of both

4) Straw

5) Compost, manure, or a mix of both

6) Straw

You can add temporary wooden sides to your beds, and these will help keep your beds in shape for the first few months. This is not necessary, however. It's quicker and cheaper to make open-sided beds, and they will have fewer hiding places for slugs, ants, and woodlice. However, you must have weed-free paths between beds for this to work and absolutely no grass, which otherwise would invade beds with no sides.

If you have a lot of compost, the easiest way to create garden paths is to mulch them with compost. You can cover your whole garden area with cardboard or newspapers in order to prevent weeds and grass from growing, then you can create your garden beds, and then you need to simply mulch the garden paths between them with compost. You would need a 2-inch (5 cm) layer of compost for garden paths.

If you don't have a lot of compost, you can use other materials, like wood chips. Wood chips are cheap, and they break down with time, enriching your soil with nutrients. You need at least a 1-inch (2.5 cm) layer of wood chips, although I would suggest making it 2 inches (5 cm). You'll need to replace or top up the wood chips every few years.

3. Make Holes for Planting

Once you have these layers, you can create little indentations of 4 inches (10 cm) into the top layer of straw, fill them with compost, and then plant seeds or seedlings in there. By having these layers, you are creating the best growing medium for your plants as your plants are growing.

It's good to have a compost pile so that you have compost when you need it. We'll look at this later in this chapter. The height of the original bed you make will shrink down as it breaks down—it will approximately halve in height in the first six months as it composts away, but you can add around 2 inches (5 cm) of mulch in the spring and top it up throughout the year to keep the soil full of nutrients. No-dig areas never need digging in the future, and when other farmers may be suffering with their land due to wet summers, no-dig areas will still do well and thrive.

You can plant in no-dig garden beds right away. The cardboard will soften within 3 months, and plants will be able to root into the soil. However, it can be a good idea to plant shallow-rooted plants early on so that the cardboard and lower layers have time to decompose before planting deep-rooted plants. Cool-season crops, like lettuce, arugula, and radishes, are perfect for this. Later on, as the layers of materials break down further, you can plant deep-rooted plants, like peas, beans, tomatoes, squash, and more. Peas and beans are also nitrogen-fixing plants, which will benefit the crops that are planted in later years.

Rejuvenating Hard or Compacted Soil

As we know from the soil structure section above, when soil is healthy, it has lots of pores between the particles of the soil, which allows air to move, water to flow, and roots to have space to grow and be able to access nutrients. However, soil can become compacted as it's pressed down, and there will be no space for oxygen, water, or for plants to grow and thrive. In this type of environment, plants would have a hard time getting the moisture and nutrients they need.

Compacted soil can be caused by a wide range of things, including intense heat, dry weather, lack of moisture, people walking on it, diseases, pests, weeds, and more. If you have hard or compacted soil in your garden, the most effective way to loosen it is to add organic matter to it. When soil is hard or compacted, all of its particles are squeezed closely together, and this doesn't allow air to circulate and water to permeate it. When you add organic matter, it "opens up" the soil and stops it from being so compacted. Adding organic matter helps soften the soil because soil-based organisms will eat their way through the organic matter and hard or compacted soil and leave their droppings (known as castings), which aerate and fertilize the soil. You would generally need to add 2–4 inches (5–10 cm) of organic matter on top of hard or compacted soil to help rejuvenate it. When you've finished harvesting a vegetable patch over winter, you can put a layer of mulch over it, and this will really help protect and improve the soil.

Ways to avoid compacted soil include not using heavy garden equipment and avoiding or limiting foot traffic on the soil. Heavy downpours can make soil become compacted, and this is especially true for clay and loam soils because they drain slowly after rain. Don't try to dig wet soil and don't mix sand in either because this can make soil harden like concrete. If you apply organic matter to the soil each year, it will prevent it from becoming compacted in the future. If you live in an area that has snow, planting cover crops is a good technique to prevent soil compaction, and this will be covered in the next section of this chapter.

Using Cover Crops to Improve Soil Quality

Using cover crops has multiple advantages, including feeding the soil with organic matter, preventing soil erosion, suppressing weeds, and enriching the soil with nutrients. They release sugars and other substances through their roots—a process which is called rhizodeposition.

Keeping your soil as healthy as possible is important, and we've already discussed keeping the disturbance of the soil to a minimum using the no-dig method. Another option to improve the quality of your soil is using cover crops.

You would typically plant cover crops over winter when the soil would be empty or between seasonal vegetables after a harvest. You can, of course, add compost or manure to help improve your soil, but you can also add organic matter by simply growing it in the place that you need it. You don't have to move anything. You can scatter the area with seeds and ensure that they are kept moist until they germinate, and then let them grow. By having a crop in place, it reduces the wind being able to erode your topsoil. When the crop is finished, you will need to kill it by cutting it or turning it into the soil, and it will decompose, giving the soil nutrients.

Cover crops are typically used to let your soil rest and rejuvenate over winter, although you can use cover crops in the summer too. Winter cover crops include winter wheat, clovers, and Austrian peas, and summer cover crops include cowpeas, soybeans, and sorghum-sudangrass hybrids.

You can plant cover crops when you don't use your garden to grow vegetables, so you need to figure out how long it will take for your cover crops to mature from the time you plant them to the time you kill them. Before you plant vegetables in the spring, you can cut your cover crops down. They will mulch the ground below and gradually turn into compost, while the roots will decompose in the ground, enriching it with nutrients. I would recommend that you allow 2–4 weeks for cover crops to be broken down by the soil before you sow any edible crops.

Some of the most popular cover crops are buckwheat, cereal rye, and crimson clover. These cover crops feed the organisms found in soil, like fungi and bacteria, and these produce nutrients that your vegetables will thrive on. Earthworms will eat the bacteria and fungi too, and they will help aerate the soil.

You can plant buckwheat in the spring to early summer, at a time when your garden area will be empty for 6–7 weeks. It establishes, blooms, and is ready for incorporation in 35–40 days, and its residue breaks down quickly. As a grain, it reaches maturity in just 70–90 days. Buckwheat helps suppress weeds and attracts beneficial insects and pollinators with its abundant blossoms.

Cereal rye can be planted in early fall, and it will germinate in mid-fall after the soil has lost its warmth. It typically takes 120–150 days to grow to maturity. You can mow down cereal rye in the spring before the plants develop seeds. Cereal rye can help increase organic matter and break up compacted soil.

Crimson clover should be planted in late summer so that the plants can become established before cold weather comes. You can plant it 6–8 weeks before the first frost at the latest. In cold climates, crimson clover can be planted in early spring instead of fall. Crimson clover is a legume, which means it can enrich the soil with nitrogen. Its roots also help prevent soil erosion and improve compacted soil. It typically takes 90 days to grow to maturity. Crimson clover will winter kill, which means that the plants will die back in the cold of winter, so you won't have to cut them down. If crimson clover survives through the winter, you can kill it mechanically (cut it down).

Oilseed radish is another good cover crop. It can be planted early in the spring to provide a quick cover for crops planted in late May or early June. Oilseed radish has a thick, deep root that can help break up compacted soil layers and scavenge nitrate that has leached beyond the rooting zone of other crops.

Mustard is another great cover crop. It can help prevent soil erosion, suppress weeds, and reduce pathogens in the soil. You can plant it in early spring or in the fall. It will reach maturity in 80–95 days depending on the variety. Mustard needs to be chopped or mowed prior to or at flowering and immediately incorporated into the soil while it is still green.

You can plant cover crops in garden beds, raised beds, and even just a small part of a garden or a raised bed. To plant cover crops, you can simply scatter the seeds and water the area well, remembering to keep them moist until they germinate. If you plant cover crops too close to the first frost date, they may not establish well. When they've grown, simply cut them, and let them mulch the soil below and turn into compost. You should kill cover crops shortly after flowering and before they set seed. This allows cover crops to grow to their maximum size and soil health benefits, but not produce seed. If you allow them to flower, they will go to seed and will become weeds themselves.

How to Make Compost and Use It

Compost is decomposed organic matter that can be used as fertilizer to grow plants and to improve soil structure and texture. Three key things that are crucial for compost are nitrogen, carbon, and water. Compost is often called "black gold" because it is so valuable to the health of your soil and your plants. It is also versatile, as it has multiple uses in the garden. You can add compost to your garden when making new garden beds using the no-dig method. You can add it to raised beds and containers when filling them, and you can also use it as mulch.

It is easy enough to make compost yourself from leaves and grass trimmings from your garden, any paper or cardboard from your house, and things like food scraps, vegetables that haven't been used, eggshells, tea bags, coffee grounds, fruit scraps, and so on.

You can purchase a compost bin or build a compost pile. This choice will depend on how much space you have and how much compost you need. If you have a small garden and not a lot of space, you should get a compost bin. Modern composters are streamlined and odor-free, and there are even small bins that you can keep in your kitchen. Or if you have the space, you can get larger outdoor versions, which are essentially a barrel with a crank that makes it easy to keep the contents mixed. If you need a lot of compost and have some free space in your garden, you can build a compost pile with wooden pallets or spare wood where you can store nitrogen items and carbon items separately, and then an area where these are layered together.

To make compost, you need to mix "green" materials (nitrogen), "brown" materials (carbon), and moisture. Green materials include kitchen scraps, like fruit and vegetable peels or waste, eggshells, and coffee grounds, as well as plants and grass trimmings. Brown materials include fallen leaves, tree branches, cardboard, newspapers, hay, straw, and wood shavings. You should have equal parts of green and brown materials. I would suggest alternating layers of green and brown materials. The final ingredient is moisture. Simply spray water on your compost to moisten it, but don't make it soggy. If it's too wet, it won't decompose properly.

There are things that you shouldn't add to compost, and this is because they will rot and smell bad and may attract rodents or larger wildlife. Do not add the following to your compost: meat or fish, dairy, fats and oils, any preserved wood, any diseased plants or invasive weeds (as these could be passed onto your plants via the compost and keep spreading and growing). Don't add charcoal ash to compost because this could kill good bacteria, and definitely don't add dog or cat waste because it could contain harmful bacteria or parasites, and you don't want that in the soil that your plants are growing in.

Compost should heat up in order to decompose at a good rate. You can start your compost pile at any point throughout the year, but it will decompose quicker in the summer than in the winter.

To keep the decomposition rate on track, you'll need to take the temperature of your compost using a compost thermometer deep enough to get about ⅔ of the way down. You can buy these online or at some garden centers. Make sure to take the temperature in several spots. The ideal temperature is between 130 and 140°F (55–60°C). If it gets up to 160°F (71°C) or more, you need to turn the pile with a pitchfork to aerate it, which will help bring the temperature down. If the temperature gets to 170°F (76°C) or above for more than several hours, this will stop microbes from working and kill the decomposing process. Try to keep the average temperature of your compost around 135°F (57°C).

If the compost starts to smell unpleasant, it could be that you have too much nitrogen (green materials), and you need to balance it with some brown materials. A properly balanced compost pile should not have any unpleasant smells. In fact, it should have a pleasant, earthy smell. If your compost starts to dry out, water it. You should it keep it moist but not soggy. You would typically need to water your compost once or twice a week. You should turn your compost every 2–4 weeks with a pitchfork. Once the compost starts to cool down and look like a black, crumbly material, then it's ready to use in the garden.

You can add compost in layers to create no-dig garden beds as mentioned previously. You can also add compost to raised beds and containers when filling them. You can mix 25% to 50% compost with the potting soil or potting mix in containers, and you can add up to 30% of compost to the soil in raised beds. When you add compost to your garden beds, raised beds, or containers, it can reduce the need for fertilizers. You can also use it as mulch in your garden as well as raised beds and larger containers (this will be covered in detail in Chapter 8). It will help keep your soil and plants' roots cool and retain moisture. You can also mulch your garden beds, raised beds, and containers to help some plants get through frosty weather. This will help keep the roots warm and will prevent the roots of tender plants from being damaged.

Using Organic Fertilizers

Synthetic fertilizers contain chemicals that have salts in them. The salts do not feed earthworms and other microorganisms in the soil. With time, the soil becomes acidic and loses important organisms that are needed to keep the soil healthy. The soil structure disintegrates, and the soil can no longer retain water. If the soil doesn't retain water and doesn't have the organisms it needs, your plants won't thrive.

Using organic fertilizers prevents this from happening. Organic fertilizers keep your soil healthy, and they're safe for you, your family, your pets, and the environment, whereas synthetic fertilizers are dangerous and can pollute the environment. Organic fertilizers are slower acting than chemical fertilizers, but organic ones are much better. Some synthetic fertilizers can burn plants because they're so harsh. Organic fertilizers are much gentler and safer. Organic fertilizers will improve your soil quality and increase good fungi and bacteria that the soil needs, whereas chemical fertilizers deplete this over time.

The key thing as an organic gardener is caring for the health of your soil. The soil needs to contain nutrients to create healthy, tasty plants. You can feed your soil with organic fertilizers. You can also make organic fertilizers at home. It is not expensive and not difficult at all. The most important nutrients plants need to grow are nitrogen (N), phosphorus (P), and potassium (K). Nitrogen is essential for photosynthesis and amino acid production. Phosphorus is required for growth and other functions, including photosynthesis and energy transfer. Potassium is used for root growth and photosynthesis.

When you have an organic garden, having organic matter and compost will improve your soil and its nutrient content, but you will also need additional organic fertilizers, such as wood ash, rock phosphate, animal byproducts, and manures (especially from animals that do not eat meat). Cow, goat, pig, and chicken droppings make great manure.

You can purchase organic fertilizers from garden centers. Organic fertilizers can be animal based (like bone meal, blood meal, fish meal, or fish emulsion), plant based (like cottonseed, alfalfa, or soybean meal, or seaweed), and there are also mineral fertilizers (like greensand or rock phosphate).

Usually on fertilizers you will see numbers shown on the side to indicate how much of each of the nutrients is in there. You may see numbers like 5-5-5 or 4-3-3. These numbers refer to N-P-K ratio, and they show how much of each of the nutrients (nitrogen, phosphorus, and potassium) the fertilizer contains. Fertilizers that have equal amount of each of the nutrients are called balanced fertilizers, and they may have formulas like 5-5-5. For example, a fertilizer with a formula of 5-5-5 is a balanced fertilizer that has 5% nitrogen, 5% phosphorus, and 5% potassium. Balanced fertilizers work well for most plants, but for plants such as tomatoes and peppers and other fruiting plants, you can use a fertilizer with a higher K number.

If you buy an organic fertilizer from a garden center, simply follow the instructions on the label. Typically, you can use organic fertilizers every 2–4 weeks during the growing season on most vegetables.

Types of Fertilizers

There are many different types of fertilizers that you can use:

Dry fertilizers: These are typically added to garden beds or raised beds before planting, but they can also be used during the growing season. You would typically spread dry fertilizers 6 inches (15 cm) away from the base of your plants and water them thoroughly so that the nutrients can soak into the soil.

Liquid fertilizers: These are easily absorbed by the roots of plants, much quicker than dry fertilizers. They are typically used during the growing season to give your plants a boost of nutrients. They are perfect for growing vegetables, and they will help vegetables that grow quickly take up the nutrients they require. Liquid fertilizers are also perfect for fruiting or flowering plants, such as tomatoes, cucumbers, roses, and more.

Growth enhancers: These help your plants absorb nutrients effectively. A good example of this is kelp (a seaweed).

Homemade Organic Fertilizers

While you can purchase organic fertilizers from garden centers, you can also make them at home using a variety of different things. If you have a compost pile, you can make compost tea, which is essentially an organic liquid fertilizer for your plants. Here's what you'll need to make compost tea:

- 3 to 4 gallons (11.4–15.2L) non-chlorinated water
- 2 to 6 cups compost
- 5-gallon (19L) bucket
- Shovel

- Strainer

Grab some compost from your compost pile with a shovel, and scoop up between 2 and 6 cups of compost. Add that to your empty bucket.

Next, you'll need some non-chlorinated water because chlorine will kill the good bacteria in your compost. You can use rainwater, or you can use tap water that has sat out for at least a day to allow the chlorine to evaporate. Add about 4 gallons (15.2L) of water to the compost in your bucket. Now you need to mix it all together. Make sure all of the compost gets completely submerged in water, and stir the mixture thoroughly so that the compost and water are combined.

Now you just need to leave the bucket in a place that's not in direct sunlight and let it sit so that the compost tea can brew. Don't leave the bucket in the sun because the heat can encourage the growth of harmful bacteria. Cold weather, rain, and snow can cause the tea to take longer to brew and can also kill beneficial microbes.

The amount of time your tea will take to brew depends on the air temperature outside. If it's above 60°F (15°C), let it sit for 12–36 hours. The lower the temperature, the longer it will take to brew. If the temperature is below 60°F (15°C), you may need to leave it for up to 72 hours. Stir the mixture once or twice a day while it's brewing.

Once the tea has finished brewing, you'll need to strain the compost from the liquid. If your compost tea isn't very dark, you don't need to dilute it. But if it's dark brown or black, you should dilute it with water to a ratio of 1:3 because it may be too strong for your plants. If you think your compost tea is not having the desired effect, you can dilute it less or even use it straight. If it's still too weak, you may need to brew the next batch longer. You can also try adding more compost to the mixture. Compost tea lasts about a week, so you'll need to use it quickly. You can use it every 2–4 weeks during the growing season as a liquid fertilizer.

Coffee grounds are a great source of nitrogen, and you can sprinkle these directly around your plants or make a liquid mix. Simply mix 2 cups of used coffee grounds with 5 gallons (19L) of water, and steep this mixture 3–4 days before using. You can use coffee grounds every 2–4 weeks during the growing season as a liquid fertilizer. Coffee grounds work especially well for nitrogen-loving plants, such as tomatoes, peppers, pole beans, blueberries, roses, and more.

You can also make Epsom salt fertilizer by dissolving 2 tablespoons of Epsom salt per gallon (3.8L) of water. Shake the mixture vigorously, and simply substitute this solution for normal watering once a month. It works because Epsom salt is made up of magnesium and sulfate, both of which are vital plant nutrients. It works especially well for magnesium-loving plants, such as tomatoes, peppers, potatoes, and roses.

Banana peels are very rich in potassium, and you don't even have to compost them. You can simply place these in your soil.

Another amazing organic fertilizer is seaweed. If you live near a beach, you can probably just collect some from there. If you collect fresh seaweed, you can dry it, then grind it, and sprinkle it around your plants.

Some weeds in your garden are full of nutrients, such as chickweed, burdock, and comfrey. You can fill a bucket ⅔ full of grass clippings and weeds and put in 2–3 inches (5–7.5 cm) of water, then let it sit for 3 days, stirring the mixture at least once a day. Keep it covered so that mosquitoes don't settle in it. Then you can spray this over plants, and it will help them grow.

If you keep chickens, goats, cows, or horses on your property, you can use their manure as organic fertilizer. You will need to compost it for best results.

We made a no-dig area in our garden. Our garden beds had sides made from wooden pallets and scrap wood we had in the shed. We cut the weeds back, put a layer of cardboard, then a layer of vegetable scraps, and then a few layers of compost and straw. We rotate crops that we grow in this area—we've grown peas, tomatoes, peppers, spinach, and more. We have had this no-dig area for over 20 years now, and it creates amazing produce year after year and is far less work than other areas of our garden.

Key takeaways from this chapter:

1. Feed the soil, not the plant.
2. Good healthy soil should be crumbly and not too compact to allow air and water to flow and roots to grow.
3. You can check the soil by digging a hole. Healthy soil should contain deep roots and earthworms and be crumbly. If the soil is clod-like and has shallow roots and no earthworms, then it's not good.
4. No-dig gardening aims to keep soil disturbance to a minimum, like in nature. It relies on using organic matter to feed the soil and help with drainage and aeration. It is easier for you and better for the environment. You can layer cardboard, newspapers, scraps, straw, and compost or manure when making no-dig garden beds.
5. Adding organic matter, such as compost or manure, to the soil is the most effective way to rejuvenate hard or compacted soils.
6. Cover crops help prevent soil erosion, suppress weeds, and enrich the soil with nutrients. Good cover crops include buckwheat, cereal rye, crimson clover, oilseed radish, and mustard.
7. You can make compost out of kitchen scraps, leaves, grass trimmings, paper, cardboard, and so on. Turn your compost periodically to add air, and water it gently to give it some moisture.
8. Organic fertilizers are better than synthetic ones because synthetic fertilizers contain salts, which make the soil acidic and make it deteriorate quickly. Organic fertilizers are slower acting, but they are much better and safer for you, your soil, and your plants. You can make fertilizer out of compost, coffee beans, and seaweed. You can also use banana peels as fertilizer.

The next chapter will look at how to start your companion garden, giving you information on how to start an in-ground garden, a raised bed garden, or a container garden. It will look at selecting and germinating seeds and transplanting your seedlings into bigger pots and eventually outdoors to grow and thrive.

Chapter 5: Starting Your Companion Garden

Starting a companion garden is super exciting! By now you have a good understanding of what companion planting is about, and you'll have given thought as to the best location for your garden, thinking about the sun requirements and exposure and many other factors, like ease of access, watering, any areas of shade, shelter from the elements, and so on. You will have given thought to the time of year you want to start your garden and which plants are best suited for growing in your area. You will also have a good understanding of what plants go well together as companions and which to avoid planting near one another. You'll have checked the structure of your soil and made amendments where relevant. You may have set up a compost pile if you didn't have one previously and started a few no-dig garden beds.

This chapter is moving on to the really practical hands-on part of starting your garden, and that can be in the ground, in raised beds, or in containers, depending on what works best for you and your space. This chapter will cover how you select and start seeds and how you grow and transplant seedlings. Starting a garden is one of my favorite parts of gardening, and I never cease to be amazed at what wonderful things you can grow from seeds. It's enormously satisfying checking on your seeds progress daily and watching them transform first into seedlings, then into plants, and finally see them produce delicious vegetables that can feed you and your family and friends. All homegrown organically and naturally without any chemicals, by you!

Starting an In-Ground Garden

Chapter 2 covered the all-important topic of choosing the perfect location for your garden that gets lots of sunlight, that is near the house so that you can access it easily, and has access to water. You don't want to start off with too large a spot if you're new to gardening. You need to ensure you're able to tend to plants without stepping on them. When you're mapping out where to have your garden, if it's on top of existing lawn, it's a good idea to use flour to sprinkle out where you want the garden bed to be, or you could place stakes there and have strings.

You need to remove rocks and weeds and create your no-dig garden beds. Starting no-dig garden beds was covered in detail in the previous chapter, but here's a short recap. First, cut the weeds at the ground level, and add them to your compost pile. Then use cardboard or newspapers to block out the sunlight so that weeds can't continue to grow. Make sure to overlap sheets of cardboard or newspapers so that no light gets through. If you're using newspapers, lay down a thick layer with 6–10 sheets. Water the cardboard or newspapers—this will help them conform to the ground better and will keep them from being blown away by wind.

After this, add a layer of kitchen scraps, consisting of fruit or vegetable peels or waste, tea bags, coffee grounds, eggshells, and so on, then a layer of manure or compost, then a layer of straw, then another layer of manure or compost, and then a final layer of straw.

It's sensible to water each layer well before adding the next layer.

The next step is to set out your plants, always checking to see how deep you should plant them, and how much space you need between plants. When you're ready to plant, make little indentations of 4 inches (10 cm) into the top layer of straw, fill them with compost, and then plant seeds or seedlings in there. Once you have planted your plants, you need to water them well, and you can also add a layer of mulch on top so that the soil retains moisture. Mulching will be covered in detail in Chapter 8.

Give Plants Plenty of Space

Ensure that there is plenty of space between plants and between rows because plants need room to grow and spread out. This will also improve air circulation around the plants, which will help prevent fungal diseases. Crowding plants is a common mistake that gardeners make. If plants are too crowded and don't have enough space between them, it means they will compete for nutrients and space. While seedlings may seem small, they will become much larger as they grow, so do consider the space that mature plants need.

Different plants need different spacing. You can usually find spacing requirements for plants on seed packets. Plant profiles in Chapter 12 will cover spacing requirements for many different plants. For companion planting to work, plants should be planted within 2–3 rows of each other. Plants that don't grow well together should be planted at least 2–3 rows apart.

If you plant companion plants in the same row and they have different spacing requirements, you can take an average spacing between the plants. If one plant needs 16 inches (40 cm) of space and the other needs 8 inches (20 cm), you can space them 12 inches (30 cm) apart. Remember to consider the height of your plants for proper shading. Try not to completely shade out any of your shorter plants.

Starting a Raised Bed Garden

If you'd like to start a raised bed garden and you're wondering what kind of wood you should use to build your raised beds, how large a raised bed should be, or how to clear a site and build a bed, this section of the book will help you.

A raised bed is essentially a frame box that has no top or bottom. It's usually raised above the ground in a sunny spot. You can build a raised bed without a frame—it can be a mound of soil—but I personally prefer framed raised beds to keep everything in place and stop the sides from crumbling and expanding.

Raised beds have quite a few benefits. They drain well and help prevent soil erosion. They also warm up more quickly in the springtime than the soil in your garden does. You have control over the soil you place in raised beds. Raised beds aren't as prone to weeds because they are elevated and you can fill them with weed-free soil. They also make tending to your garden more convenient because you don't have to bend down so far, so they are great for people with mobility issues. If you only have a small space, raised beds could be a great solution for you.

Raised beds can look attractive and neat too. Having raised beds makes it very easy to separate and rotate crops. Raised beds are perfect for companion planting. The minimum size for a raised bed is usually 4x4 feet (1.2x1.2 m), and they should be a minimum of 6 inches (15 cm) tall, but they'll need to be taller for plants that have a deeper root structure—18 inches (45 cm) is usually enough for most plants.

You can make raised beds using anything you have to hand: wood, stones, bricks, or cement blocks. Avoid treated wood because chemicals from it could leach into your soil. If you choose pine, it is inexpensive but may rot after a few years. You can get rot-resistant wood, like cedar or redwood, but it's more expensive. You can also use railroad ties or pallets. Concrete may increase the pH of the soil over time. Cinder blocks are a great material for building raised beds and will retain heat too. Rocks and stones work too, and they look great.

Raised beds should not be wider than 4 feet (1.2 m) so that you can easily reach everywhere without having to step on them. If you're putting a raised bed against a fence or a wall, you might want it to be only 2–3 feet (60–90 cm) wide since you can only access it from one side. Length is not as important. You can make a bed that is 4x4 feet (1.2x1.2 m), or 4x8 feet (1.2x2.4 m), or 4x12 feet (1.2x3.6 m). It can be as long as you want, but I personally find it easier to have multiple shorter beds rather than one really long bed.

How deep your raised beds should be depends on what plants you want to grow. Shallow-rooted plants, such as lettuce, leafy greens, spinach, onions, leeks, basil, chives, radishes, strawberries, chives, dill, mint, cilantro (coriander), parsley, thyme, oregano, and marigolds, need a minimum soil depth of 6 inches (15 cm). Deep-rooted crops, such as carrots, parsnips, beans, beets, broccoli, Brussels sprouts, cabbage, cauliflower, cucumbers, melons, garlic, kale, Swiss chard, turnips, potatoes, squash, rosemary, sage, borage, lavender, calendula, nasturtiums, snapdragons, and sweet alyssum, need a minimum soil depth of 12 to 18 inches (30–45 cm). If you want to grow peppers, tomatoes, okra, eggplants, pumpkins, watermelons, or winter squash, they need the soil to have a depth of 18 inches (45 cm). If plants don't have loose soil to this depth, the roots won't be able to go down deep enough to access nutrients.

Usually, lumber comes in a standard size that is 6 inches (15 cm) in height. You can stack several boards to make your beds 12 or 18 inches (30 or 45 cm) tall or even taller. But keep in mind that the added weight of the soil will add pressure to the sides. You'll need to add cross-supports to any bed that is over 12 inches (30 cm) tall.

You'll need to prepare the area where you plan to build a raised bed before building it. Here's what basic site preparation for a raised bed looks like. First, outline the spot where you plant to build your raised bed. If you have grass in the area, mow it short, and dig out the clumps. Loosen the soil in the bed, flip the clumps of sod upside down, and add them to the bed. You can also scrape the soil from the pathway around the outside and add that to the bed.

Or you may decide to go for a no-dig method, as mentioned in Chapter 4, which is what we do. Mow the grass or weeds as close to the ground as possible. Then cover the area with cardboard or newspapers, which will smother the grass and weeds and eventually rot down into the soil as well. Be sure to overlap the cardboard or newspapers by about 6 inches (15 cm) to make sure no weeds slip through cracks. Next, add 6 inches (15 cm) of compost on top of the cardboard. If your raised bed will be 6 inches (15 cm) tall, the compost will be your growing medium. But if it will be taller, you'll need to fill the bed with topsoil and other materials, and the compost will go on top of that.

You can plant your raised beds right after setting them up. By the time the roots reach the cardboard, it will have started to break down, and the roots will be able to grow deeper below that cardboard layer. You can top up your raised beds with an inch or two (2.5–5 cm) of compost each fall or winter. This will help improve the quality and fertility of the soil not only in your raised beds but below them too.

How to Build a Raised Bed

Building a raised is not difficult at all and requires minimal DIY skills. You are essentially building a box with no top and bottom. Most lumber stores can cut the planks for you. Here's what you'll need to build a raised bed:

Tools

- Drill/driver and bits
- Screwdriver
- Hand saw and tape measure if cutting the planks yourself

Materials

- For a 4x8-foot (1.2x2.4 m) bed, get 3 pieces of 8-foot (2.4 m) long 2x6 in. (5x15 cm) lumber. If they have 2x8 in. (5x20 cm) or 2x10 in. (5x25 cm) lumber, that's even better. For a 4x4-foot (1.2x1.2 m) bed, get 2 pieces of lumber. This will make 6-inch-tall (15 cm) beds if you get 2x6 in. (5x15 cm) planks. If you want a taller bed, you'll need to double the amount of planks for a 12-inch-tall (30 cm) bed and triple it for an 18-inch-tall (45 cm) bed.
- You can get pine stakes for extra bracing.
- If you don't have a saw, ask the guys at the lumber yard to cut the pieces in half. For a 4x8-foot (1.2x2.4 m) bed, cut one of the pieces in half, which will give you two 4-foot (1.2 m) lengths to use for the ends. For a 4x4-foot (1.2x1.2 m) bed, cut both pieces in half.

Deck/Exterior Screws

To make your bed stronger, use a piece of 2x4 in. (5x10 cm) or 4x4 in. (10x10 cm) lumber in the corners to give you something stable to nail or screw into rather than the end grain of the board.

And here's how you build your raised bed:

1. If your 8-foot-long (2.4 m) boards were not pre-cut at the lumber store, mark off the half way point, and cut as many planks as you need for the 4-foot (1.2 m) sides of the bed.

2. Screw the planks together using decking screws. Two holes at the end of each plank is enough. Drill pilot holes using a drill bit slightly thinner than the screws themselves. One end of each plank will overlap the end of the next and screw directly into it, so position your pilot holes correspondingly. It will be easier if you have a helper to hold it while you fasten the corners.

3. If you'd like extra bracing and a sturdier frame, cut your pine stake into 4 pieces, and use them to nail the boards at the corners for bracing.

4. With all the wood cut to size and the holes drilled, you can start putting the bed together.

5. Lay down the beds. The walls need to be laid out so that each plank overlaps the next with the pilot holes located at the overlapping end.

64   COMPANION PLANTING FOR BEGINNERS

6. Screw the walls together with long screws so that each wall is properly secured to the next.
7. Congratulations, you've just built your raised bed, and it's ready to be filled!

You could decide to bury the base of your raised bed slightly to stop weeds from encroaching. You can make your raised bed last longer by putting a heavy plastic liner inside the boards. You could put hardware cloth at the base of your raised beds if you're putting them on soil to prevent things like gophers and moles from getting into your raised beds.[7]

You can fill your raised beds with topsoil and then top it off with 6 inches (15 cm) of compost. If you want to know how much soil your raised beds require, you can use the formula of length x width x depth, and this will give you how much soil you need in cubic feet or cubic meters.

Apart from just topsoil and compost, you can add things like vermiculite, worm castings, coconut coir, peat moss, and grass clippings. Below you will find a recipe for mixing soil for raised beds. I've been using it for years, and we've gotten some of the best harvests using this mix. It's a bit more complicated but definitely worth it. The amounts are for one 4x4-foot (1.2x1.2 m) raised bed. You can multiply the amounts for larger beds.

- 4 cubic feet (113 L) of topsoil
- 3 cubic feet (85 L) of coconut coir (you can use peat moss instead)
- 2–3 cubic feet (56.5–85L) of compost or composted manure
- 2-inch (5 cm) layer of shredded leaves or grass clippings

If you use grass clippings, make sure they are not from a lawn that has been sprayed with herbicides or been fertilized with food that contains granular herbicides to kill weeds. They both persist and will kill plants up to 3 years after the initial application. Simply mix all the materials with a hoe or a cultivator and water well. Now you're ready to fill your raised beds. If you use this recipe, you probably won't need to fertilize your raised beds much in the first year. But in the following years, you can add an inch or two (2.5–5 cm) of compost.

Starting a Container Garden

You will need containers, potting soil or potting mix, seeds or seedlings, and water to start a container garden. Generally, the bigger the container, the better. The main advantage of having large containers is that they dry out slower than smaller ones. However, tall and narrow pots dry out quicker than short and wide ones. So, unless you have a deep-rooted plant, I'd suggest getting wider and shorter containers.

One tip for choosing the correct size of a container is that you should pick a container that is ⅓ of

---

[7] Image from https://www.almanac.com/content/how-build-raised-garden-bed

the height of the plant, measured from the soil to the highest leaf. This is generally true for above-ground plants, but may not be true for root crops. If you want to grow multiple plants in one container, the container needs to be big enough for all the plants to have space to grow. Plant profiles in Chapter 12 cover container size requirements for a variety of different plants.

Most plants won't thrive in standing water, so it's important that your containers have drainage holes at the bottom. If you want to use a container without drainage holes for decorative purposes, use it as a cachepot that holds the pot that the plant is growing in. This technique is known as double potting. A cachepot doesn't need drainage holes, and it should be large enough to accommodate a saucer that fits the growing pot.

If you plan to leave your containers out all year round, then you'd be better off with frost-safe containers made from wood, cement, or stone. Fiberglass and resin containers can also be left outside in the winter. Some plastic pots can survive the winter fine, but they can become brittle over time. If you need to move your containers around a lot, then they need to be light so that you can lift them.

When you're considering potting soil, one of the key choices will be whether you use a purely soilless growing medium or whether you decide to mix in some garden soil. This may come down to budget because using a purely soilless growing medium is more expensive, but it's sterile and less prone to pests and diseases. When you go to buy potting soil, you will find there's potting soil and potting mix available. Even though these terms are often used interchangeably, there is a difference between the two. Potting soil may contain soil. Potting mix is completely soilless and sterile, which makes it safer for plants because it doesn't contain pathogens that can cause plant diseases.

Potting mixes are typically light and fluffy and have good aeration and drainage, while potting soil is heavy and dense and has worse aeration and drainage than potting mixes. Potting mixes have worse longevity than potting soil, though. They contain peat moss and other organic matter that will eventually decompose, leading to soil compaction and nutrient depletion, and you would typically need to change your potting mix every 6–12 months and repot the plant. Potting soil will also degrade and become compacted over time, but you would typically need to change it every 12–18 months. Another thing to consider is that potting mixes are more expensive than potting soil. But once you know what is needed to mix your own growing medium, this can help reduce costs. I personally prefer using potting mix in containers. I make my own potting mixes, and you will learn how to make your own potting soil or potting mix later in this section.

It is important to have good soil in your containers because nutrients in potting soil don't regenerate like in garden soil, and the roots of the plants can't go beyond the container and explore further afield like they can in the ground to find the nutrients they need. Plants in containers are entirely dependent on the nutrients that you provide for them.

Do not use just garden soil in containers because it's often too compacted, and this can lead to root rot because the soil can't drain effectively. Garden soil just doesn't offer enough air, water, or nutrients to container plants.

It's also never a good idea to solely use compost in your containers. It would be fine to add compost to potting mix, vermiculite, or perlite, but just on its own it's not a good idea. Investing in good potting soil is a worthwhile investment because you'll get an abundance of delicious vegetables and fruits that are full of vitamins and minerals.

There are different types of potting soils and potting mixes for different purposes. There is an all-purpose potting mix that you can use indoors and outdoors in different types of containers—this is a good all-rounder to grow different plants in, and this is what I would suggest to a beginner to container gardening.

You can make your own potting soil or potting mix, and this can help you save quite a bit of money if you need to fill a lot of containers. Here's my favorite recipe for mixing potting soil. We've been using it for years and have always had great success with it:

- 2 gallons (7.6L) of peat moss
- 2 gallons (7.6L) of perlite
- 2 gallons (7.6L) of compost
- 2 gallons (7.6L) of garden soil
- ½ cup of dolomitic limestone
- ½ cup of soybean meal
- ½ cup of greensand
- ½ cup of rock phosphate
- ½ cup of kelp powder

Simply mix all the ingredients together and ensure everything is mixed. Then you can use it for all your container plants.

If you want a soilless potting mix, here is my favorite recipe. It was devised by Cornell University, and I adapted it for organic gardening by substituting synthetic fertilizers with organic ones.

- 1 bushel (8 gallons or 35.2 L) of peat moss
- 1 bushel (8 gallons or 35.2 L) of perlite or vermiculite
- 1 lb (454 g) bone meal
- ½ lb (227 g) ground limestone
- ½ lb (227 g) blood meal

Again, this should all be mixed together. It's sensible to wet the mixture as you stir to make it easier to mix everything together.

Always make sure to measure the pH level of your potting soil or potting mix. You can purchase pH testing kits online or at your local garden center. The instructions are easy to follow, and you will likely have to mix a sample with water and other ingredients and put in a test strip. If the level is outside of the range, you may need to adjust or change the soil.

You can use sulfur or aluminum sulfate to lower the pH level of your soil (make it more acidic). You can also use peat moss or fresh pine needles to make your soil more acidic, but these are usually not as effective and don't work as quickly as sulfur or aluminum sulfate. To increase the pH level of your soil (make it less acidic), you can add finely ground agricultural limestone. The amounts of sulfur, aluminum sulfate, or lime should be carefully measured before adding, so I would suggest checking with your local garden center—they should be able to help you with that.

If you can master making your own potting soil and potting mixes, you will be able to fill up your containers with high-quality growing medium much more cheaply than buying commercial potting soil.

You can put some filler at the bottom of larger pots so that you won't have to add so much expensive potting soil and to help with drainage. You could crush aluminum cans, use plastic milk cartons, or some other non-biodegradable packaging. You can fill either a quarter or up to a third of a container with this material, then top it with landscape fabric. Then you can put your potting soil on top of it. The fabric acts as a barrier to stop the potting soil from mixing with your filler, but it allows the water to drain through, and there should still be sufficient space for your plants' roots.

Selecting and Starting Seeds

Gardening would be super expensive if you were to buy all your plants as already established. Generally, the more established a plant is, the more expensive it is to buy because of all the work that has gone into getting it to that state. It is much cheaper to grow your own plants from seed. Growing plants from seed is not difficult, and it's so rewarding and enjoyable to see your plants grow from seed to finally gathering harvest from them. I can still remember the very first time I grew tomatoes, basil, and marigolds from seed. Checking on their progress is one of the first things I did every day, and I bored my family and friends with constant updates on how they did, but I was so proud and excited to have grown actual plants from seed.

Ensure that you buy your seeds from a reputable company. I strongly suggest getting organic seeds. Organic seeds are seeds taken from plants grown without the use of synthetic fertilizers and pesticides, which means they are better for you and for the environment. Plants grown from organic seeds are also naturally better at fending off pests on their own.

Check the seed packet to see if the plants you want to grow would grow well in your location. You could look for regionally based companies with seeds that thrive in your area. Regional suppliers are less likely to offer seeds that are unsuited to your growing conditions.

When you are choosing vegetables to plant, do look on the back of seed packets or in the seed catalog for seeds that have characteristics of being disease resistant because this will give you better quality vegetables and may reduce pests that come into your garden. While you can keep seeds for a few years, it is preferable to buy new seeds each year to ensure you get a better crop.

Also, check the seed packet for details about the best time to sow them and what conditions the plants like to grow in. Most seed packets will tell you if they should be started indoors or sown directly in the garden. They will usually tell you how long it will take for the plants to produce edible produce (days to maturity), and they should tell you their light and water requirements. Some may give information about the type of soil the plant likes.

Make a list of the vegetables and herbs that you enjoy eating, and then think about where these would grow in your garden. If you're a complete beginner to gardening, I would suggest starting out with vegetables that are easy to grow. Lettuce, green beans, peas, radishes, carrots, cucumbers, kale, Swiss chard, beets, and zucchini are all relatively easy to grow. Tomatoes and peppers require a bit more care, but they are not terribly difficult to grow. Eggplants, cauliflower, celery, and watermelons can be more difficult to grow.

If you don't like certain vegetables, don't grow them because if you don't enjoy eating them—it'll probably be just wasted time and food unless you plan to sell them. Look back at Chapter 3 with regards to which vegetables and herbs do well together from your list. Remember that if you're growing peas, pole beans, cucumbers, tomatoes, or other vining plants, you'll need to have trellises to support them when they grow, and also remember that they may create shade as they grow, so take this into consideration. If you're planting pumpkins and watermelons, they need a lot of space to spread.

You can start seeds indoors—usually before the last frost—so that your seedlings are ready to be transplanted outside to the garden when the weather is warmer. Seed packets may say things like "plant inside 6 to 8 weeks before last frost". You would typically start seeds in a seed starting tray or in small containers and then transplant the seedlings into bigger containers when they grow too big before finally transplanting them to your garden, raised beds, or growing containers if you have a container garden.

Some plants can be started indoors and then be transplanted outside. Plants that can be started indoors include artichoke, basil, broccoli, Brussels sprouts, cabbage, cauliflower, celery, chard, chives, collard greens, eggplants, kale, leeks, mustard, parsley, peppers, and tomatoes.

Some plants don't transplant well and should be planted directly in the soil or in containers that you plan to grow them in (this is called direct sowing). Plants that should be started directly in the soil or in containers include beans, beets, carrots, corn, garlic, okra, parsnips, pumpkins, radishes, squash, turnips, watermelons, and zucchini.

Some vegetables are grown from root divisions or bulbs. Some examples include asparagus, garlic, horseradish, onions, potatoes, rhubarb, and sweet potatoes. This will be covered in more detail in Chapter 12 in individual plant profiles.

You can grow seeds in any containers, and this could be a good way to recycle butter or margarine tubs or yogurt pots. The container needs to be 2–3 inches (5–7.5 cm) deep with some drainage—you can simply poke a drainage hole at the bottom. You can also purchase seed starting trays especially for this purpose, and it does make transplanting seedlings easier when you need to.

You can start seeds in potting mix, but most seeds, especially smaller ones, do better when started in seed starting mix, and it should be a fresh, sterile mix. I would advise against starting seeds in potting soil and especially in garden soil because this can lead to fungal diseases and kill your seeds. Seed starting mix is a special form of soilless potting mix that typically uses smaller particles of vermiculite and sand and omits organic materials found in standard potting soil. You can loosen and dampen the seed starting mix before planting seeds, but don't soak it. If you start seeds in seed starting mix, you'll generally need to transplant the seedlings into a standard potting mix or potting soil when they begin to develop into larger plants.

You can make your own seed starting mix by mixing equal parts of coco coir, perlite, and vermiculite. Simply combine all the ingredients in a clean tub or bucket, and water the mixture well. Stir the mixture with your hands or a trowel until it's moist but not soggy (like a wrung-out sponge). You can fill your seed starting trays or pots with this mix and sow your seeds right away.[8]

You can also make your own potting mix for transplanting your seedlings into when they grow. You can make a basic potting mix or an enriched one with compost. To make a basic potting mix, mix 6 parts coco coir, 1 part perlite, and 1 part vermiculite. Enriched potting mix is made by mixing 4 parts coco coir, 2 parts compost, 1 part perlite, and 1 part vermiculite. Simply combine all the ingredients in a clean tub or bucket, and water the mixture well. Then stir it until it's moist but not soggy.

Look at the packet instructions diligently for how deep you should plant your seeds. Some small seeds just need to be scattered over the surface of the soil, while others need to be planted in a hole. If you don't have a dibber (a tool for making holes to plant seeds into), you can simply use an old pencil to make a hole, drop the seed in, and then cover it with soil if you're sowing directly or seed starting mix if you're starting seeds indoors. It's a good idea to plant 2–3 seeds per hole because not every seed you plant will germinate. There isn't anything you're doing wrong—it's just nature.

If more than one seed grows, you can thin them out. It simply means you should let the strongest looking one grow and cut the rest at the base. You should thin out seedlings when they have developed 1–2 true leaves. The very first leaves that plants grow from seed are called seed leaves or cotyledons. They are long and narrow in some plants, but in others, they are heart shaped. True leaves come after seed leaves. They have the same shape as the adult foliage, just baby sized.

You will need to keep the soil or seed starting mix moist but not soggy. You would typically need to water your seeds daily, and you can spray your seed starting mix with a spray bottle if you're starting seeds indoors, or you can spray the soil with a fine spray hose nozzle or water it with a watering can if you're direct sowing seeds in the garden.

If you're starting seeds indoors, you can keep the seeds covered with a clear plastic dome or wrap, and this will help them to germinate more quickly. You can purchase heating mats to germinate seeds because most seeds germinate well in temperatures between 65 and 75°F (18–24°C). Your seeds will need to be watered more if you use a heating mat. You could also place a fan near them to improve air circulation.

Once the seedlings emerge, remove the plastic dome or wrap you had covering them. When the seedlings have started to grow, keep watering them the same way. Keep the soil or seed starting mix moist but

---

[8] Image from https://www.thespruce.com/successful-start-seed-indoors-1402478

not soggy—it should feel like a damp sponge. You would typically need to water your seedlings daily.

If you're starting seeds indoors, put the tray in a place where your seedlings will receive lots of sunlight. If they're too far away from light once they've germinated, they'll start to get long and leggy because they reach for the light, but this will make them weaker. The only way to prevent seedlings from becoming leggy is to provide more light. You can do that by getting grow lights for your seedlings.

Having adequate lighting is essential for growing seedlings successfully. When I was just starting out with gardening decades ago, I tried starting plants from seed indoors without artificial lighting. I was lucky to have a massive south-facing window in my living room, and that's where I first tried starting seeds. That worked okay, but my seedlings were thin and leggy, especially compared to the ones you'd find in a garden center. Also, at least half of the seeds didn't sprout at all. And things got only worse when I tried starting different plants from seed. It was clear that they didn't get enough light from my large windowsill. That's when I decided to splurge on grow lights, and I was amazed at the difference it made! Almost all of my seeds started sprouting, and the seedlings became much stronger and healthier, and they had no problem surviving the transition to my in-ground garden, raised beds, containers, and even hydroponic systems.

You would typically use fluorescent or LED (light-emitting diode) grow lights for starting seeds. Metal halide (MH) and high-pressure sodium (HPS) lights produce lots of heat and can burn seedlings. Fluorescent grow lights are cheaper than LEDs; however, LED grow lights have a few benefits over fluorescent grow lights. They are more energy efficient and last longer than fluorescent grow lights. They also don't lose their effectiveness over time.

If you get grow lights for seedlings, you shouldn't leave them on all day long. Seedlings need 14–16 hours of light per day, so you should have your lights on a timer for convenience. Some people grow seedlings with 12 hours of light daily, but it's usually not enough in my experience. You can try that, but you should monitor your seedlings closely in this case. If they start getting tall and growing sideways, you should add 2 more hours of light per day.

How high you should have grow lights above your seedlings depends on the type of lights you have. I'd suggest following the height recommendations provided by the light manufacturer. However, if that information isn't provided, fluorescent grow lights should be kept 2–3 inches (5–7.5 cm) above seedlings, and LED grow lights should be at least a foot (30 cm) above. You'll need to move your grow lights away from the seedlings as they grow.

Issues with Seeds

If not all your seeds germinate, it's worth having another read of the back of the seed packet to see if you did everything it suggested in terms of temperature, light, and water. Have the seeds rotted because the soil was too moist? Or was the soil too dry, and the seeds dried out? Try again and try to follow the instructions and be consistent with how moist your soil is.

If your seedlings are tall, leggy, and spindly, it could be that they aren't getting enough light, so they're growing to try to reach the light. They should get 14–16 hours of bright light per day, which you can help along with grow lights. If the temperature is too warm, this can cause plants to be leggy too. If that's the case, you could reduce the temperature in the room and also use a little less fertilizer.

In the picture below, it shows the difference between the seeds on the left, which were grown under grow lights, and the seeds on the right, which were grown on a windowsill and have become leggy.[9]

If your seedlings looked good, and then suddenly they toppled at the base, this could be due to a soil-borne fungus known as damping off. Damping off can affect most seedlings, particularly under conditions of high humidity, poor air circulation, and if seeds were sown too thickly. It is mainly a problem when starting seeds indoors. Damping off is mainly caused by overly moist soil, which is ideal for the growth and spread of fungal pathogens.

There is no cure for plants that have damping off. If you have it in the soil, I would recommend getting rid of it and using a soilless growing medium instead because you can't get rid of it once it's there. This is why I recommend using seed starting mix, which is a soilless growing medium, for starting seeds in the first place. Also, try not to overwater your seed starting mix and sow the seeds more thinly because overcrowding can lead to damping off.

When I first tried to grow cucamelon seeds, I had this happen, and it was so frustrating to see little seeds starting to sprout and then just die for what seemed like no good reason. I then started using seed starting mix to start seeds and never had this problem again.

If you have mold growing on the surface of the seed starting mix or potting mix, this is a sign that the growing medium is too wet. It may not harm the plants too much, but definitely stop watering them for a few days, and you could put a fan nearby too, which will help with air circulation. You can scrape off the mold or put the seedlings in fresh potting mix, but be really careful and try not to damage them.

Growing and Transplanting Seedlings

When you're growing seedlings, the growing medium needs to be kept moist but not soggy. The best indicator that your seeds or seedlings need water is how dry their growing medium is. When you touch the potting mix or soil, it should feel neither soggy nor too dry. Instead, it should feel like a moist sponge. When watering your seedlings, use a mister or a very gentle spray bottle to water the top of your seed starting tray or container. If you sowed seeds directly, you can water your seedlings carefully with a fine spray hose nozzle or a watering can.

If you have grow lights, remember to raise them as the seedlings grow so that you don't burn them. You could also have a fan in the room to keep air circulating well. You should fertilize seedlings with an

---

[9] Image from https://www.gardeners.com/how-to/how-to-start-seeds/5062.html

organic liquid fertilizer when they grow to 3 inches (7.5 cm) and then weekly after that.

One of the best ways to determine if a seedling is ready to be transplanted outside is to look at how many true leaves it has. The very first leaves that plants grow from seed are called seed leaves or cotyledons. They are long and narrow in some plants, but in others, they are heart shaped. True leaves come after seed leaves. They have the same shape as the adult foliage, just baby sized. You will need to wait until your seedlings have at least 3–4 true leaves before transplanting them to your garden or containers outside.

However, if the weather is still too cold or you have a container garden, you can continue growing seedlings indoors. You will have to pot them up as they grow, though. Potting up seedlings, whether you've grown them yourself or have purchased them from a nursery, just means putting them into larger containers so that they can grow, thrive, and produce wonderful vegetables, fruits, and herbs for you to enjoy eating. Seedlings need to be put into larger containers so that they have room for their roots to grow and don't become root bound.

If you haven't seen a root-bound plant before, the picture on the right shows what one looks like. This is a tomato seedling that has been in a small container much too long. You can see how the roots have just grown into the container shape because they had nowhere else to go.[10]

You can sometimes gently massage a root-bound plant before you transplant it into a bigger pot, but you need to be careful not to damage the roots when you do this.

When you pot up seedlings, their roots will become bigger and will take up more water. Seedlings are always very thirsty and need lots of water to thrive. When you've put seedlings into their new containers, do remember to feed them because they'll want to take in as many good nutrients as they can to grow strong.

You can plant seedlings when plants are starting to look cramped and overgrown in their small seed starting trays. If plants have started out in 4-inch (10 cm) pots, then around 6–8 weeks after germination they can be moved into 6–8-inch (15–20 cm) pots.

The time for planting seedlings into bigger pots can depend on the plant too. Tomatoes will outgrow their pots very quickly, but herbs can take a bit more time. Tomatoes grow faster than peppers, for example, so they will need to be planted sooner than peppers. Vegetables like squash grow fast and like a lot of room, so it can be fine to start squash in 6-inch (15 cm) pots.

If your seedlings are starting to have their roots poke out of drainage holes, this is a key sign that they

---

[10] Image from https://homesteadandchill.com/potting-up-seedlings/

need to be transplanted into larger containers. You can pot up seedlings before this happens, but this is just a sign they're definitely ready to be put into larger containers.[11]

One helpful tip when you're potting up seedlings is to make a "dummy hole" or placeholder with the existing container in the new container that the seedling is being transplanted into. You can fill the new container with potting soil, then place the existing container in it and check that things are at the right level. Ensure the soil in the new container is moist. When you do this, it will help ensure that there are no air pockets around the plant, and it saves you having to tip in extra soil, which can get all over the leaves of the plant and be a bit awkward. It also means that transplanting of the seedling goes smoothly and stops the plant from being jostled about. Prior to learning about this tip, we often had over- or underfilled containers and had to mess about with soil levels.

When it comes to transplanting seedlings into the garden or containers outdoors, don't put them directly outside—the transition to being outside needs to be gradual. You can start by putting them in a protected place outdoors for a few hours while they are still in containers, but bring them back inside at night because it might be too cold for them. Over 10 days, gradually let them get used to being outside more and more. After that, you can transplant them into your garden, or if you're growing in containers, leave the containers outside. A cold frame is also a good place to harden off seedlings.

When you eventually reach the day when you transplant your seedlings into the garden, it could be a good idea to choose an overcast day to reduce the stress for the plants because if they've been indoors or in a greenhouse and then they are placed in the harsh outside world, it can be a shock. Ensure that you water them well, and it can be a good idea to add 2 inches (5 cm) of mulch to keep back the weeds and retain moisture (this will be covered in Chapter 8). Think about how big the plant will be at its mature size because this is the space it will eventually need. Don't be tempted to fill every space. Give your plants room to grow and thrive. Different plants need different spacing. You can usually find spacing requirements for plants on

---

[11] Image from https://homesteadandchill.com/potting-up-seedlings/

seed packets. Plant profiles in Chapter 12 will cover spacing requirements for many different plants.

When you come to transplant seedlings, simply poke a hole in the soil, carefully remove the seedling from its container trying not to disturb the roots, put the seedling into the hole you've made, firm the soil around it, and water it thoroughly.

Propagating Plants from Cuttings

If you're just starting out with vegetable gardening, you'll likely have to start plants from seed or purchase seedlings from a nursery. There is another way to start plants, however—from cuttings. It's exactly what it sounds like—you can use cuttings from existing plants to grow new plants. Taking cuttings from plants is a great way to propagate them. It is also called cloning. Some plants can be difficult to start from seed, so you can purchase a plant from a nursery and then propagate it via cuttings.

I have always adored taking plant cuttings. I love the fact that from one plant you can create numerous others and watch them grow. I do this with all my house plants, and I have done this with plants that I grow in my garden too.

When you propagate plants this way, often the plant has done a lot of the growing work, and the new plants grow much quicker than from seed. Only take cuttings from healthy, strong plants. Take a few more cuttings than required because sometimes not all of the cuttings survive.

Here's what you'll need to propagate plants from cuttings:

- Existing plant (parent plant)
- Razor blade or scissors
- Rubbing alcohol
- 4–6-inch (10–15 cm) containers or a seed starting tray
- Clear plastic cover for seed starting tray or a plastic bag
- Soilless potting mix
- Pencil or stick
- Rooting hormone
- Water
- 2 small plastic cups

You'll need a porous, soilless growing medium. You can make your own by mixing equal parts of sand, perlite, peat moss, and vermiculite. Do not add fertilizers or manure to this because they can burn cuttings.

You can start cuttings in seed starting trays, but larger plants may need a 4–6-inch (10–15 cm) deep container. You can also use Styrofoam coffee cups or large paper cups, but make sure to poke a drainage hole at the bottom.

Here's how you propagate plants from cuttings:

1. Choose a healthy parent plant to take cuttings from. Don't take cuttings from diseased or wilting plants. The parent plant should have good, green growth and be large enough to take cuttings from.
2. Next, fill your seed starting tray or container with the growing medium, and poke a hole in it with the pencil.
3. Now you'll need to find suitable stems for cutting. They should be green and non-woody. Newer growth is easier to root than older or woody stems. Find a stem with a node—a bump along the stem where a leaf or a flower bud attaches. New roots will emerge from it.

4. Sterilize your razor blade or scissors with rubbing alcohol, and make a clean cut just below the node. The cutting doesn't need to be long, 4–6 inches (10–15 cm) is enough, but it should have at least 2 leaves and 1 node.

5. Once you've taken the cutting, you need to make a partial slice through the middle of the node with a sterilized razor blade. This will increase the chances of roots emerging from this spot. If your cutting has more than 1 or 2 leaves—cut them off. The cutting only needs 1–2 leaves to continue photosynthesis. Having too many leaves will consume energy that would otherwise go to root creation. If the leaves are very large in relation to the stem, you can cut off the top halves of the leaves too.

6. Next, you'll need to dip the cutting in the rooting hormone. Rooting hormones are typically not organic; however, you can find organic options made with willow extract. I find gel or liquid rooting hormones to be more effective than powder. This step is optional, but rooting hormone can help promote root growth, and I would recommend doing it. Fill one plastic cup with water, and place some rooting hormone into the other one. Dip the node end of the cutting into the water and then into the rooting hormone. Tap off any excess hormone—too much can hinder the chances for successful rooting.

7. Carefully place the cutting into the hole you made in the growing medium, and gently tap the growing medium around the cutting. You can fit several cuttings into one container, but space them out so that the leaves don't touch one another.

8. Place the container with the cutting into a plastic bag, or cover the seed staring tray with a clear plastic cover. It will keep the humidity high and hold in heat. Don't seal the bag completely because cuttings need some airflow to prevent fungal rot. You can remove the cover from the seed starting tray once a day to let the moisture escape. Keep the cuttings in a warm, sunny spot, but don't put them in full sunlight until new leaves start to appear along the stem.

9. Keep the growing medium slightly moist but not so wet that condensation forms on the inside of the plastic bag or seed starting tray cover until the roots form. After 2–3 weeks, you can start checking for roots by tugging gently on the cutting. When you begin to feel resistance, it means the roots have developed. At this point, you can transplant the cutting into your garden or a container.

You can even grow fruit trees from cuttings. The process is essentially the same, but you'll need to take either softwood or semi-hardwood cuttings from branches. Softwood cuttings are generally taken in the spring when new branches are green and no blossoms have appeared. They are flexible but will snap if you bend them hard enough. They dry out pretty quickly, so you'll need to plant them as soon as possible after taking the cuttings. Softwood cuttings usually root in about a month. Semi-hardwood cuttings are harvested in early summer when the new growth is beginning to harden and the green is starting being overtaken by bark. They should still be a little pliable, and they also dry out quickly, so you'll need to plant them as soon as possible. Semi-hardwood cuttings usually root in about 6 weeks.

Cuttings from trees should be between 6 and 12 inches (15–30 cm) long. You'll need to remove leaves from the bottom half of the cutting, and any fruit or buds should be taken off as well. Then you'll need to dip the cut end of the cutting in rooting hormone and plant it just like you would plant a cutting taken from a plant. Once the cuttings have roots that are about 1¼ inches (3 cm), you can transplant them into 4-inch (10 cm) planters if you're going to transplant them into the garden or into the desired containers if you're going to grow them in containers. You'll need to grow fruit trees indoors for the first year. You can transplant them or move the container outside the following spring season. You should slowly harden off your young trees to outdoor conditions before transplanting them into your garden. Of course, it takes years for trees to mature, but if you want to grow a fruit tree from scratch, growing them from cuttings is the best way to go about it. Growing fruit trees from seed can be tricky, and it's much easier to grow them from cuttings.

You can grow a lot of different plants from cuttings, including tomatoes, peppers, celery, sweet potatoes, fennel, basil, rosemary, lemon verbena, lavender, and mint as well as fruit trees, such as lemon, lime, apple, peach, and pear trees, and more.

I remember when I first started my in-ground garden using the no-dig method. I chose a sunny area in the garden and started preparing my no-dig garden beds by putting down cardboard on the grass, then compost, vegetable scraps, straw, more compost, and more straw. I made indentations in it, filled them with compost, and planted seedlings in there that I had grown from seed indoors 8 weeks earlier. When they were bigger and had grown 3–4 sets of true leaves after germination, I started bringing them into the garden throughout the day, but kept them inside at night. I did that for 10 days before planting them in the no-dig area of my garden. I carefully planted tomatoes and basil together with marigolds nearby too. All of these plants get on really well with one another and have lots of benefits. Marigolds repel nematodes, tomato worms, and whiteflies. Basil repels flies and mosquitos and enhances the flavor of tomatoes. And tomatoes create shade, which helps the soil keep the moisture in, and that's great for basil because it prefers moist soil.

We also had raised beds in a different part of our garden that had potatoes and sweet alyssum growing in them. It was important not to plant the potatoes near the tomatoes because potatoes and tomatoes can be attacked by the same blight. Sweet alyssum smells great, looks beautiful, and attracts wasps, which eat pests.

Key takeaways from this chapter:

1. When you start a companion garden, think about sunlight, water, ease of access, and shelter.
2. With raised beds, you can choose what soil to put in there. There will be no soil compaction. You don't have to bend or kneel. They need to be at least 6 inches (15 cm) tall, but they can be up to 18 inches (45 cm) tall for plants that have deeper roots. You can put hardware cloth at the bottom of raised beds to prevent moles and gophers from getting into your raised beds.
3. With container gardens, you can control the soil. You can easily move the containers. If you lack garden space, they're a perfect solution. You can

use fillers at the bottom of containers to use less potting soil.
4. Seeds are less expensive than seedlings or established plants. Ensure the seeds you use are organic, fresh, and are from a reputable company.
5. Plant seeds for vegetables that you would like to eat and that you know grow well in your area.
6. Use trellises to support climbing or vining plants.
7. Some plants do better when started indoors, whereas some plants don't like to be transplanted and are better sown directly outside or in the desired containers.
8. You can get disease-resistant seed varieties.
9. You can start seeds indoors before the growing season starts and then transplant them into the garden later in order to get a head start on the growing season.
10. Grow seeds in seed starting mix that is sterile and contains no organic material to avoid fungal issues.
11. Cover seeds with a plastic dome or plastic wrap. Remove the cover once the seedlings have emerged.
12. You'll need to water your seeds daily and keep the soil or seed starting mix moist but not too wet. Once they sprout, you can water the seedlings daily too. You can give your seedlings liquid fertilizer once they are at least 3 inches (7.5 cm) tall.
13. You can use grow lights to provide more light for your seedlings. Keep them on for 14–16 hours a day on a timer.
14. When seedlings have 3–4 sets of true leaves, they are ready to be transplanted outside. Transition to the outside should be gradual, though. You can move your seedlings outside during the day while they're still in containers, but bring them back inside at night. Do so for 10 days before planting your seedlings outside.
15. Transplant seedlings into your garden on an overcast day so that it is less stressful for them.
16. Give seedlings space and think about their size when they are fully grown.
17. You can also start plants from cuttings (which is also called cloning), and it's a great way to propagate plants.

The next chapter will cover everything you need to know to maintain your garden properly, looking at how to water it and maintenance tasks you need to do daily, weekly, and monthly to keep your plants healthy and producing a good quality crop and to keep your garden looking its best.

Chapter 6: Maintaining Your Garden

Once you've started your vegetable garden, it does need some care and maintenance to ensure that your plants thrive. You will need to water your plants and fertilize them. You will need to keep the area free from weeds and mulch the soil with compost to provide nutrients and keep the weeds down. You will also need to prune some plants. It is important to follow the guidance for care on the back of each seed packet. So, this chapter will cover everything you need to know about maintaining your garden.

Watering In-Ground Gardens

How Much You Should Water Your Plants

People can be unsure about how much water they should give their plants and how often they should water them. Watering your garden can depend on the type of soil you have, the climate you live in, the time of year, and the type of plants you are growing.

Having an outside source of water really eases the pressure of having to carry watering cans through your house. And you'll need a lot of watering cans even if you have a small garden. So, if you have access to an outside tap, this is a treasure! If you have a well, you could hook a hose directly to the well for watering. If you don't have an outside tap or a well, you could consider getting a water butt. It's not that expensive, and it will collect lots of delicious rainwater to feed your plants, which they'll love. It would also help you save on your water bill, so it's a win-win situation. If you don't have either of these, you could think about running a hose from a tap in your house out to the garden. Hose reels are very easy to manage. They're convenient and don't take up a lot of space and will make life much easier.

In-ground gardens should ideally get an inch or two (2.5–5 cm) of water each week, and they prefer good, deep watering rather than frequent, shallow watering. When you water more often but not as deeply, you get weak root growth and evaporation. Therefore, watering in-ground gardens about 1–2 inches (2.5–5 cm) or so once a week is preferable. Most plants typically need 1 inch (2.5 cm) of water per week, although during peak summer you should increase that to 2 inches (5 cm). If it rains, you'll need to water your plants less. You should also consider the type of soil you have. Sandy soil dries out quicker than clay soil, so you'll need to water it more frequently. To determine when you need to water your plants, you can simply place your finger about an inch (2.5 cm) into the soil, and if it feels dry, you need to water it.

An inch of water is a 1-inch-deep (2.5 cm) layer of water over the entire soil surface in question. Your garden will get some water from rain, so you can make a rain gauge from a straight-sided container, like a used tuna can. Measure 1 and 2 inches (2.5 and 5 cm) up from the bottom, and put lines on the inside at these levels using a permanent marker. Next, add additional marks every quarter of an inch or 5 mm—this will help you determine how much water your garden needs. Place this can on a level spot in the garden where it will be completely exposed to the rain. Check it every week to see how much water your garden got from rain and how much you need to water it. You can purchase a rain gauge from a garden center, but a simple marked container works perfectly fine too.

To measure the volume of water your garden needs, you can simply multiply your garden beds' length by width in inches or centimeters and then by 1 or 2 inches (2.54–5.08 cm, but you can round that up to 2.5–5 cm for convenience) depending on how much water your garden needs. Next, divide the result by 231 if your measurements were in inches and by 1000 if they were in centimeters to get the number of gallons or liters of water your garden needs, respectively. For example, if you have a 4x8-foot garden bed, and your garden needs an inch of water, multiply 48 by 96 by 1, then divide by 231 to determine how many gallons you need. The answer would be 19.95 (you can round that up to 20 for convenience). Or let's say you have a 1.2 by 2.4 m garden bed that needs 2.5 cm of water. You'll need to multiply 120 by 240 by 2.5, then divide by 1000 to determine how many liters you need. In this case, your garden will need 72 liters of water.

When You Should Water Your Plants

First of all, you should water plants once you plant them. For already established gardens, watering them once a week with 1 or 2 inches (2.5–5 cm) of water is OK. However, if the weather is really hot, you may need to water them more frequently—twice a week or even more is the heat scorching. Some vegetables are thirstier and dry out quicker too. In my experience, tomatoes need a lot of water, and their soil can dry out quickly. You can check how moist your soil is by simply placing your finger about an inch (2.5 cm) into the soil. If it feels dry, you need to water it.

When you water your plants, you should aim to water them near the base. Watering your garden in the morning is best unless there has been heavy rain. Plants absorb moisture more effectively in the morning and become hydrated before the weather heats up. If you water your plants in the morning, this allows any water that may get on leaves to dry or evaporate throughout the day rather than just sit there overnight. If your plants remain wet for extended periods of time, this can lead to fungal diseases. Another thing that can happen if you water your plants in the midday sun and get water on the leaves, the water droplets can act like a magnifying glass and scorch the leaves of your plants.

What Happens if Plants Don't Get Enough Water?

If your plants don't get enough water, this is known as drought stress, and this can cause your plants to produce small fruit or none at all. Vegetables like cabbage and turnips can become tough, bitter, or fibrous. Some may have a flower stalk but then not grow anymore. Or plants could just have wilted leaves, shrivel up, and die.

You can look for signs that plants are underwatered. If they have dry, brown leaf edges, slow leaf growth, leaf curl, yellow leaves, wilted leaves, or branch dieback, these are all signs they may need more water. Don't wait to water your plants if they feel dry, even if the weather forecast says it will rain the next day. If your plants look dry or look like they're suffering from heat, water them. Leafy greens, such as lettuce, kale, and spinach, have shallow root systems and don't hold moisture well, so they do need to be watered regularly to thrive.

What Happens if Plants Get Too Much Water?

It is possible to overwater plants, and this often leads to root rot. Roots need oxygen from the soil, but if it's saturated with water, there's not enough oxygen there. Plants can collapse or have bland fruit if that's the case. If you are growing vegetables with the intention of storing them, they won't store well when it's been really wet—this applies to potatoes, onions, winter squash, and rutabaga.

If plants have any leaf diseases, this will be worse in a wet season. You can't do much if it's rainy, but one solution could be to build raised beds—they offer better drainage because the soil is raised. You can check for signs that a plant is overwatered. If plants look wilted, have brown leaves or yellow falling leaves, if new growth is dropping off, or if a plant is floppy, slimy, or has smelly roots (which is a sign of root rot), this means your plants are likely overwatered.

Drip Irrigation

While watering your plants can be a relaxing experience, it can take quite a bit of time and effort, especially if you have a bigger garden. You can make watering less of a chore by installing a drip irrigation system.

There are different automatic watering systems, like soaker hoses, sprinklers, and drip irrigation systems. Drip irrigation is the most effective way of watering your plants in my opinion. Soaker hoses can often get clogged or crack. Sprinklers can get the leaves wet, and if plants stay wet, they can get fungal diseases. Drip irrigation lines water the soil at an even rate, and you're not wasting water like with sprinklers due to evaporation.

Drip irrigation is a great solution because it helps prevent diseases by minimizing water contact with the leaves, stems, and fruit of plants. It also allows the rows between plants to remain dry, improving access and reducing weed growth. Drip irrigation systems will help you save time, money, and water because they are incredibly efficient.

You can buy drip irrigation kits from garden centers or home improvement/hardware stores. Many kits are modular in design, which allows you to change your drip irrigation system as your garden changes. I would suggest making a plan of your garden and taking it to a store so that they can suggest a kit that would fit your needs best. Drip irrigation kits are relatively affordable and are not very difficult to install, so you can certainly do it yourself, or you can always hire someone to install the system for you.

Watering Raised Beds

You can water your raised beds using a watering can, a garden hose, sprinklers, or drip lines. Watering raised beds with a watering can is very time consuming and can take quite a lot of effort. A garden hose would speed up the process, but don't blast young plants with a hose because this can damage them. You can also place a hose on the soil and let water drain into your raised beds. The soil should never become fully dry in your raised beds. Keep an eye on the weather because your plants may need more (if it's hot) or less water (if it's rainy or cold) as it changes.

Drip Irrigation for Raised Beds

You can get drip irrigation kits for raised beds. Just like with in-ground gardens, this is a great solution for watering your plants. If you have an automatic watering system, it's a good idea to let it water when you are naturally in the garden so that you can check that it's working correctly and there aren't any issues, like a dead battery, a faulty timer, or leaks, and that your raised beds are not being over- or underwatered. Raised beds should be watered evenly and consistently, which is why an automatic watering system can be a good idea. To retain the moisture in your raised beds, you can mulch them, and this will reduce water evaporation and will also help reduce weeds.

Watering Containers

You will need to water plants in containers a lot, in fact, daily on most days because containers dry out really easily. This will vary depending on the time of year. You will need to water your plants more during the summer months—you may need to water them twice a day if it's really hot and sunny.

People not watering their containers regularly is definitely the number one reason why container plants die. If your containers are drying out really quickly, this may be a sign that you have more plants in the container than the soil can support, so you could consider taking out some of the plants and putting them in a different container, or pruning plants back, or moving the container to somewhere where it gets slightly less direct sunlight.

As with in-ground gardens and raised beds, having an outside source of water really eases the pressure of having to carry watering cans through your house. If don't have access to an outside tap, you can get a water butt to collect rainwater, or you could run a hose from a tap in your house out to the garden.

Another thing to think about regarding containers is their size. The smaller the container, the faster it will dry out. So, if you can have larger containers, they will be easier to look after. You can also mulch larger container to help keep the moisture in, and this will be covered in more detail in Chapter 8.

Touch Soil to Determine How Moist It Is

You can purchase a wide variety of different water meters, but in all honestly, these are probably never as effective as looking at the plant yourself, placing your finger in the soil, and making a judgement call as to how dry or moist the soil is. You need to water plants regularly because otherwise they will start to wilt. When you place your finger in the soil, if the first inch (2.5 cm) you feel is dry, then it needs watering.

You should water your containers until water starts flowing out of the drainage holes—this shows you have got the whole container wet. This will also leach the soil, which can help wash away any soluble salts in the soil that may accumulate from fertilizers or water.

If you are using a soilless potting mix and it starts to pull away from the edge of the pot, this is a sign that it has dried out a lot. You will need to repeatedly water this in order to fully hydrate the soil. It can be a good idea to place the container in a bucket or a sink with water until you can see water on the top of the container—then the soil is fully moist.

Built-in Reservoir

You can get containers that have a built-in reservoir to ensure your plants have a water supply—these are called self-watering pots. The reservoir may need filling on hot summer days, but it does make watering easier. You can either buy containers that already have reservoirs, or you can make your own. Reservoirs often work via a wick. You could use capillary matting or terrycloth for the wick and have a piece of material that is approximately 6 inches (15 cm) wide that goes from the reservoir into the bottom of your plant pot. When the plant needs water, it will draw it up through its roots and growing medium.

It is better to use this wick method rather than just sitting containers in a tray of water. If plants just sit in water, they can become waterlogged, and their roots may rot, which will cause them to die eventually.

Drip Irrigation for Containers

Another technique you can use is the drip method. Take a plastic bottle and cut out the bottom. Drill tiny holes in the bottle cap. Then stick the bottle into the soil cap side down and fill it with water. You may need to experiment with the size of the holes so that the water doesn't all come pouring out too quickly or too slowly. This can be a great way to deliver water to hanging baskets too.

You can also get terracotta ollas. If you place these in the soil next to your plants, they will draw water from them when required. These look prettier than plastic bottles, but they obviously cost more, so it depends on the budget you have available.

If you need to go away on holiday and don't have anyone to water your plants for you, you can set up automatic watering systems, such as a drip irrigation system with a timer, using a garden tap or a water butt. You can use a container with a reservoir and connect this to a water butt. You could make a much larger reservoir (using something like an old bath) and use wicks from this to plants suspended above. All of these suggestions take a bit of setting up and some expense. But it could keep your lovely crop of vegetables, fruits, and herbs thriving if you need to go away and there's no one there to water them.

Moisture Crystals

There are various moisture crystals you can add to your potting soil. They look like rock salt when they are dry, but when they absorb water, they take on a jellylike consistency—these will act as reservoirs of moisture that plants can draw upon when the soil dries out. These don't detract from the fact that you will need to water your containers frequently. But it will just give you a bit of a buffer until you do to help protect your plants a little.

There are some simple things you can do to help ease the load of watering your containers. A really simple tip is to purchase containers that are light colored because they won't absorb as much heat as dark-colored containers and won't dry out as quickly. Also, you can purchase non-porous containers, such as plastic or glazed terracotta ones. They won't absorb the moisture out of the soil.

Garden Maintenance and Care

If you want your plants to thrive throughout the growing season, you will need to schedule in some time to maintain your garden. As mentioned previously, one of the key tasks is watering, and this is essential to the health of your plants. Watering regularly will prevent plants from being stressed, and when plants are stressed, they're more prone to diseases and pests. If you don't water your plants regularly, you won't get a great harvest.

Apart from watering your plants, there are a few things you need to keep on top of, such as fertilizing your garden, pruning your plants, removing weeds, removing dead/straggly plants and composting them, and attracting pollinators, all of which will be covered below.

Fertilizing

You will need to add nutrients to your soil as the growing season progresses because your plants will use these. Chapter 4 has covered using organic fertilizers and making homemade organic fertilizers, so you can refer back to it to find all the information you need in regards to fertilizing your garden. Organic fertilizers, like kelp, bone meal, fish meal, or alfalfa meal, will help your plants thrive. If you got your organic fertilizer from a garden center, simply follow the instructions on the label. You would typically need to fertilize your garden every 2–4 weeks during the growing season, and this is also true for most homemade fertilizers.

You can also mulch your garden beds, raised beds, and larger containers with compost, and this will help enrich your soil with nutrients while also helping your soil retain moisture and preventing weeds from growing. This will be covered in more detail in Chapter 8.

It's worth remembering that you can take care of your soil even when you aren't growing vegetables to eat by planting cover crops and mowing them down to give the soil nutrients. Plants like clover, alfalfa, and ryegrass all make great cover crops and will improve your soil structure and feed beneficial microbes. Again, this was covered in more detail in Chapter 4, so you can refer back to it to learn more about using cover crops to improve your soil quality.

Weeding

When weeds grow near your vegetables, they will compete with your vegetables for sunlight, water, and nutrients. You want your vegetables to get all the benefits of sunlight, water, and nutrients so that they grow strong and healthy and taste delicious. You need to pull up weeds weekly to stop them from developing thick and deep roots.

In a no-dig garden, mulching is used to control weeds. Mulching will be covered in-depth in Chapter 8, but it's essentially topping the soil with organic matter, such as leaves, newspapers, compost, and so on. If mulch areas have thinned, you could top them up, and the mulch will prevent weeds from growing and will also help retain moisture in the soil.

Other techniques for weeding include hand weeding, shallow hoeing, and using contact weed killers.

Hand weeding is self-explanatory—it means simply pulling the weeds up with your hands. It's an effective method of weed control, but it can take quite a bit of time and effort, especially if you have a larger garden.

Shallow hoeing is hoeing that "fluffs" the soil on the surface. Stirrup hoes (shuffle hoes) are ideal for shallow hoeing. Shallow hoeing works on newly germinated weeds. It kills them and stirs up the weed seed in the top ½ inch (1.2 cm) of the soil. "Fluffing" the soil makes it harder for the next bunch of weed seeds to germinate.

Contact weed killers are organic herbicides that kill weeds on contact. Organic options are non-selective, however, which means they will kill any plant they touch, so you should be careful when applying them. They work best on annual weeds (the ones that complete their lifecycle in a year). They are not as effective against perennial weeds (the ones that die back seasonally but grow back in the spring), but they can weaken them after repeated applications. They typically come in liquid form, either pre-diluted or as concentrates that you need to dilute yourself. You simply need to spray a weed killer on the leaves and stems of weeds for it to work. As mentioned previously, organic contact weed killers are non-selective, and they will kill any plant they touch, so make sure none of it gets on your plants.

These are the 3 main weed management techniques. Chapter 8 will cover weed control in more detail.

Plant Growth Stages

Perhaps one of the most useful things I've learned about plants over the years is how to observe the stages of plant growth. All plants follow the same basic pattern of growth on their way to maturity, and knowing at which growth stage your plants are can help you know their needs better. Plants go through the following stages during their life cycle:

- Sprout
- Seedling
- Vegetative
- Budding
- Flowering
- Ripening

Plants start their life cycle as seeds. Depending on the type of plant, seeds can take anywhere between a few days to a few weeks to germinate and sprout. Seeds need air, water, and warmth to germinate and grow into seedlings.

As roots develop, sprouts grow into seedlings. They start growing true leaves, which look like baby versions of mature leaves. The main thing that seedlings need to grow is lots of light. If you grow seedlings indoors and they become leggy because they are not getting enough sunlight, you can get grow lights to provide more light to them. This will help them grow stronger and will help prevent legginess. Seedlings also need to be watered regularly because they can't store water for very long, so you'll need to keep the soil moist. They can also benefit from fertilizing. You can fertilize seedlings when they are at least 3 inches (7.5 cm) tall with a mild dose of liquid balanced fertilizer.

When seedlings move into the vegetative stage of their life cycle, plants focus on developing sturdy stems and green, leafy growth. From this point, plants need light, water, air, nutrients, and the right temperature to grow. You'll need to water your plants regularly and fertilize them to provide them with the nutrients they need. Regarding the right temperature, plants are divided into cool-season and warm-season crops. This will be covered in detail in plant profiles in Chapter 12. When plants are in the vegetative stage, they need nitrogen, which provides the nutrients that energize the building of new cells. You can use a balanced fertilizer at all growth stages for most plants with good results. However, you may consider using a fertilizer with a higher first number (nitrogen) during the vegetative stage.

As plants grow, they transition from the vegetative stage to the budding stage when they start shifting away from green growth toward producing buds, flowers, and then fruit. In this stage, plants need more phosphorus to help encourage budding. You might consider using a fertilizer with a higher second number (phosphorus) when plants are in the budding stage.

The next stage is flowering, and this is when buds become flowers and fruiting plants begin forming fruit where flowers grew. In this stage, nitrogen becomes less important, and plants need more potassium. Potassium is important for flowering, fruit production, and overall plant health. You may consider using a fertilizer with a higher third number (potassium) when plants are in the flowering stage.

The final stage is ripening, and this is when flowers and fruit ripen and mature. In this stage, plants no longer need added nitrogen for leafy growth because they focus their energy on finishing flowers and fruit. I would recommend that you stop fertilizing your plants in the ripening stage because when flowers and fruit are verging on full maturity, they need a week or two of just water without nutrients so that they can use up all the nutrients they have already absorbed. This process is known as flushing.

Plant Growth Stages

① Sprout
Seeds contain all the nutrients they need to germinate and grow their first pair of leaves.

② Seedling
As roots begin to develop and spread, plants need a boost of quickly absorbed, well-balanced nutrients.

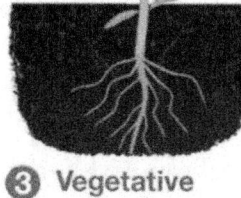

③ Vegetative
Nitrogen is most important for plants when their energy is directed into growing stems and foliage.

④ Budding
Full-grown plants need extra phosphorus during the transition to the blooming stage.

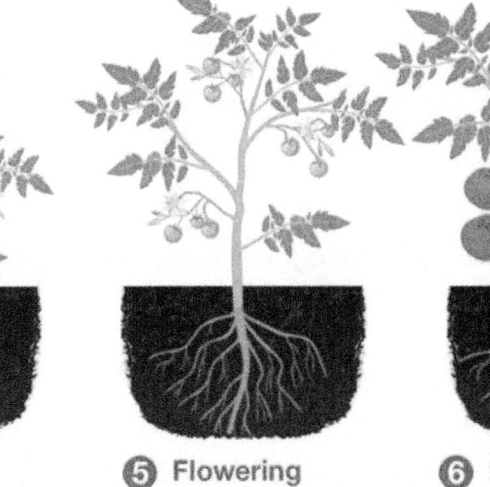

⑤ Flowering
Potassium is essential for the development of healthy flowers and fruit.

⑥ Ripening
As flowers or fruit reach full maturity, the plants no longer need nutrients--just water.

Deadheading, Pinching, and Pruning Plants

Deadheading means getting rid of a dead flower head of a plant. When flowers look brown and shriveled or have gone floppy and brown, you can pull these flowers off, or pinch the head off, or some will require you to cut the stem with some secateurs. When you deadhead plants, they will grow fuller and produce more flowers too. They will also continue to bloom for longer because they won't be wasting energy sending it to the dead parts of the plant. Also, when you deadhead a plant, you get rid of dead parts that are taking up space, so more oxygen can circulate around the plant, and more sunlight can get to the leaves when these are removed.

Pinching a plant means removing the end of the plant just above a node on the stem where the leaves are attached. When pinching a plant, you remove the end set of leaves or buds, and in response, the plant sends out two new branches (also known as lateral stems), which results in more leaves and flowers. Pinching encourages branching on plants. It works especially well with herbs because it allows them to produce more desirable stems and leaves. It can also help keep plants compact. By pinching stems, you force the plant to focus on regrowing lost stems rather than growing tall. You can pinch your plants once they have formed a few pairs of leaves on the stem. You don't need to pinch your plants often—most plants can benefit from one or two pinching sessions during the growing season.

Pruning is removing parts of plants, trees, or vines that are not essential to growth or production and are no longer visually pleasing. If you prune any dead, damaged, or diseased bits of plants, this will help them to be healthy. When you're pruning a shrub or a tree, it's advisable to use varying lengths when cutting to make it look more natural, and you should be cutting branches just above buds or where a branch unites with another.

It's worth checking the guidelines for plants because some plants prefer to be pruned in late winter or early spring, whereas others should be pruned after they have bloomed in the spring. When you go to prune your plants, don't prune them in the hottest part of the day. If you're pruning deciduous plants (plants drop their leaves at the end of every growing season), early spring is a good time for this because the cuts will have plenty of time to heal before winter.

If your plants have grown really well, but your garden beds, raised beds, or containers are overcrowded, and the plants don't have room to grow, then pruning the plants can help. It will do wonders for plants in containers because it will tidy the plants up and also encourage new bits of the plants to grow, and the plants will be bushier and more compact rather than tall and straggly.

Herbs should be given a regular trim. Some herbs will grow flowers, such as basil and cilantro (coriander). When they grow flowers, this changes the leaves and how the herb tastes. It can make herbs taste bitter, so herbs are typically harvested before they flower. A really good tip is that if you trim your herbs but don't intend to use them immediately and don't want them to go to waste, you could consider either drying them or putting them into ice cubes to use when you need them. Mint can look nice when its flowering, so you could leave a bit of this to give some nice aesthetic appearance to your garden and also attract pollinators, such as bumblebees, moths, and butterflies.

Support

As part of maintenance, you need to ensure that plants that require supports have them. There are trellises for cucumbers, raspberries, and blackberries. You can get bean wigwams, pea sticks, and obelisks for climbing plants and flowers. You can also get supporting hammocks for pumpkins, melons, watermelons, and other heavy vegetables and fruits.

Vegetables need sturdier trellises than vining flowers because they have heavy fruit. You can buy A-frame trellises—they are quite sturdy and durable. Another option is tomato cages, which are good for tomatoes, peppers, and bush squash. They can also be used for pole beans, cucumbers, and grapes. Vining plants will usually climb and wrap themselves around trellises of their own accord.

You can stake tall plants so that the wind doesn't blow them over and snap them. This works well for many vegetables, including tomatoes, eggplants, beans, peas, and more. It's best to place a stake when a plant is still young so that it can climb up the stake. You can put stakes in at the same time you are planting your plants, and you can stake plants in containers or raised beds too.

You can buy stakes made of bamboo or vinyl-coated metal in most garden centers. Push the stake into the soil beside the plant. Make sure it's not taller than the plant itself. If you're staking plants in containers, I would suggest placing the stake near the edge of the container and not in the center. This will give plants more room to grow. Once you've placed the stake, you'll need to tie your plant to the stake about ⅔ of the way up the stem, but be careful not to tie it too tight. This can damage your plant as it grows because the tie can cut into the plant's stem. Use stretchy ties to prevent this, such as special plant ties or strips of nylon. You can also use plant clips—they're easier to use than garden ties. Taller plants may need several ties at different points along the stems.

General Welfare

As mentioned previously, you will need to water and fertilize your plants regularly. You will also want to ensure that all your plants look the best they are able to by pruning and deadheading plants to get rid of dead flowers and dead or overgrown stems or branches. If plants have grown too tall (leggy) and aren't blooming, you'll need to cut them down. You'll have to take out any plants that are dead or not doing well and replace them with new plants. Most importantly, you'll need to check your plants for pests and any signs of diseases regularly. Dealing with pests and diseases will be covered in the next chapter.

Preventing Animals from Eating Plants

Depending on where you live and what wildlife comes into your garden, you may need to take action to protect your beloved plants. The most obvious choice is putting up a fence, especially if there are large animals, like deer, getting into your garden. Of course, fencing your whole lot is not always feasible or desirable, and motivated critters can find openings in any fence. But putting up a fence is an effective way to stop unwanted critters from getting into your garden.

You can spray your plants with liquids that have an offensive odor or taste, and this is perhaps the least expensive way to repel critters. There are commercial products like Deer-Off (based on eggs, hot peppers, and garlic) or Plantskydd (a blood meal solution) that you can spray directly on plants to make them unpalatable. There are also products that contain predator scents, such as coyote urine, that can be placed strategically around the yard.

You can make a homemade spray that's quite effective in my experience. Mix 1 ounce (30 ml) of hot pepper sauce (the hotter the better), 4 drops of natural dish soap, and 1 cup of aromatic leaves, such as marigolds. Put all the ingredients in a blender, add a cup or two of water, and mix until smooth. Strain the mixture to remove any solids, and put it in a spray bottle. Spray the mixture on your plants once a week, and reapply it after every rain. Make sure to label the bottle, and store it in the fridge.

Critters can often be kept at bay with scare tactics—usually a surprise burst of water or a loud noise works well. You can buy a scarecrow with a motion detector and a sprinkler that sprays water when critters cross its path. Placement is important with such products, so you might need to observe where critters come from. If you have a dog—that's great. Dogs are good at scaring away various critters.

You can also try adding plants that animals don't like—these are usually bitter-tasting or aromatic plants that have a strong fragrance. Marigolds don't need much maintenance, and they can help repel critters. Herbs, such as mint and lavender, can also help keep pests and critters away due to their taste.

Repotting Plants That Have Outgrown Their Pots

When your plants outgrow the container they're in, you'll need to put them in a bigger container, which will give more room for their roots to grow and help the plants to thrive. If you can see your plant's roots start to poke out of the drainage holes, the plant needs to be repotted as soon as possible. You can also check if a plant is root bound by removing the plant from its pot and looking at the roots. Repotting plants is essentially the same as potting up seedlings as they grow, which was covered in Chapter 5. You can refer back to that chapter to find out more about repotting your plants.

If you repot plants into containers that are typically two to two and a half times the size of the outgrown one, this may mean you won't have to repot them too often. When repotting a root-bound plant, try to loosen the roots by massaging them very gently before putting the plant into a new container with fresh potting mix and fertilizer.

Caring for Potted Plants During Winter

If you have the room, it can be a good idea to bring your potted plants inside your house over winter. You can cut them back to half their size, and they will produce new shoots. Then in the spring, you can put the containers back outside when it becomes warm again.

Hardy perennials, trees, and shrubs will not be able to survive if their roots become completely frozen. With shrubs and trees, it's a good idea to wrap some chicken wire around the pots and stuff this with mulch and straw and then place them in a garage or a basement over winter so that these plants are not killed off in the freezing conditions.

If you have terracotta or ceramic pots, these can crack during the winter. You can store empty pots that have been cleaned and sanitized in places like a garage, a cellar, or a shed to prevent these from cracking in the winter.

Each morning, I go out into my vegetable garden, and I absolutely love tending to it—it's peaceful and calm, and much of the world hasn't woken up yet. There are no phones ringing, no emails pinging, and no chatter. I love the beautiful smells coming from the flowers. I love hearing birds chirping or seeing them come down onto the fence (blackbirds are fearless and happy to be in the garden at the same time as me).

Maintaining my vegetable garden is second nature to me, and it is a part of my daily morning routine and a part of the day that I really look forward to. I make myself a cup of green tea with lemon and head out to take a walk around the garden, noticing new flowers that have bloomed and new vegetables that have started to fruit. I water the vegetables if they require it, and I pull up any weeds as I go. I check the health of the plants and ensure there are no signs of pests or diseases. I check that plants are correctly supported and encourage climbing plants with the trellises I have for them. After I've watered the plants, I take a basket and harvest any vegetables or fruits that are ready. I have them in a plastic basket that I can hose to wash off any debris before taking the produce I've harvested into the house.

Once I have watered and checked the plants, weeded the garden, and harvested vegetables and fruits, I sit at my table in the garden and finish my cup of tea, just relaxing for a few moments before heading in and putting away the harvested produce. Doing this each morning, I feel this is the best way to start my day. It's good for my physical and mental health, and I think it's more of a therapeutic experience rather than a chore. I love my garden and how it develops, and for a relatively small amount of maintenance it requires, I feel I get much more back.

Key takeaways from this chapter:

1. To maintain your garden, water it, fertilize it, remove weeds, mulch your garden beds, raised beds, and larger containers, check plant health, check your plants for any signs of pests or diseases, and ensure that plants that need supports have them.
2. You can use things like outside taps, water butts, a hose reel, or you can hook up a hose to a well to help water your garden.
3. Many variables affect how much water your vegetable garden needs, such as soil, climate, weather, the type of plants you're growing, and more.
4. Stick your finger 1 inch (2.5 cm) deep into the soil to feel the moisture. If it is dry, water it. If it feels moist, wait.
5. Too little or too much water can be damaging for plants. Check for signs if your plants are underwatered or overwatered.
6. It is best to water plants in the morning. Water your plants at the base, and don't splash the leaves.
7. If you have raised beds, drip line irrigation is ideal. You can have it on a timer, which is really convenient.
8. Water containers daily (sometimes twice a day in the hot summer months).
9. Fertilize your plants with a liquid organic fertilizer during the growing season.
10. You need to weed your garden regularly so that weeds don't compete for sun, water, and nutrients with your vegetables.
11. You can mulch your garden, raised beds, and larger containers to prevent weeds. Keep on top of weeding so that it is quick maintenance and not an onerous chore.
12. Deadhead, pinch, and prune plants so that they bloom for longer. Check pruning guidelines for when to prune plants and don't prune at the hottest part of the day. Prune back herbs—this will help make them taste less bitter after flowering.
13. Support climbing plants with trellises, canes, wigwams, obelisks, poles, and so on. This applies to peas, beans, raspberries, cucumbers, and other plants.
14. Check your plants for any signs or pests or diseases.
15. Deter animals from eating your plants.

16. Repot plants when they become too large for their containers.
17. Bring potted plants indoors over winter to stop pots cracking and plants from freezing and dying.

The next chapter will look at pest control and dealing with diseases. It will discuss various organic options to deal with pests rather than using chemical pesticides. The chapter will also look at dealing with diseases and using companion planting for pest control and disease prevention.

Chapter 7: Pest Control and Dealing with Diseases

Once you have established a wonderful vegetable garden, you want to be able to see it grow, develop, and come to fruition, and you deserve to reap the harvest of lovely, fresh vegetables filled with vitamins to help you live a healthy, sustainable lifestyle. So, naturally, the last thing you want is your crop getting eaten and damaged by pests and diseases.

To prevent your vegetables from getting damaged by pests, insects, or animals or them becoming diseased, you need to inspect your plants each week. If you have spaced your plants with plenty of room between them, this will make them less prone to fungal diseases, like powdery mildew.

This chapter will cover how you can spot common garden pests. It will discuss a wide variety of organic pest control options so that you can maintain a sustainable garden. It will show you how you can use polyculture to create diversity. It will give you information on using trap crops to control pests. This chapter will give some brief information about attracting beneficial insects to your garden to assist with pest and disease control (Chapter 9 will cover attracting beneficial insects in more detail). Also, common garden diseases will be covered as well as disease prevention. This chapter will cover how companion planting can help prevent diseases and specific companion plants for disease management. And finally, this chapter will conclude with information about crop rotation to prevent pests and diseases.

Common Garden Pests

Pests can damage your plants in a variety of ways. Some will target the roots, some may chew up the leaves, some pests feed on other pests, and some will spread diseases through plants in your garden. This section will cover some common types of pests you should look out for, and the next section will cover how you can deal with them using organic options.

Aphids

Aphids are a common garden pest. They are small, 1/16- to 1/8-inch-long (2–4 mm), pear-shaped, soft-bodied insects. They can be a variety of different colors, including green, black, red, yellow, brown, or gray.

---

[12] Image from http://www.balconycontainergardening.com/wildlife/633-tips-for-aphid-control

They attack a lot of different plants, including tomatoes, lettuce, kale, and cabbage, and they especially love fruit trees and flowering plants. They suck the sap out of stems and new leaves.

If your plants ever look yellow or brown or if they curl or wilt, do check to ensure there are no aphids on your plants. Because aphids leave behind honeydew (a sugary liquid that is released as they eat your plants), this can cause sooty mold on your plants. If your garden also has ants, this will exacerbate the aphid issue because ants and aphids work hand in hand. Ants will protect aphids because ants like honeydew. A great biological control to deal with aphids is to stop ants first, and this will be discussed in the next section of this chapter that covers dealing with pests.

Ants

Having some ants in the garden is nothing to worry about, but if there are lots of them, they might become a problem. Ants especially like containers because they can find food, water, and shelter in them. If you have other pests, such as aphids, soft scales, mealybugs, and whiteflies, ants love them because all these pests produce honeydew, which is one of their favorite things to eat. Ants often protect these pests from predators and parasites so that they can continue to produce honeydew. Dealing with ants can help reduce the abundance of honeydew-producing pests.[13]

Asparagus Beetles

These only feed on asparagus plants. So, if you're growing asparagus, it's something to look out for. If you're not, they shouldn't bother your other vegetables. They will chew asparagus spears and ferns and make the foliage go brown. It can prevent good growth the following year. Ensure that you cut down ferns and clean up fallen leaves after fall to prevent asparagus beetles from living there over winter.[14]

Birds

Birds are beautiful, and I do love them, but they can act like "pests" in the garden sometimes. They can eat your fruits and vegetables that are ripening up, and they can also pluck seeds out of the soil to eat and dig holes (probably looking for worms) in your garden, raised beds, and even containers.

---

[13] Image from https://www.gardeningknowhow.com/plant-problems/pests/insects/ants-in-flower-pots.htm

[14] Image from https://www.gardeningknowhow.com/edible/vegetables/asparagus/spotted-asparagus-beetle.htm

Cabbage Worms

These are green caterpillars that turn into yellow-white butterflies sometimes with up to 4 black spots on their wings. You will find these on cabbage, kale, cauliflower, broccoli, turnips, radishes, Brussels sprouts, and kohlrabi. They will chew holes in leaves and flowers. Birds (while they can be pests too) will eat cabbage worms.[15]

Carrot Rust Flies

Carrot rust flies are small, shiny, and black, and they have an orange head and legs. Their larvae look like tiny maggots. These can affect carrots, parsnips, celeriac, celery, and parsley. They will leave tunnels in your vegetables and scar them.

Caterpillars

Caterpillars can rampage over your garden, munching up leaves, stalks, and stems and making your plants look tatty and damaged. They often show up around late summer and early fall, and they can be a really annoying pest of fall vegetables, like cabbage, kale, collards, broccoli, and cauliflower.[16]

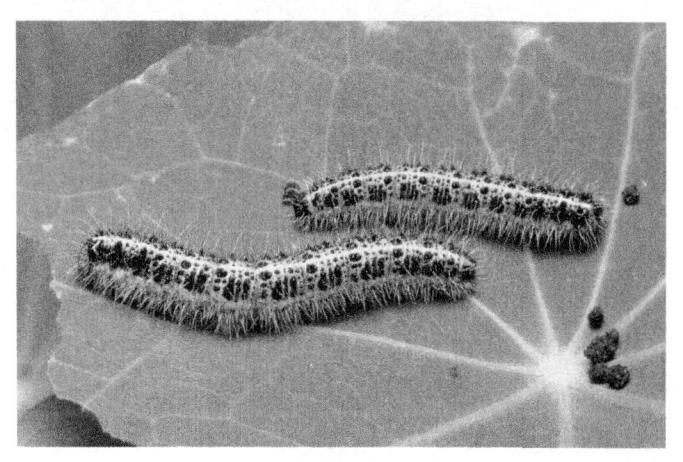

Codling Moths

If you have apple trees, you'll need to look out for codling moths. They chew and bury into apples and leave their larvae inside them. If you see a brown worm in an apple, it is probably a larva of a codling moth.[17]

Colorado Potato Beetles

These beetles are about ⅜ of an inch (1 cm) long, with a bright yellow/orange body and five bold,

---

[15] Image from https://kellogggarden.com/blog/gardening/how-to-get-rid-of-cabbage-worms/

[16] Image from https://www.nature-and-garden.com/gardening/organic-treatment-caterpillars.html

[17] Image from https://www.growveg.co.uk/pests/uk-and-europe/codling-moth/

brown stripes along the length of their bodies. They will eat tomatoes as well as potatoes and other garden crops, like peppers, tomatillos, and eggplants. They will strip the leaves of plants until they look like skeletons. They tend to eat the top of plants first.[18]

Cucumber Beetles

These beetles are yellow, have yellow wings, and they have 3 longitudinal black stripes. They'll go on melons, cucumbers, gourds, squash, and sometimes on corn, beans, beets, and other vegetables. They will make holes in leaves and can transmit bacterial wilt.[19]

Cutworms

These turn into brown or gray moths. In the caterpillar stage, they can be yellow, green, brown, or gray. They love to eat young seedlings, especially broccoli, tomatoes, cabbage, and kale.[20]

Flea Beetles

These beetles jump like fleas. They damage young plants by leaving holes in the leaves, and their larvae eat plants' roots, which can destroy a plant completely. They can be found on radishes, potatoes, tomatoes, corn, and eggplants.[21]

Leaf Miners

You can often tell that your plants have leaf miners if you see trails on the leaves. The trails wind round and may look silver or beige. They appear on vegetables, shrubs, bushes, fruit trees, and perennials. These are caused by larvae of a small dark fly. A female fly

---

[18] Image from https://uwm.edu/field-station/colorado-potato-beetle-redux/

[19] Image from https://extension.usu.edu/pests/research/cucumber-beetles

[20] Image from https://gardenerspath.com/how-to/disease-and-pests/control-cutworms/

[21] Image from https://extension.usu.edu/vegetableguide/cucumber-melon-pumpkin-squash/flea-beetles

will make little cuts in the leaf surface and lay her eggs there, and the larvae will tunnel inside the leaf just under the surface. They will feed there, and after 2–3 weeks they'll emerge as adults.

This mostly just makes the leaves of your plants look unpleasant, but if there's a lot of damage to leaves, then the plant could become weak and even die. One of the most effective ways to get rid of this is to remove infected leaves as soon as you see the trails and dispose of them. Don't add these leaves to compost. Bag them up and dispose of them in the trash.

Mealybugs

Mealybugs look like white, cottony masses that appear on the leaves, stems, and fruit of plants. They have a sucking mouthpart that draws sap out of plants. Plants will turn yellow, curl, and become weak. Mealybugs produce honeydew, which can encourage sooty mold to grow and attract ants. They attack a lot of different plants, including asparagus, beans, beets, cabbage, cucumbers, lettuce, peppers, pumpkins, tomatoes, and more.[22]

Mexican Bean Beetles

These are a common garden pest. These beetles are copper in color and have 16 black spots. Their larvae are yellow with bristly spines. They love all types of beans: green beans, pole beans, snap beans, runner beans, lima beans, and soybeans. They will eat leaves until they look like skeletons.[23]

---

[22] Image from https://wallygrow.com/blogs/feature/how-to-get-rid-of-mealybug-on-houseplants

[23] Image from https://val.vtecostudies.org/projects/lady-beetle-atlas/mexican-bean-beetle/

Pill Bugs

Pill bugs aren't really going to harm your plants, so if you see some near your plants, you shouldn't worry too much about it. However, if you see masses of them, then you may need to do something about it. There are a number of ways to get rid of pill bugs, and one way is to ensure you have food for them that is away from your garden. For example, you could have a compost pile out of the way, and this should keep pill bugs happy and away from your plants.

Pill bugs love dark and damp conditions, so they often live under debris in the garden. Cleaning up the debris from leaves, grass clippings, pieces of wood, and so on can help reduce their population. A top tip is that you can put a toilet paper tube around seedlings, and this will stop pill bugs from reaching them.[24]

Root-Knot Nematodes

Nematodes are parasite worms that burrow into roots, and this stops the roots from absorbing the necessary water and nutrients. You can check the roots of your plants by pulling out one plant and looking at the roots to see if there are little balls or knots in the roots. To treat nematodes, once you have harvested the crop, you can bring the roots out into the sun, and direct sunlight will kill nematodes. You can also put French marigold plants near plants with nematodes because French marigold roots release a chemical that is toxic to nematodes.

Slugs and Snails

These will eat plants in your garden, especially low hanging plants in the shade or where it's damp. Slugs and snails can carry lungworm, which can be dangerous to pets.[25]

They will attack any young seedlings and a great variety of plants. They will leave holes in leaves. They eat at night and love rainy days. You won't see them often throughout the day.

Spider Mites

Spider mites are very common. They're extremely small, and they have 8 legs and can be red, green,

---

[24] Image from https://www.thoughtco.com/fascinating-facts-about-pillbugs-4165294

[25] Image from https://ucanr.edu/blogs/blogcore/postdetail.cfm?postnum=46093&

yellow, or brown. They emerge in the spring and eat plants, which makes the plants weak and susceptible to diseases. They attack a lot of different plants, but they're especially attracted to strawberries, tomatoes, melons, and fruit trees. A female spider mite can lay hundreds of eggs and infestations grow really quickly. Definitely look under the leaves of plants because they will hide there. If the infestation is really bad, remove infested leaves and dispose of them in the trash. Don't add these infested leaves to your compost because the infestation could spread.

Springtails

Springtails love moisture, and they swarm together in clouds that you can see in the air. They can be brown, gray, black, or white. They like wet soil, rotting straw, decaying leaves, and other damp organic matter. They feed on mold, fungi, and algae. They are mostly a nuisance pest and won't damage plants or harm people or pets. They will chew roots in the soil where they're located, which can inhibit plant hardiness, but they rarely do significant damage. If the soil dries out, they will likely find a new home.[26]

Squash Bugs

Squash bugs feed on cucumbers, squash, melons, pumpkins, and zucchini. They suck juice from the leaves and stems of plants. Leaves damaged by squash bugs will be mottled with yellow, and they may go crispy and die.[27]

Thrips

Thrips are tiny insects—they are usually 2 millimeters in length. They attack a variety of different vegetables, including onions, beans, carrots, squash, and more. When they're young, they are pale yellow. When they're adults, they are brown or black. If your plants' leaves are looking dull or have a silver mottling, you may have thrips. If you look really close at the leaves, you may see little black dots on them.

Certain plants tend to get thrips more often, and these include onions, peas, tomatoes, cucumbers, beans, carrots, and many flowers, especially gladioli and roses. Thrips like dry and hot conditions, so if you

---

[26] Image from https://www.planetnatural.com/pest-problem-solver/houseplant-pests/springtail-control/

[27] Image from https://www.purdue.edu/hla/sites/yardandgarden/dont-let-sap-sucking-squash-bugs-get-old/

increase humidity around your plants, this can discourage them. If you get rid of dead leaves and fallen flowers off plants, this can discourage thrips too.[28]

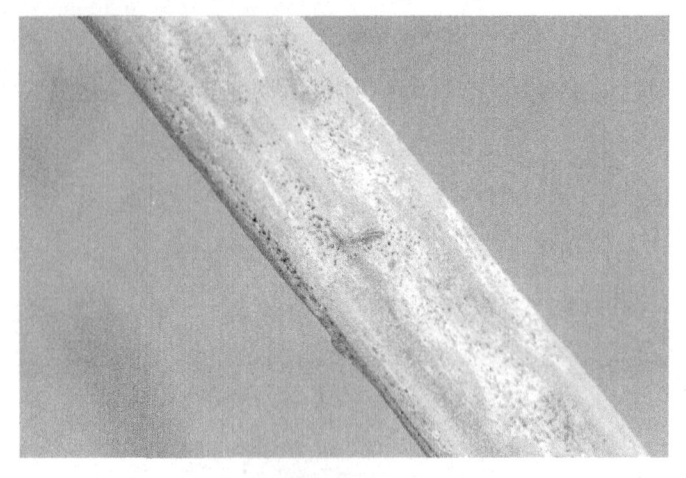

Tomato or Tobacco Hornworms

Hornworm caterpillars turn into brown or gray moths. They will attack tomatoes, potatoes, peppers, eggplants, and tobacco. They eat the leaves, usually the tops of plants, and leave dark pellets of excrement behind.

Vine Weevils

This beetle will eat the leaves of plants in the summer, and its larvae will attack the roots of plants, which can cause the plants to die. Vine weevils attack a wide variety of plants, but they are especially attracted to flowers, like cyclamen, fuchsias, polyanthus, primulas, and also strawberries.[29]

Whiteflies

Whiteflies are sap-sucking pests, and they target vegetables, such as tomatoes, eggplants, peppers, okra,

---

[28] Image from https://www.gardenersworld.com/how-to/solve-problems/thrips/

[29] Image from https://luv2garden.com/identify-and-control-black-vine-weevils/

and brassicas, as well as ornamental plants. They produce honeydew, which can lead to sooty black mold and attract ants. Look for yellow leaves and white ovals under leaves which may be whitefly eggs.[30]

Organic Pest Control Methods

Using organic pesticides is less damaging to the soil and environment rather than using chemical pesticides. Organic methods of pest control do work and can even be more effective than chemical pesticides in some cases. It was mentioned in the introduction to this chapter, but it is super important to regularly check your plants for pest damage because the sooner you identify it, the sooner it can be dealt with. A few holes in plants is nothing to worry about, but if damage is getting out of hand, you may need to do something about it.

Organic Pesticides/Sprays

You can purchase organic pesticides from garden centers to help control pests. Make sure to check the packaging carefully to make sure the spray you're purchasing is organic. They will contain *Bacillus*, which is a bacterium. They may have neem oil and copper in them too. You can also make your own organic pesticides from household products or plants. It is advisable to spray both store bought and homemade pesticides on a small part of a plant rather than the whole thing at first just to check it doesn't damage it. Also, don't spray pesticides in really hot sun because this can burn plants.

You can make sprays for pest control at home. Here are some of my favorite recipes:

Neem Oil Spray

Neem oil is typically used when you have a pest infestation, but you can spray your plants with a neem oil solution every 2–3 weeks as a preventative measure. This is good to get rid of soft-bodied insects, such as aphids, fungus gnats, whiteflies, scales, squash bugs, Colorado potato beetles, and mealybugs. Neem oil also works well for treating leaf miners. Pests won't lay eggs after being sprayed, and they will eat less and grow more slowly. Neem oil spray would sadly work on beneficial insects too, so you could spray early in the morning or late in the afternoon, and then cover your plants with a row cover to stop them from being affected. It can also prevent powdery mildew. It does have quite a strong smell. Simply follow the instructions on the label, make a spray, and spray your plants every 3–4 days until pests are gone, and reapply the solution after it rains.

Insecticidal Soap

You can buy insecticidal soap or make homemade insecticidal soap by mixing 1 tablespoon of liquid soap with a quart (0.95L) of water. Just like neem oil, insecticidal soap works well against soft-bodied insects. Simply follow the instructions on the label, make a spray, and use it to spray your plants once or twice a week until pests are gone. Don't forget to reapply it after it rains.

Chili Pepper Spray

This spray is effective against most insects and pests attacking your plants. Mix half a cup of chopped hot peppers, 2 cups of water, and 2 tablespoons of

---

[30] Image from https://www.naplesgarden.org/container-gardening-bugs-friends-or-foes/

dish soap (with no bleach). Let this sit overnight, strain it, then put it in a spray bottle and spray on plants. Spray your plants every 3–4 days until the infestation is gone. Reapply the spray after it rains.

Garlic Spray

This is great for getting rid of pest and insect infestations. You can make this out of a head of garlic, a tablespoon of dish soap (with no bleach), 2 tablespoons of vegetable oil, and 2 cups of water. Mix the ingredients together, and allow the mixture to sit overnight. Then put it in a spray bottle and spray on plants. Garlic has fungicidal effects, and it's good for getting rid of aphids, squash bugs, whiteflies, and other pests. Spray your plants every 3–4 days until pests are gone. Reapply the spray after it rains.

Oil Spray

This solution is super easy to make. It works great against aphids, mealybugs, mites, leaf miners, whiteflies, and beetle larvae. Simply mix a tablespoon of vegetable oil, 2 tablespoons of baking soda, 1 teaspoon of dish soap, and 2 quarts (1.9 L) of water. Put the mixture into a spray bottle, and spray it on affected plants. Spray as necessary until pests are gone.

Soap Spray

This will help get rid of pests and insects and will keep your plants safe. Soap spray works well against aphids, whiteflies, mealybugs, thrips, spider mites, and other soft-bodied pests and insects. It doesn't work well against larger insects, such as caterpillars, sawflies, and beetle larvae, however. Simply mix 2 teaspoons of dish soap with a quart (0.95 L) of water. The insects become dehydrated and die when you spray them with this. You will need to spray your plants every 4–7 days until pests are gone, and don't forget to reapply the solution after it rains.

Tomato Leaf Spray

Because there are alkaloids in tomato leaves, this will repel leaf eaters and aphids. You can take some leaves from the bottom part of tomato plants. It will also attract predatory insects that will eat the unwanted bugs. You can chop 2 cups of tomato leaves and let them sit in a cup of water overnight. Then strain the mixture, and add 2 more cups of water before spraying it. Use as necessary until pests are gone.

Apart from sprays, there are other organic methods to deal with pests:

Water

You can spray your plants with a hose to remove pests like aphids, spider mites, and thrips, but don't blast your plants with water because this can damage them.

Remove Pests by Hand

You can pick off some pests by hand. This is easy to do this with snails, slugs, caterpillars, Colorado potato beetles, and squash bugs. Most insects won't harm you, but you can wear rubber gloves just in case. You will need to kill the insects or place them in a plastic bag or a container with a lid that they can't escape from. Keeping your garden clean also helps prevent pests. While fallen leaves and fruits will decompose and enrich the soil with nutrients, they can also attract pests. You can clear away any dropped or fallen leaves or fruits and add them to your compost pile if they are not diseased.

Nip Off Infected or Infested Parts of Plants

One of the best organic prevention and control methods for pests and diseases is to regularly inspect your plants and physically remove any pests or diseased areas. You can nip off infected or infested leaves or buds or pull up infected crops. You can prune off parts of plants that look like they have a disease or pests.

Diatomaceous Earth (DE)

You can use a shaker to pest-proof plants with this powder. This absorbs the moisture from the bodies of insects and pests. It will work against slugs, aphids, caterpillars, and thrips. It will, however, also kill beneficial insects, so be careful with it. You can put it on the soil around your plants. If you have any leaves that show signs of an infestation, then you can put it underneath the leaves.

Exclusion

You can use exclusion methods to keep pests and diseases away from your plants by covering plants with floating row covers, which are made from lightweight spunbonded fabric. These are effective to keep away aphids, tomato hornworms, cabbage moths and worms, Colorado potato beetles, and squash bugs. If plants don't need pollinating, you can keep the covers on all the time. The fabric is generally sold in 4 or 8-foot rolls, and it comes in lightweight and heavyweight versions (for summer and fall, respectively), which also offers some frost protection.

If you live in an area where there are a lot of deer, tall fencing should keep them out. If you have trouble with rabbits, then having mesh at the bottom of your fence that goes into the ground should keep the rabbits out. If you have raised beds, you can put galvanized wire on the bottom of it, and this will keep out moles and groundhogs. You can put netting and mesh over plants to stop squirrels, birds, and deer from eating your vegetables and fruits before you do.

To protect young seedlings from being attacked by cutworms, you can put a toilet paper tube around them and bury it ½ an inch (1.2 cm) into the ground. This works well to protect cabbage seedlings from cabbage root flies and cabbage maggot flies too.

Another exclusion technique is to put abrasive strips of materials on the soil around plants, which can help repel slugs, snails, and caterpillars. You could create barriers with sawdust, wood ashes, crushed eggshells, seashells, or coffee grounds, and all of these will break down and feed the soil with time too.

You can also set up copper or steel wires around your raised beds and have 2 wires close together connected to a 9V battery to create an electric fence for slugs and snails. While this may prevent any further snails getting in, the ones that are already there will continue to eat your plants. You could put copper around your garden beds too because copper has a chemical reaction with snail and slug slime, which repels them.

Mulch helps protects plants from soil splashing on their leaves, and it will also stop pests from laying eggs on the surface of the soil.

Dealing with Ants

If you spot a lot of ants in your garden, try to find ant trails and follow them to see where they lead you. Ant trails usually lead to ant mounds, where all the ants live alongside their queen ant. You need to kill the queen ant to destroy a colony. You can pour boiling water onto the mound, and it may reach the queen through the tunnels. However, it may sometimes not work because even boiling water cools down quickly on contact with earth, or the queen may be deeper underground, and water might not reach her.

Using borax is a much more effective way of dealing with ants. Mix ½ cup sugar, 1.5 tablespoons of borax, and 1.5 cups of water. Soak some cotton balls in the mixture, and put them in places where you see lots of ants. Sugar will attract the ants, and they will take borax to their home, where they will eat it later. Eating borax will kill the ants.

If you have ants in containers, get a bucket or a tub that is larger than the container and place the container inside the bucket or tub. Make up a water solution that is two tablespoons of insecticidal soap per quart (0.95L) of water. Fill up the bucket or tub until the solution just covers the surface of the potting soil, and leave it to soak for 20 minutes.

Attracting Beneficial Insects for Pest Control

This section is just a short summary of how to attract beneficial insects to your garden to help with pest control, and this will be covered in much more detail in Chapter 9.

Ladybugs are good insects to have. They are natural predators to aphids, chinch bugs, asparagus beetle larvae, alfalfa weevils, bean thrips, grape root worms, Colorado potato beetles larvae, spider mites, whiteflies, and mealybugs, among other insects, which means they will eat them. You could grow flowers and herbs, such as cilantro (coriander), dill, fennel, caraway, yarrow, tansy, angelica, scented geraniums, coreopsis, and cosmos, to attract them.

Lacewings are great to have in your garden. In their larval stage, they look like small ½-inch (1.2 cm) alligators, and they will happily eat aphids, caterpillars, mealybugs, leafhoppers, whiteflies, and insect eggs.

You can plant cilantro (coriander), dill, yarrow, cosmos, and tansy to attract them. Hover flies are also great to have around. They may look like a small bee, but as they move through the air, they are more fly-like in their appearance. Planting dill, parsley, yarrow, caraway, and lavender will help attract them to your garden.

If you're unsure about which are good insects and which are bad, try to see whether the bugs are eating your garden or defending it by eating other insects. Look to see whether the bugs are chewing holes in your leaves or eating other bugs. You could use a folding 10x power hand lens to help you see the bugs better. If you see bugs in your garden, you can make a description of the bug and then do an Internet search on it or ask in gardening groups on Facebook or gardening forums. You need to find out if it's beneficial or harmful and attract more of the beneficial ones to your garden.

Beneficial nematodes will control soil dwelling pests. The most common ones are *Steinernema carpocapsae* and *Heterorhabditis bacteriophora*. These nematodes search for insects they can use as hosts, and they release bacteria that kill the hosts once inside. If you are suffering from carrot flies, you can release beneficial nematodes into the soil near your carrots, and they will eat the larvae. *Steinernema* is a good nematode to use. You can also use a microbial pest control agent called Bt (*Bacillus thuringiensis*). There are different types of Bt. For example, Btk (*Bacillus thuringiensis kurstaki*) is a subspecies of Bt that targets mosquitoes, fungus gnats, and black fly larvae as well as caterpillars, like cabbage worms, tomato hornworms, cabbage loopers, and gypsy moth. Bt var. san diego (*Bacillus thuringiensis var. san diego*) are used to get rid of Colorado potato beetles. Bt var. san diego has a manufacturing process that includes genetic engineering, however, so it's not approved by the National Organic Program (NOP). Bt and Btk are organic are certified for use in organic agriculture and gardening.

Companion Plants for Pest Control

Companion planting can be used for pest control, and fewer pests usually means fewer diseases. Pests make plants unhealthy by attacking them and letting diseases in. Below you will find companion plants that can help repel pests.

Basil repels asparagus beetles, carrot flies, mosquitos, and whiteflies. Basil is a great companion plant for tomatoes, peppers, root vegetables, like carrots, beets, potatoes, radishes, parsnips, and turnips, as well as asparagus, borage, chives, and oregano. Do not plant basil with cucumbers, fennel, sage, and rue.

Borage repels aphids, asparagus beetles, and tomato hornworms. Borage can be grown with virtually any plant, but it works especially well with strawberries, tomatoes, peppers, eggplants, pumpkins, zucchini, cabbage, corn, radishes, squash, beans, peas, basil, and marigolds.

Catnip repels ants, aphids, cabbage loopers, cockroaches, Colorado potato beetles, flea beetles, Japanese beetle, squash bugs, and vine weevils. You can grow catnip with almost any plant, except parsley. Catnip works especially well with beans, beets, broccoli, Brussels sprouts, cabbage, carrots, cauliflower, collard greens, cucumbers, eggplants, hyssop, lettuce, potatoes, pumpkins, radishes, squash (including winter squash), strawberries, tomatoes, turnips, and zucchini.

Chives repel aphids, carrot flies, cucumber beetles, Japanese beetles, and spider mites. They grow well with tomatoes, peppers, carrots, beets, potatoes, rhubarb, kohlrabi, parsley, broccoli, cabbage, eggplants, mustard, and strawberries, and they can also enhance their flavors and growth intensity. Do not plant chives near asparagus, peas, spinach, and beans because they will compete for the same nutrients, and avoid planting it near oregano, sage, thyme, and rosemary because they prefer drier soil, while chives prefer more moist conditions.

Cilantro (coriander) repels aphids, Colorado potato beetles, and spider mites. Cilantro (coriander) grows well with beans, asparagus, sunflowers, onions, spinach, celery, mint, sage, and alyssum. Do not plant it near carrots, dill, lavender, thyme, and rosemary.

Dill repels aphids, spider mites, and squash bugs. Plant dill with asparagus, cucumbers, corn, onions, broccoli, cabbage, Brussels sprouts, kohlrabi, and basil. Do not plant it near carrots, celery, tomatoes, potatoes, eggplants, peppers, and lavender.

Garlic repels aphids, bean beetles, fleas, Japanese beetles, potato bugs, and spider mites. Garlic pairs well with beets, cabbage, spinach, potatoes, carrots, tomatoes, fruit trees, dill, and rue. Do not plant it with beans, asparagus, strawberries, sage, parsley, and other alliums, like onions and leeks.

Horseradish repels aphids, caterpillars, Colorado potato beetles, and whiteflies. Horseradish grows well with asparagus, potatoes, sweet potatoes, rhubarb, spinach, fruit trees, and strawberries. Do not plant it with brassicas, like broccoli, Brussels sprouts, cabbage, cauliflower, kale, turnips, and others. Once you harvest brassicas, pests that they attract tend to move to horseradish if it's nearby. So, it's best to avoid planting them near horseradish.

Lavender repels bean beetles, cabbage moths, carrot flies, and ticks. Lavender is a good companion plant for alliums, rosemary, thyme, basil, oregano, yarrow, marigolds, zinnias, and roses. Do not plant it with mint, impatients, camellias, and hostas.

Marigolds are one of the best plants for pest control, and it repels most pests, including bean beetles and nematodes. Marigolds are a great companion plant, and they go well with everything, including asparagus, broccoli, kale, cabbage, lettuce, cucumbers, gourds, kale, potatoes, carrots, onions, squash, tomatoes, eggplants, pumpkins, melons, dill, and rosemary.

Mint repels ants, aphids, cabbage moths, and flea beetles. Mint grows well with tomatoes, peppers, eggplants, carrots, beets, radish, onions, beans, peas, cabbage, kale, marigolds, and roses. Do not plant it near lavender, rosemary, sage, oregano, parsley, thyme, and basil.

Nasturtiums repel ants, bean beetles, squash bugs, and striped pumpkin beetles. Just like marigolds, nasturtiums go well with everything, including tomatoes, potatoes, beans, onions, cucumbers, squash, melons, pumpkins, zucchini, broccoli, cabbage, cauliflower, kale, and spinach.

Oregano repels cabbage moths, cucumber beetles, and mosquitoes. You can plant oregano with eggplants, peppers, cucumbers, asparagus, beans, cabbage, broccoli, Brussels sprouts, cauliflower, kohlrabi, squash, turnips, rosemary, thyme, and strawberries. Do not plant it near mint, chives, basil, and cilantro (coriander).

Pennyroyal repels ants, fleas, flies, gnats, and mosquitos. You can plant it next to any plant that needs protection from pests. It's especially beneficial when planted near cabbage, kale, and cauliflower.

Rosemary repels bean beetles, cabbage moths, carrot flies, and mosquitos. You can plant rosemary near any plants in the brassica family, like cabbage, broccoli, cauliflower, kale, Brussels sprouts, turnips, kohlrabi, rutabaga, and radishes, as well as carrots, beans, chives, onions, strawberries, sage, oregano, thyme, and alyssum. Do not plant it near tomatoes, cucumbers, pumpkins, mint, and basil.

Rue repels cucumber beetles, flea beetles, and Japanese beetles. You can plant it near roses, fruit trees (especially fig trees), raspberries, and lavender. Do not plant it near cucumbers, cabbage, sage, and basil.

Sage repels bean beetles, cabbage moths, and carrot flies. Sage works well with brassicas, like broccoli, cauliflower, cabbage, Brussels sprouts, kohlrabi, and others, as well as tomatoes, carrots, collard greens, strawberries, rosemary, parsley, thyme, and oregano. Do not plant it with cucumbers, rue, and basil.

Tansy repels ants, beetles, cabbage moths, Colorado potato beetles, cutworms, flies, and squash bugs. Tansy in a great companion for most crops, including beans, cabbage, kale, broccoli, cauliflower, cucumbers, squash, corn, and potatoes.

Thyme repels cabbage moths, cabbage worms, cabbage loopers, whiteflies, tomato hornworms, and corn earworms. Thyme grows well with cabbage, potatoes, eggplants, tomatoes, shallots, strawberries, lavender, and roses. Do not plant it with basil, chives, and cilantro (coriander).

Tomatoes repel asparagus beetles. Asparagus and tomatoes make good companions because tomatoes produce solanine, which is toxic to asparagus beetles, and asparagus produces a substance that deters nematodes, which can damage tomato roots.

Using Trap Crops to Control Pests

Trap crops are plants that are used to attract pests away from your vegetable crops so that they go on the trap crops (also known as sacrificial plants) and ignore your vegetables. Trap crops are planted as a decoy to lure pests away from vegetables. While pests are feeding on trap crops, your vegetables are safe. You can plant trap crops around the perimeter of the area where your main crops are planted. Because there will be a lot of pests on trap crops, this will attract predatory insects, like ladybugs, lacewings, and parasitic wasps, and these predatory insects will eat them and restore the natural balance in the ecosystem.

Squash bugs and squash vine borers are known to cause trouble to cucurbit crops. If you're growing cucurbits, such as cucumbers, pumpkins, zucchini, squash, and so on, you can plant blue Hubbard squash as a trap crop. If you're growing 100 cucurbit plants, 6–7 blue Hubbard squash plants are enough to control squash bugs.

Radishes make a great trap crop because they grow really quickly and attract things like flea beetles away from brassicas, zucchini, and summer squash, plus they also attract beneficial insects. Nasturtiums have been mentioned a lot in this book, and that's because they make a great companion plant. They are great in a vegetable garden, and they are edible too, but they also can act as a trap crop for flea beetles and aphids. They're great around cucumbers and squash. Marigolds are excellent as a companion plant, but they also make a great trap crop. French marigolds will attract slugs, thrips, and nematodes. They also repel a lot of different pests and attract beneficial insects. Mustard plants can also be a good trap crop for brassicas. You can have stinging nettles near your garden (but not actually within a vegetable plot), and they will attract aphids away from your plants, while also attracting beneficial insects, such as ladybugs and lacewings.

You can plant trap crops around the perimeter of your garden or between the rows (which is called intercropping). If you plant around the perimeter, this is good for insects that don't fly very well, such as thrips. They'll get side-tracked by the perimeter crops and won't go into the middle of larger fields. Intercropping is better for pests that can fly well and nematodes.

In a companion garden, intercropping is a better option in most cases because you'll have a mix of plants in there. You can aim to plant 10–20% of trap crops compared to your main crop. You can plant trap crops before your main crops. You need to know what pests may attack your crop, and then you need to plant the appropriate companion plant to act as a trap crop to lure the pests away from your vegetables. You can look back at Chapter 3 for good examples of companion plants. Dill and lovage will lure hornworm larvae away from tomatoes. Horseradish and tansy will lure Colorado potato beetles away from potatoes. Marigolds will keep nematodes away from vegetables. Basil and marigolds are good to keep thrips away from garlic. Chervil will keep slugs away from vegetables. Ensure that your trap crops are kept healthy too. If you see that lots of pests have congregated on your trap crops, dispose of infested plants in the trash, and try not to let pests escape.

You need to have trap crops ready for the right time of year when you'll need them. Aphids tend to invade in May or early June, so your trap crops need to be ready then. It is best to combine trap cropping and companion planting to attract beneficial predatory insects, like lacewings and ladybugs, to feed on pests.

Using Polyculture to Create Diversity

Polycultures take the idea of companion planting one step further. Companion planting is simply planting at least one plant as a companion to another. In a polyculture, several different plants are grown together. Rather than thinking in terms of a primary crop grown with companion plants or a secondary crop, polyculture planting involves thinking about each growing area as a whole ecosystem.

From the pest management point of view, having more diverse crops increases the number of beneficial insects and pollinators, and it also brings in more natural predators, which help control pests. Plants in the same family are often attacked by the same pests, so things like crop rotation (which will be covered later in this chapter) can break up pest cycles that occur when one crop is planted continuously in the same spot. Having mixed crops can slow the buildup and spread of pests in a growing season.

Research has shown that having French marigolds in a greenhouse with short vine tomatoes reduced the number of whiteflies there. It was the limonene in the marigolds that did this. African marigolds also release thiophenes from their roots, which repel nematodes. When rosemary, lavender, and basil were planted together with peppers in a greenhouse, they were able to protect the pepper plants from aphids (Hicks-Hamblin, 2021, online).

Calendula or cosmos will attract wasps, and they will eat aphids. Garlic is a fantastic thing to plant for pest control and disease prevention. Many pests, such as aphids, onion flies, ermine moths, Japanese beetles, and many others, really dislike the smell of garlic. Garlic is perfect to plant between rows of potatoes or near lettuce, cabbage, or fruit trees. Mint is another great thing to plant to repel aphids, ants, and flea beetles. You may want to put mint in its own pot or garden area because it's invasive, which means it grows very quickly and will spread into any space it can. Nasturtiums are great to help prevent pests such as caterpillars from eating cabbage, kale, and broccoli, and they'll also keep blackflies from attacking fava beans. Sage is a great herb to plant near carrots because it repels carrot flies. You can also plant it near cabbages to prevent cabbage moths from attacking your cabbages.

If you are just starting out as a beginner and would like a nice little collection of plants to reduce the number of pests in your garden, you could plant some calendula, nasturtiums, basil, and borage. This will help repel pests and attract beneficial insects and pollinators, like bees, butterflies, and hummingbirds.

Dealing With Diseases

Diseases in plants are usually caused by fungi, bacteria, or viruses. If you have rain showers and warm temperatures, look for fungal and bacterial diseases. In the summer, look for viral diseases. Nematodes love warm weather but can impact the roots of plants all year round.

Because you'll be maintaining your garden on a daily basis, it's generally quite easy to spot if your plants are suffering from any diseases. You should try to tackle these swiftly before they become a big issue and spread.

If you buy plants from a nursery, check that they're healthy. Ensure your plants have enough water, sunlight, and enough space for air to flow around them. You can save plants from some diseases, especially if you catch them early on, but if your plants are beyond saving, you'll have to remove them and dispose of them in a plastic bag in the trash. Never put infected plants in a compost pile.

If you have been working with diseased plants, then ensure you wash your hands, tools, and gardening gloves before handling any other plants to avoid spreading diseases. If you don't live in a tropical area but are growing tropical plants, these may be more prone to diseases because they're not native to the area and haven't built up resistance to local garden pests.

Fungal Diseases

If you see that your plants are wilting, or you have noticed spots on your plants' leaves, or if you can see rotten plant stems, this could be due to a fungal disease. Fungi thrive in dark and damp conditions, so too much rainfall can cause fungal diseases in plants. To prevent fungal diseases from occurring, water your plants at the base, and make sure that plenty of air can circulate around your plants and that all your plants get a good amount of sunlight.

Fungicides are used to treat fungal diseases, although not all diseases can be treated by fungicides. You can purchase organic fungicides, such as neem oil, horticultural oil, copper, sulfur, bicarbonates, and others, from garden centers. If you use copper fungicides for an extended period of time, copper levels can build up in the soil and kill earthworms and other beneficial organisms. Neem oil fungicides affect beneficial insects, so try to use them in the evening when bees are not active. You can also make homemade organic fungicides with baking soda or apple cider vinegar.

To make fungicide with baking soda, mix 4 teaspoons of baking soda and 1 teaspoon of mild soap with a gallon (3.8L) of water. This fungicide recipe works especially well for stopping powdery mildew. Mix all the ingredients together, and put the mixture in a spray bottle. Spray all infected leaves top and bottom, and make sure to cover all the leaves with a thick layer of the mixture so that it drips off the leaves. It can be a good idea to spray the entire plant and not just infected leaves because fungus could be hiding where you can't see it.

To make apple cider vinegar fungicide, mix 4 tablespoons of apple cider vinegar with a gallon (3.8L) of water. This simple recipe has helped me save dozens, if not hundreds, of plants. Try to spray this mixture early in the day so that the sun and acid don't burn your plants. This also works well as a preventative spray. You can spray it every 2–3 weeks just in case.

You can also mix 1 quart (0.95L) of warm water, 1 teaspoon of mouthwash, and 1 tablespoon of hydrogen peroxide to make another good homemade fungicide. Mix all the ingredients together, and spray your plants until the fungus is gone.

Below you will find a list of fungal diseases and their symptoms:

Anthracnose

This fungal disease attacks tree leaves and garden vegetables, including beans, tomatoes, cucumbers, spinach, and watermelons. It is caused by a fungus and cool, wet weather. If your plants have anthracnose, their leaves will have black, tan, or red spots as well as lesions, and the leaves may become yellow and drop off. This is a fungal disease that tends to happen in late spring and early summer. Remove infected leaves, and collect and destroy any fallen leaves. Thin your plants so that air can circulate around them. You can spray the leaves with a copper or neem oil fungicide too.[31]

Black Spot

Black spot displays itself as black spots on leaves that go yellow and then die. If plants are in the shade and too close together, this can cause this fungal disease. To prevent black spot, ensure your plants have plenty of space so that air can circulate around them. Also, make sure you water your plants at the base, get rid of infected leaves, and spray them with a sulfur, copper, or neem oil fungicide if you notice this. Homemade baking soda fungicide works well against black spot too.[32]

Blight

Blight refers to a specific symptom affecting plants in response to infection by a pathogenic organism. It is caused by fungi, which survive on infected plants or in plant debris. This can impact tomatoes, potatoes, and eggplants. There will be dark spots at the soil level of plants that will climb up toward the leaves of plants.

---

[31] Image from https://www.gardentech.com/disease/anthracnose

[32] Image from https://www.gardentech.com/disease/black-spot

If your plants have blight, act quickly to prevent it from spreading. Remove all affected leaves and burn them, or put them in a plastic bag and dispose of them in the trash. Blight is difficult to treat once it's established, but you can spray your plants with a copper fungicide in early stages of the disease.[33]

Clubroot

This is a soilborne fungal disease that can attack broccoli, cauliflower, cabbage, Brussels sprouts, radishes, and turnips. Plants don't grow well when they have it, and if you pull them up, they will have bulky roots. Leaves may go yellow and drop.

Fungicides will not treat clubroot, and once it's in the soil, it can stay there for 20 years. It only attacks most brassicas, so you can rotate crops to get rid of it.

Clubroot prefers acidic soil, so you can amend the pH level of your soil by adding hydrated lime, which will make the soil less acidic (increase its pH level). Determining the amounts of lime you need can be quite complicated, but your local garden center should be able to help you with that.[34]

Damping Off

This is a soilborne fungal disease that kills seedlings. Their stems and roots will rot if they have damping off, and healthy-looking seedlings can just keel over and die. It mostly happens when starting seeds indoors. There is no cure for plants that already have damping off. However, you can reduce the chances of it happening it by starting seeds in fresh, soilless seed starting mix. Having proper ventilation also helps avoid damping off. A small fan or simply cracking the lid of your seed starting tray will suffice.

Downy Mildew

Downy mildew is an umbrella term for a large number of plant diseases. It is caused by a fungus-like organism called oomycetes or water molds. By the time plants show symptoms, it is already too late, so prevention is key.

This disease likes damp and cold conditions. It spreads through air and water splashing soil onto plants. Different plants can have different symptoms; however, one common symptom is yellow spots on the upper leaf surface between the leaf veins. These spots spread everywhere except the veins and eventually turn brown. Plants cannot photosynthesize on these yellow or brown spots, and when a leaf becomes

---

[33] Image from https://www.planetnatural.com/pest-problem-solver/plant-disease/early-blight/

[34] Image from https://ucanr.edu/blogs/blogcore/postdetail.cfm?postnum=42974

totally brown, it drops. If a plant loses too many leaves, it will die.[35]

Preventing downy mildew is much easier than controlling it. Water your plants at the base, and make sure they have good air circulation around them. Downy mildew spores overwinter in plant debris. After your crops are done, rake up all leaves and plant debris and dispose of them to help prevent the disease.

If your plants are seriously damaged, remove them and dispose of them in the trash. You can use copper or neem oil fungicides to control downy mildew in early stages. Homemade baking soda fungicide works well against downy mildew too.

Gray Mold

This fungal disease is also known as botrytis blight. If your plants or their fruit appear to be misshapen and have gray fungal spores, this may be due to gray mold. Gray mold causes a dark brown to black blight of flowers, buds, leaves, and stems. Wounded and old plant tissue and flowers are easily infected by gray mold. Gray mold thrives in cool and wet conditions. However, many flowering plants can recover from gray mold when warm, dry conditions return.[36]

The best way to prevent gray mold is to space out plants so that they have good air circulation around them and can dry out after rain or watering. You need to remove infected fruit, flowers, stems, or leaves from the plant and dispose of them, and if need be, thin out the plants so that plenty of air can circulate around them. You can use fungicides to control gray mold. Mycostop is an organic fungicide that works well against gray mold.

Powdery Mildew

Powdery mildew is a fungal disease that affects a wide variety of plants. There are many different species of powdery mildew, and each species attacks different plants. Plants that are commonly affected by powdery mildew include cucurbits (squash, pumpkins,

---

[35] Image from https://www.planetnatural.com/pest-problem-solver/plant-disease/downy-mildew/

[36] Image from https://www.planetnatural.com/pest-problem-solver/plant-disease/gray-mold/

cucumbers, melons), nightshades (tomatoes, eggplants, peppers), legumes (beans, peas), and roses.

Plants infected with powdery mildew look as if they have been dusted with flour. This disease usually starts off as circular, powdery white spots, which can appear on leaves, stems, and sometimes fruit. It usually covers the upper part of leaves.

To help prevent powdery mildew, water your plants from the base, and make sure they get enough sunlight and plenty of air can circulate around them. You can protect plants from powdery mildew by making a spray with 1 part milk and 2–3 parts water and spraying it on your plants every 10–14 days. This works especially well on cucumbers, zucchini, and melons.

If your plants have powdery mildew, you should remove all infected leaves, stems, and fruit and dispose of them. There are a few organic fungicides that work well against powdery mildew, including sulfur, lime-sulfur, neem oil, and potassium bicarbonate. Homemade baking soda fungicide works well too.

Rust

Rust is a common fungal disease spread by wind in wet conditions. Spores land on plants and breed. Plants that can be affected by rust include potatoes, sweet potatoes, carrots, onions, beans, peas, corn, eggplants, okra, artichokes, and asparagus. Plants affected by rust disease will have rust-like spots on their leaves.[37]

This strips the nutrients out of plants and stunts their growth. It thrives in the summer when it's warm and humid. If your plants have rust, remove all infected parts and dispose of them. Also, clean away all debris in between plants to prevent rust from

---

[37] Image from https://www.planetnatural.com/pest-problem-solver/plant-disease/common-rust/

spreading. There are a lot of organic fungicides that can treat rust, so you can ask your local nursery what they have in stock. Neem oil fungicides work well against rust. Homemade baking soda fungicide works well too.

Verticillium Wilt

Verticillium wilt is a soilborne fungal disease that enters plants through the roots. Plants' leaves will discolor and curl, then wilt, and plants may die when they have this. It can impact tomatoes, peppers, eggplants, cucumbers, pumpkins, and potatoes.

Verticillium wilt can be spread in contaminated soil, so if you suspect your plants might have it, be careful not to spread the soil from around the affected plants on tools or muddy boots. Weed control is important for prevention of this disease because some weeds are hosts, and in some cases, they will not show any visible signs of infection. There is no effective treatment for verticillium wilt. You will have to remove and dispose of infected plants. The best protection against verticillium wilt is growing plants with resistance or immunity to the disease.[38]

Bacterial Diseases

Plants are typically resistant to bacterial diseases. If your plants are healthy, they shouldn't get bacterial diseases. If pests have attacked plants' leaves or stems, then this could allow bacteria to enter and cause rot in the plants, and the plants may look slimy. There are no treatments for most bacterial diseases, so it is best to get rid of infected plants if this occurs and disinfect gardening tools to stop the bacteria from spreading.

Here is a list of bacterial diseases and their symptoms:

Bacterial Leaf Spot

Bacteria can get into the leaves of your plants and cause spots on the leaves, discoloration, and can cause leaves to die. Bacterial leaf spot spreads in warm and wet conditions. Some of the plants commonly affected by this are lettuce, beets, eggplants, and peppers. You can pick off infected leaves, but if a plant has been systemically infected, you'll need to remove it and dispose of it in the trash. There are no treatments for bacterial leaf spot, but you can use copper fungicides to control the disease in early stages. Baking soda and

---

[38] Image from https://content.ces.ncsu.edu/verticillium-wilt-of-tomato-and-eggplant

neem oil fungicides will work too. Remove plant debris, and do not plant new crops where host plants were once growing.[39]

Bacterial Soft Rot

Bacterial soft rots are a group of diseases that cause more crop loss worldwide than any other bacterial disease. Bacterial soft rots affect a wide variety of plants, including lettuce, brassicas, cucurbits, tomatoes, peppers, potatoes, carrots, herbs, and more. Symptoms include wet, slimy, soft rot that affects all parts of vegetable crops, including heads, curds, edible roots, stems, and leaves. There is no treatment for bacterial soft rot. If your plants have this, immediately remove all infected plants or plant parts and dispose of them.[40]

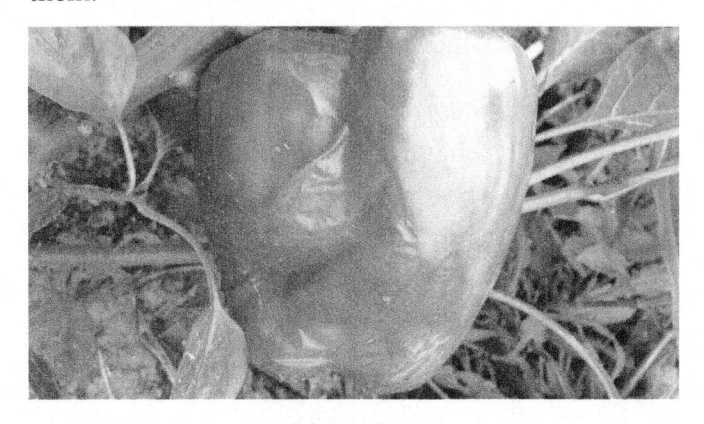

Black Rot

Black rot is a potentially lethal bacterial disease that affects most brassicas. Symptoms include light-brown or yellow V-shaped lesions on leaves, and the leaves become brittle and dry with age. This disease thrives in warm and wet conditions. There are no treatments for black rot, but you can use copper fungicides to control the disease in early stages. You can remove infected leaves, but if a plant has been systemically infected, you'll need to remove the whole plant and dispose of it.[41]

Viral Diseases

Viral diseases are spread by insects, and you may notice yellow leaves that twist, crinkle, and then die. There is no treatment for viral diseases, so the best solution is to pull up infected plants, bag them up, and dispose of them in the trash. Viral diseases are spread by pests, so pest control is key to prevention. Make sure to weed your garden regularly too because some weeds can be hosts for viral diseases.

Below is a list of viral diseases and their symptoms:

Mosaic Virus

Mosaic viruses are a group of viral diseases that are spread by aphids. There are a lot of different varieties of this virus that affect different plants, for example, cucumber mosaic virus, bean common mosaic virus, potato mosaic virus, and others. It can affect brassicas, cucurbits, beans, potatoes, tomatoes, peppers, celery, and other plants. If your plants have this, their leaves

---

[39] Image from https://www.gardeningknowhow.com/plant-problems/disease/bacterial-leaf-spot.htm
[40] Image from https://www.growingproduce.com/vegetables/more-vegetables/take-hard-line-bacterial-soft-rot-pepper/
[41] Image from https://ag.umass.edu/vegetable/fact-sheets/Brassicas-black-rot

may curl, they won't grow well, and you won't get a bountiful harvest.[42]

There is no treatment for mosaic virus, so you'll need to remove and dispose of any infected plants, including the roots, and also any plants near those affected. Since mosaic viruses are spread by aphids, pest control is key to prevention. Weeds can be hosts for mosaic viruses, so make sure to stay on top of weed control. You can also plant virus-resistant plant varieties in your garden.

Tobacco Mosaic Virus

Tobacco mosaic virus is a tobamovirus. Other tobamoviruses include tomato mosaic virus and pepper mild mottle virus. Tobamoviruses are not transmitted by insects. They are highly infectious and very stable in the environment. They can survive on plants, root debris, seeds, tools, and contaminated clothing, which means they can be transmitted by a gardener who has touched an infected plant. It can affect eggplants, tomatoes, bok choy, bitter melon, long melon, Chinese mustard, snake beans, and Chinese cabbage. Symptoms include leaves having a mosaic pattern on them, mottling, leaf distortion, and sometimes leaves may die and fall off infected plants.

If your plants have this, remove and dispose of them. Burn them if you can, or double bag them and dispose of them in the trash. To help prevent this virus, do not smoke and handle plants or allow tobacco products near the garden. If you notice your plants have this, avoid handling other plants, remove and dispose of infected plants as soon as possible, wash your hands, sanitize your tools, wash your clothes, take a shower, and change your clothes before handling other plants.

Tomato Spotted Wilt Virus

This virus is spread by thrips. It can affect peppers, tomatoes, eggplants, lettuce, celery, peas, potatoes, and sweet basil. Plants infected with this will have bronzing of the upper sides of young leaves, which later develop distinct necrotic spots. Other symptoms include ring spots, line patterns, mottling, and chlorotic blotches on leaves. If your plants have this, remove and dispose of them. Make sure to control thrips and weeds to help prevent it from happening in the future.

Other Diseases

Some diseases can be caused by environmental factors, such as drought, freezing, and other stressors. One of the most common diseases of this type is blossom-end rot.

Blossom-End Rot

Blossom-end rot is an environmental problem, which is typically caused by uneven watering or

---

[42] Image from https://www.planetnatural.com/pest-problem-solver/plant-disease/mosaic-virus/

calcium deficiency. This can mean your tomatoes, peppers, eggplants, or cucumbers have rotten bottoms. Blossom end rot will not spread from plant to plant. To prevent blossom end rot, try to keep your soil evenly moist, and add bone meal or oyster shells to your soil to enrich it with calcium.[43]

Disease Prevention

Prevention is better than cure, and that's true with plant health as well. Below are some things you can do to help prevent diseases in your garden:

1. Water plants at the base, and avoid splashing water on leaves or splashing soil on plants. Water plants in the morning to allow any water splashes to dry. This will help prevent fungal diseases.
2. Ensure your plants have sufficient airflow around them and get a good amount of sunlight. If the environment around plants is dark and moist, this is an ideal breeding ground for diseases.
3. Clear any weeds or dead plants because they can house pests and diseases. If you notice any leaves are diseased, remove them and dispose of them in the trash. Do not put them in compost.
4. Wash your hands and tools in between tending to different crops so that you don't spread diseases like the mosaic virus unknowingly.
5. If you think you have experienced damping off with seedlings, then get rid of the soil they were grown in and start again with fresh, soilless seed starting mix.
6. Check any plants you purchase for signs of diseases before you plant them in your garden.
7. Purchase good quality plants and seeds from reputable suppliers that look healthy (and not spindly).
8. You can also purchase disease-resistant varieties of plants. The seed catalog will generally let you know which varieties are disease resistant. Sometimes when you buy disease-resistant plants, they will have abbreviations such as F2 or F3, which means Fusarium resistance. N stands for nematode resistance. AB means resistant to early blight, and LB means resistant to late blight. PB is resistant to powdery mildew, and DM resistant to downy mildew. A means anthracnose resistant. S means scab resistant. BMV is bean mosaic virus resistant.
9. Rotate crops (put your crops in different parts of the garden each year), and avoid rotating plants from the same family, for example, tomatoes, eggplants, and peppers or cabbage, broccoli, and cauliflower.
10. Don't put your plants out too early if it's still cold. They won't grow as well and may be more prone to pests and diseases.

---

[43] Image from https://morningchores.com/blossom-end-rot/

11. Mulch your garden, raised beds, or larger containers because this will prevent soil from splashing onto the plants. It will also help retain moisture and reduce weeds.
12. Try to prevent pests from damaging your plants because disease-causing organisms can get inside plants through holes and cuts and infect them.

Companion Plants for Disease Management

As we now know, companion planting is about growing certain plants near each other so that plants are healthier and can produce a better yield. They can support each other physically with shade or actual support to grow up like a trellis, and they can enrich the soil with nutrients. They can help one another in many ways, and one of them is controlling pests and diseases.

Herbs are excellent companion plants because they help repel pests, which can spread diseases and also damage your plants and make them more vulnerable to diseases.

As mentioned previously, asparagus and tomatoes make good companions because tomatoes produce solanine, which is toxic to asparagus beetles, and asparagus produces a substance that deters nematodes, which can damage tomato roots.

Planting garlic, onions, borage, and horseradish among your vegetables can help make them more disease resistant. Garlic contains sulfur, which is a naturally occurring fungicide. If you plant chives near apple trees, they will prevent scab, and if you plant them near rose bushes, they will help prevent black spot. If you put onions with strawberries, it will make strawberries more disease resistant. Borage is good for preventing diseases with strawberries and tomatoes. Horseradish makes potatoes more disease resistant and also repels Colorado potato beetles. Putting chamomile next to any plants or shrubs that are ailing may help heal them, as they are naturally anti-fungal.

Using Crop Rotation to Prevent Pests and Diseases

Crop rotation means planting different crops sequentially on the same plot of land, and it helps improve soil health, optimize nutrients in the soil as well as combat pests and weeds. By rotating crops, you can also prevent the buildup of large populations of soilborne pathogens. If you kept the same crop in the soil year after year (a monoculture), the pathogens would build up, and you would have a lot of losses to your crop. Growing the same crop year after year in the same soil allows pests and diseases to get really well established there. It would also deplete the soil of the nutrients that type of crop needs. Planting crops year after year would mean that they would grow slowly and be not as healthy, and you'd get less yield from them.

But if you change your crops to something that isn't a host for that soilborne pathogen, the pathogen will die out, and you'll get a better yield come harvest time. Many soil pathogens die out after a few years if there are no suitable hosts, so rotating crops can help eliminate pathogens in the soil.

It's not a good idea to rotate crops that belong to the same family, as they are often affected by the same pathogens. For example, broccoli, cabbage, turnips, and mustard are all part of the brassica family, so do not rotate these because it won't help reduce pathogens in the soil. Your vegetables would be more prone to black rot, fusarium wilt, and clubroot.

Some pathogens, such as *Rhizoctoinia solani*, *Sclerotium rolfsii*, and *Pythium* species, attack a lot of different vegetables, so if you suspect you have these pathogens in your soil, it would be best to include small grains in your crop rotation.

If you're growing potatoes and they got potato rot, this will also affect other plants in the nightshade family, such as eggplants, tomatoes, and peppers. If your potatoes were impacted by Colorado potato beetles and you planted potatoes there for another year, the beetles would multiply and lay even more eggs. Whereas if you planted a completely different plant from a different family in there, potato beetles would die off and you'd stop that cycle.

Some pests will stay in the soil for 5 years or more, so rotating crops isn't going to get rid of them. Clubroot spores can stay in the soil for up to 20 years, and white rot (which affects alliums) can survive for up to 40 years. It's good practice to rotate crops, and this can act as a preventative measure for some pests that are poor fliers, like carrot rust flies and flea beetles. It's best if you can pick a site that is downwind from the previous crop location too. If you plant things like carrots after early June, that is after the mating cycle of carrot rust flies, which means there will be a lot of them, but since they are poor fliers, planting downwind can help protect your crop.

Even though crop rotation won't eliminate all pathogens and prevent all diseases, it's still a good method of disease prevention and managing soil fertility. It does take a bit of planning and organizing, but it is well worth it. When you rotate crops, different crops improve the soil and give it nutrients that other plants can use, such as legumes fixing nitrogen in the soil. A full crop rotation cycle lasts 3 to 4 years. Do not plant an area with crops from the same plant family before that cycle is up. You can plan out your crop rotation cycle and keep track of this in a garden journal with a sketch as to your current year and next year's planting. I have created a garden journal that will help you keep all the important information about your garden and plants in one convenient place. If you'd like to find out more about it, please check page 5 of this book.

We had an infestation of ants in our vegetable garden, and we also had aphids. They often go hand in hand because ants like honeydew that is left from aphids sucking the sap out of leaves and stems. Ants can damage things like corn, cucumbers, watermelons, potatoes, and okra. First, we sprayed plants that had aphids on them with a hose to remove them. Then we made a neem oil spray to spray on plants infested by aphids. We knew that once the aphids are gone, the ants would go too. We sprayed the infested plants every 3–4 days for a few weeks, just to be sure we dealt with the infestation, and aphids indeed disappeared. Shortly after, ants were gone too.

Key takeaways from this chapter:

1. Common pests include aphids, caterpillars, carrot rust flies, codling moths, Colorado potato beetles, Mexican bean beetles, slugs, snails, tomato or tobacco hornworms, and whiteflies.
2. You can make organic sprays to repel pests with chili peppers, garlic, neem oil, vegetable oil, and soap.

3. There are repellant plants that repel pests with their small flowers, such as garlic, onions, leeks, sage, rosemary, tansy, and nasturtiums.
4. You can nip off leaves and buds that show evidence of pests and/or diseases and dispose of them in the trash. You can also pick off pests by hand.
5. You can cover plants with floating row covers, netting, or mesh and have barriers, such as sawdust, wood shavings, or eggshells, to keep pests away from your plants.
6. Some insects, such as ladybugs and lacewings, are natural predators to pests and will eat them. You can attract predatory insects by planting flowers and flowering herbs.
7. You can use polyculture to attract beneficial insects and pollinators.
8. You can plant trap crops around the perimeter of the area where your crops are planted, or you can plant them between the rows of vegetables, which is called intercropping. Some examples of traps crops include radishes, horseradish, dill, marigolds, and nasturtiums.
9. Plant diseases can be caused by fungi, bacteria, or viruses.
10. To prevent diseases, water your plants at the base, and avoid getting water on the leaves or splashing them with soil. You can thin your crops out to improve air circulation. If your plants have signs of diseases, you may need to remove and dispose of diseased parts, like leaves, or sometimes whole plants. Check plants from nurseries before buying them. Buy disease-resistant plant seeds. You will find code letters on them that indicate which diseases they are resistant to.
11. You can use companion planting to help repel pests and improve the disease resistance of your plants.
12. Avoid planting potatoes and tomatoes together because they are prone to blight.
13. You can do crop rotation to reduce pests and pathogens in the soil. Don't rotate crops of the same family. If you plant crops from different families every year, pathogens in the soil will die off because they won't have any suitable hosts.

The next chapter will look at weed management in the garden. It will cover organic options for weed control, how you can use mulch to control weeds, and finally, how companion planting can help with weed management.

Chapter 8: Weed Control

At the start of spring, I think most gardeners promise themselves they'll keep on top of the garden and weeds in particular. But weed management takes a lot of work, and there are always things to do in the garden, and life has a way of getting in the way of gardening plans.

Weeds are plants that interfere with your crops. For example, if you're growing beets and the area has lots of dandelions, they will be taking space and nutrients from your beets, so you'll want to remove them. But if dandelions are not growing near your vegetables, you can view them as a flower that will help attract pollinators, and it's not such an issue.

When you have weeds, your crops won't produce such a good yield because weeds compete against your plants for water, light, nutrients, and space. Weeds are taking up all the good stuff and taking it away from your vegetables. Weeds can also be hosts to diseases and provide shelter to pests. Pulling up weeds gives you some good exercise and will help your plants thrive. This chapter will cover organic weed control options, using mulch to control weeds, and using companion planting for weed management.

Organic Weed Control Methods

When you try to control weeds organically, it is more about preventing weeds rather than treating them. Organic gardening tries to create healthy soil for your whole garden. When your soil and plants are healthy, there is less opportunity for weeds to grow.

Organic options for weed control include hand weeding, shallow hoeing, and contact weed killers.

Hand weeding means simply pulling the weeds up with your hands. It's an effective method of weed control, but it can take quite a bit of time and effort, especially if you have a larger garden.

Shallow hoeing is hoeing that "fluffs" the soil on the surface. Stirrup hoes (shuffle hoes) are ideal for shallow hoeing. Shallow hoeing works on newly germinated weeds. It kills them and stirs up the weed seeds in the top ½ inch (1.2 cm) of soil. "Fluffing" the soil makes it harder for the next bunch of weed seeds to germinate.

Contact weed killers are organic herbicides that kill weeds on contact. Organic options are non-selective, which means they will kill any plant they touch, so you should be careful when applying them. They can also damage lawn grass. They work best on annual weeds (the ones that complete their lifecycle in a year). They are not as effective against perennial weeds (the ones that die back seasonally but grow back in the spring), but they can weaken them after repeated applications. They typically come in liquid form, either pre-diluted or as concentrates that you need to dilute yourself. You simply need to spray weed killers on the leaves and stems of weeds for them to work. Since organic contact weed killers are non-selective, they will kill any plant they touch, so make sure none of it gets on your plants.

You can make an organic herbicide at home using vinegar, salt, and dish soap. To make it, mix 1 gallon (3.8L) of vinegar, 1 cup of salt, and 1 tablespoon of dish soap. The acidity in the vinegar destroys the cells of plants, the salt attacks the tissue, and the soap helps this mixture to stick to the plant. Like all organic herbicides, it is non-selective, which means it will kill all plants, not just weeds. It can also damage lawn grass. So, be careful when spraying it, and make sure it only gets on weeds.

Here are some more things you can do to control weeds organically:

1. **Don't give weeds room to grow.** If you have chosen disease-resistant plants, you can safely plant these closer together and make no room for weeds. You can use plants of varying height, and taller plants will shade the soil, which means weeds will get less sunlight. You can also use plants that cover the soil, such as pumpkins or squash.

2. **Crop rotation can be used for weed control.** Crop rotation was covered in the previous chapter, and it can be used to break weed cycles. By rotating your crops, you're reducing the likelihood that specific weeds will become adapted to the growing environment and become problematic. You can also use cover cops at times when the soil would otherwise be bare.

3. **Don't let weeds flower.** Remove them before they manage to spread any of their seeds.

4. **Use a flame torch.** Another way to kill weeds is using a flame torch, but you need to be careful not to damage other plants or lawn if you do this. If you have weeds that are growing in the cracks of a patio or a driveway, this technique can be useful. You could opt to use boiling water too.

5. **Use allelopathy to combat weeds.** This is where plants release chemicals from their roots that stunt the growth of other plants. If you choose allelopathic crops in places where you have weeds, these will stunt the growth of the weeds. Crops that have allelopathic properties include barley, oat, wheat, rye, canola, mustard species, buckwheat, red clover, white clover, sweet clover, hairy vetch, creeping red fescue, tall fescue, and perennial ryegrass. These crops are often used as cover crops, and they may suppress weeds in subsequent crops.

Using Mulch to Control Weeds

Mulching means covering the soil with a layer of mulch, which is any material that is spread or laid over the surface of the soil and used for a covering. Mulching helps retain moisture in the soil, reduce weeds, keep the soil and plants' roots cool, and make garden beds, raised beds, and containers look more attractive.

You can use different materials for mulching. Some are more aesthetically pleasing than others, while others are more functional and can add nutrients to the soil. There are two categories of mulch: organic and inorganic, and both have their advantages and disadvantages. Organic mulch is made of natural materials. It will decompose over time and add beneficial nutrients to your soil. It can reduce weeds, but it doesn't always fully block weeds. Inorganic mulch is made of synthetic materials. It can fully block weeds, and it's better at retaining moisture than organic mulch, but it won't add nutrients to the soil. No-dig gardening uses organic mulch.

Organic mulch materials include compost, shredded leaves, wood chips, pine needles, straw, grass clippings, newspapers, peat moss, and coconut coir. As mentioned previously, organic mulch will decompose, so it will need to be replaced after some time. But while it's decomposing, it will add nutrients to the soil as well as help improve the soil structure, texture, and drainage. The drier and woodier the mulch, the slower it will decompose and the fewer nutrients it will give to the soil.

I personally like using compost, shredded leaves, and coconut coir for mulching. Compost is one of the best materials for mulching, and it is commonly used in no-dig gardening. It will break down over time and provide beneficial nutrients to the soil and improve its structure, texture, and drainage. Shredded leaves are great for mulching too, and they are essentially free. Coconut coir is affordable and can last a long time. It also breaks down and improves the soil quality over time.

If you decide to use pine needles, keep in mind they can reduce the pH level of the soil and make it slightly more acidic, but usually not enough to cause any problems to plants. Also, make sure to use needles that have been dried, or they can rot and cause mold to grow otherwise. Most newspapers should be fine to use for mulching because they use soy-based black inks and hydrogen peroxide for bleaching pulp. But don't use glossy magazines or newspapers with colored or glossy inks because they may contain chemicals that are toxic to plants.

Inorganic mulch materials include plastic or landscape fabric and gravel or stone. Inorganic mulch materials are good at holding in moisture and blocking weeds. Since they don't decompose, they don't add any nutrients to the soil, but at the same time they don't need to be replaced as often as organic mulches.

You can mulch in-ground gardens, raised beds, and larger containers. You can't mulch small containers because you need to leave some space at the base of plants. You can mulch containers that are at least a gallon (3.8 L) in volume. Don't add mulch if you've just planted the seeds. The best time to mulch your garden or containers is when the seedlings are at least 3–5 inches (7.5–12.5 cm) tall.

To mulch your garden, simply place your chosen mulch material on the soil, but keep it 3 inches (7.5 cm) away from the base of plants. For trees, leave a 1-foot (30 cm) open ring of space around the tree trunk or 4 to 6 inches (10–15 cm) from each side. Make sure the mulch is dry, and it should be in small pieces. Mulch should be placed on top of the soil but not in it because this will prevent your plants' roots from getting enough water, air, and nutrients they need for healthy growth. You would typically need a 2–3-inch (5–7.5 cm) layer of mulch for in-ground gardens and raised beds. For containers, a 2-inch (5 cm) layer is sufficient. Make sure the mulch doesn't touch the leaves of your plants because this can spread diseases.

When you water mulched garden beds, raised beds, or containers, aim the water at the base of plants. Drip irrigation works great with mulched gardens. When watering mulched containers, you might need to separate the mulch from the base of plants before watering to avoid watering the mulch. If you pour water directly on the mulch, it may lead to water retention and root rot. After watering your containers, you need to put the mulch back on the potting soil. You can use drip irrigation in mulched containers, and you don't need to remove the mulch when using it because it drips water into the potting soil over time and won't soak the mulch.

If you're going to grow cover crops, you should remove mulch when the growing season ends.

However, if you're not planning to grow cover crops, you can leave it and let it decompose and enrich your soil. Organic mulches can last up to 5–6 years. When mulch seems to be too dry and brittle, you'll need to remove it and replace it with fresh material. If mulch becomes too compacted and starts blocking water flow to the roots, again, you'll need to replace it. If you notice any fungi or any signs of diseases on your plants, you'll need to remove your mulch, bag it up, and dispose of it in the trash. Some pests can use mulch as shelter, and if you notice pests in mulched areas of your garden, you can turn the mulch with a rake or spray it with an organic pesticide. If that doesn't help, you'll need to replace it.

Using Companion Planting for Weed Control

Companion planting can really help with weed management in a variety of ways. If you companion plant your vegetables with herbs, flowers, or other vegetables, weeds won't have as much room to grow because there are plants occupying the available space already. Mint is really invasive, but you can use that to your advantage. Its roots, properly called rhizomes, run underground and can send up shoots many feet away from the mother plant. It lies low to the ground and spreads, which helps prevent weeds from growing, and it smells fantastic too.

You can plant plants of varying heights, using layers to fill space. The Three Sisters planting method, which involves planting corn, pole beans, and squash together, is a great example of using plants of varying heights. Corn creates shade and provides support for beans, which means weeds will get less sunlight, and squash has big leaves that cover the ground, which further robs weeds of access to sunlight.

You can grow cover crops over winter or when you're not using your garden to grow vegetables, which will prevent weeds from growing and give the soil some nutrients. You can use crop rotation to break weed cycles too. When you rotate crops, you're reducing the likelihood that specific weeds will become adapted to the growing environment and become problematic. You can plant fast-growing crops between rows of slower growing crops. For example, you could plant lettuce or radishes between rows of Brussels sprouts or parsnips.

There is an interesting take on having some weeds as companion plants. There is a farming method called agroecology, where the presence of weeds enhances the biological control of pests. There have been studies in Columbia which found that if there were more weeds, it helped reduce the presence of leafhoppers, which are a major bean pest. Beans that were grown with pigweed didn't have as many bean beetles as beans that were grown in monocultures. If apple orchards had a lot of weedy undergrowth beneath them, this encouraged more parasitic wasps, so the apple trees weren't attacked by pests as much. Finally, when there were weeds like ragweed, goldenrod, smartweed, and pigweed in a peach orchard, this helped reduce the presence of oriental fruit moths.

Certain weeds host a lot of insects, and many of them are beneficial. Golden rod supports 75 species of insects, and pigweed supports 30 species. You could have some strips of weeds in a large vegetable plot or allow them to grow in ditches at the side of the garden—things like dandelions, pigweed, goldenrod, and evening primrose. But it is essential to know which are good weeds and which are bad. It's best to have wild annuals and biennials in your vegetable garden and leave perennials at the perimeter so that you can mow them down if you want. Annuals and biennials have smaller roots, so they don't complete for water and nutrients as much as perennial weeds may. It's best to avoid weeds like chickweed, horse nettle, jimsonweed, and ragweed because these could bring in fungal diseases. Weeds can be beneficial, and they don't need much attention because they seem to thrive anywhere. If you do get fed up with them, you can remove them.

When I first started out with gardening, I used to remove weeds by hand initially. They would grow back quite quickly, and it seemed like a never-ending task. It was my least favorite part of gardening because it took quite a bit of time and effort. I then started using mulch and organic herbicides, and this worked much better and really cut down on the time that I had to spend pulling up weeds. I mulch my garden beds, raised beds, and containers with compost mostly, but I also sometimes use shredded leaves and coconut coir as mulch. Because I mulch my garden, this means there are no bare patches where weed seeds can land, and even if there were weed seeds, they wouldn't be able to grow through the thick layer of mulch. I also use cover crops in the winter to help prevent weeds and enrich the soil with nutrients.

Key takeaways from this chapter:

1. Weeds compete with your plants for water, light, nutrients, and space.
2. Weeds can host diseases, and they can shelter pests.
3. Using organic herbicides is much better for the soil, environment, people, and animals than using chemical herbicides.
4. You can make an organic herbicide at home using vinegar, salt, and dish soap.
5. Other ways to get rid of weeds organically include removing them by hand, filling your growing space so that there is no room for weeds to grow, crop rotation, using a flame torch, using allelopathy, and mulching.
6. Use mulch to control weeds—it blocks out sun, prevents weed seeds from germinating, retains moisture, and organic mulch breaks down and enriches the soil with nutrients.
7. You can use compost, shredded leaves, shredded or chipped bark, grass clippings (non-treated), pine needles, straw, or newspapers as mulch.
8. Mulch your garden before weeds germinate, and get rid of any weeds that are already there.
9. You should use a 2–3-inch (5–7.5 cm) layer of mulch for it to be effective.
10. Companion plant to fill your growing space so that there is no room for weeds to spread. Use sprawling plants and plants of varying heights. Use cover crops over winter. Rotate crops to break weed cycles. Plant fast-growing crops in between slower crops. You could also have weeds as companion plants to decrease pests.

The next chapter will look at which insects are beneficial and how you can attract them to your garden. It will cover how companion planting can help attract beneficial insects. The chapter will also cover other beneficial creatures, such as birds, bats, and frogs.

Chapter 9: Attracting Beneficial Insects

It is far better to attract beneficial insects to your garden to sort out pests for you than it is to use pesticides. Chemical pesticides will get rid of beneficial insects as well as bad ones and can put chemicals on vegetables and fruits that you'll consume, as well as impacting the environment—water, air, and wildlife. Even organic pesticides will affect beneficial insects, so it's best to spray them early in the morning or late in the afternoon and then cover the plants with a row cover to stop beneficial insects, such as bees and ladybugs, from being affected. If you create a good environment for beneficial insects, they will come to your garden and eat pests, which is cheaper and safer than using pesticides. Insects are becoming more resistant to chemical pesticides, but beneficial insects can get rid of them by eating them or laying eggs on them, which kills the host.

We often think of all insects as being creepy and a nuisance if they crawl or fly near us. We tend to brush or swat them away. But insects play a vital role in our gardens, and there are beneficial insects that work to make our gardens a much healthier place. This chapter will look at beneficial garden insects and how to attract them to your garden. It will cover how companion planting can help attract beneficial insects. It will also cover other useful creatures, such as birds, bats, frogs, and more.

Beneficial Insects in the Garden

There are approximately 1 million insects that have been discovered and classified, and less than 1% of these are pests. So, a far greater number of insects in your garden either won't harm it or are actually beneficial to your garden. Beneficial insects are the ones that eat pests that would otherwise munch upon your delicious vegetables. These are known as predators and can include ladybugs, lacewings, and praying mantises. There are also beneficial parasitic insects. They lay their eggs on pests, and when the eggs hatch, the larvae eat the host. And there are also pollinators who pollinate flowers in the garden, and these include bees, moths, butterflies, and flies. This chapter will focus on predatory and parasitic beneficial insects, and pollinators will be covered in detail in the next chapter.

Most of us dislike wasps. Naturally, we don't want to be stung by them, and they hover round if you have sugary drinks or eat outside. But parasitic wasps are tiny, and they will defend your garden from caterpillars, including corn earworms, tomato fruit worms, cabbage worms, and tent caterpillars. Parasitic wasps will also lay eggs in butterfly or moth eggs. There are other wasps too, such as braconid wasps (these lay eggs on tomato hornworms), Trichogramma wasps (these lay eggs in over 200 different pests), as well as chalcid wasps and ichneumon wasps that lay eggs on caterpillars and aphids.

Flies can be annoying too, but some of them can be beneficial. Tachinid flies lay eggs on corn borers, gypsy moth caterpillars, grasshoppers, Japanese beetles, Mexican bean beetles, squash bugs, and green stinkbugs.

Ladybugs are pretty to look at, but their larvae eat a lot of aphids—up to 40 of them per hour. Green lacewing larvae eat caterpillars and aphids. Praying mantises eat grasshoppers, but they'll also eat beetles, moths, flies, butterflies, bees, and each other. Spiders (which are technically arachnids, not insects) are great at pest control, and they eat bugs, aphids, fruit flies, roaches, grasshoppers, and mosquitoes. Ground beetles eat nematodes, caterpillars, slugs, thrips, silverfish, and weevils both in their adult and larva form. Soldier beetles eat Mexican bean beetles, Colorado potato beetles, caterpillars, and aphids. Hover fly larvae will kill aphids, caterpillars, beetles, and thrips. Other beneficial insects include twice-stabbed lady beetles that prey on euonymus scale and vedalia beetles that prey on cottony cushion scale.

A key bit of advice is that beneficial insects are harmed by any pesticides or insecticides you use for pests or insects. So, try to encourage beneficial insects who will naturally take care of pests to your garden and try to use pesticides or insecticides as little as possible and only when absolutely necessary. It's OK to have a few pests remaining because if you got rid of every single aphid, then ladybugs wouldn't have anything to eat. If you see you have some pests, try to tolerate them because beneficial insects will come and sort them out—just stay patient.

Attracting Beneficial Insects to Your Garden

While you can purchase and release beneficial insects into your garden, if you plant your garden with the right things, they'll be attracted there naturally. Also, if you don't have the right things in your garden, any beneficial insects you specifically purchase wouldn't stay there anyway. You can support beneficial insects in your garden by ensuring they have food, water, and shelter. Having diverse plants will increase the range of insects you get in your garden. Insectaries are plants that attract predatory and parasitoid insects, who use either the nectar, pollen, or shelter provided by these plants.

Here's what you can do to attract beneficial insects to your garden:

1. **Have a diverse garden** with different nectars and pollens to attract a variety of insects, which in turn will attract wildlife—birds, amphibians, reptiles, and small mammals. Many predator insects use pollen and nectar for food. Plants in the carrot or aster family are ideal for this. Insects like protection from the weather, heat, and rain, and they will want to hide from birds or wildlife who will try to eat them, so plants can provide them with shelter. Beetles like mulch or leaf litter. Flying insects like shrubs. They also hide underneath leaves and in marigold petals. Creating a hedgerow with early flowering shrubs would be a great place for beneficial insects to dwell year-round. You can plant a border that has fruiting and flowering trees, shrubs, and perennials so that something is in bloom throughout the year.

2. **Have a water source.** Beneficial insects need water, so make sure to keep any watering holes topped up. You could also have a bird bath or simply place a few small containers with water around your garden—this will attract birds and beneficial insects.

3. **Have early bloomers with tiny blossoms.** Alyssum is good, and plants like carrots or parsley can be left to bloom and will help attract beneficial insects in the spring. Other plants with tiny flowers

include angelica, cilantro (coriander), clover, fennel, dill, Queen Anne's lace, rue, and yarrow.

4. **Use specific plants to attract specific insects.** For example, paw trees will attract zebra swallowtail butterflies. Daisies, chamomile, mint, and catnip attract predatory wasps, robber flies, and hover flies. This will be covered in more detail in the next section of this chapter.

5. **Some weeds can help attract beneficial insects.** You could have some strips of weeds in a large vegetable plot or allow them to grow in ditches at the side of the garden—things like dandelions, goldenrod, and evening primrose.

6. **Let some of your herbs flower.** Herbs lose their flavor when they flower, so they are usually harvested before that. But you can leave a few plants to flower, and this will help attract lots of beneficial insects to your garden.

7. **Plants with flowers in an umbrella shape** have clusters of flowers, and parasitic wasps like these. They will eat aphids, caterpillars, thrips, flies, and other pests.

8. **Layer plants**, like alyssum and catmint, under roses. Adult beneficial insects will consume pollen, and their larvae will eat pests.

9. **Leave ants unless they become problematic.** Ants should be left alone as much as possible because they will disperse seed and extend the life of your plants.

10. **Earthworms** aren't insects, but they will aerate and enrich your soil. You can attract worms by adding organic matter, like compost or manure, to your garden. Watering your garden deeply also helps attract worms.

11. **Mulch your garden.** Insects dislike dust, so having the soil covered with mulch is a good environment for insects.

12. **Try to limit the use of pesticides and insecticides** because they affect beneficial insects too.

13. **Plant an insectary.** This is a garden plot especially for insects. You could have a separate bed close to your vegetable garden or small clumps of plants interspersed among your vegetables. In your insectary, have early bloomers, plants of varying heights, use low-growing herbs, like thyme and oregano, for ground beetles and taller flowers, like cosmos and daisies, for parasitic wasps and hover flies. Umbellifers, like yarrow, fennel, wild carrots, and dill, as well as composite flowers, like zinnias and sunflowers, are good to have too.

Companion Plants for Attracting Beneficial Insects

Plants with flowers (especially small flowers) are great for attracting beneficial insects. Wherever possible, let some plants flower and go to seed. Earlier, I've mentioned how well basil goes with tomato, and if you have this companion planting combination, let some of your basil plants flower, and it will attract lots of beneficial insects.

You may be surprised to learn that ants are a beneficial insect—they can aerate your soil just as efficiently as earthworms. Ants are natural composters, and they'll turn any dead insects into fertilizer. Ants can help spread seeds too. So, never panic if you see ants in your garden. Ants can keep insects away from some plants. Ants love flowers, so if you want to attract ants, plant lots of flowers.

Different beneficial insects are attracted to different plants, and below you will find a list of beneficial insects and plants that can help attract them. You can research online what pests may attack the plants you're growing in your area and see which beneficial insects are predators to these pests, and then plant some plants that attract them.

Aphid midges: Plant dill and plants with lots of pollen and nectar, like alyssum, yarrow, or cosmos. They'll eat aphids.

Braconid wasps: Plant fern-leaf yarrow, common yarrow, dill, lemon balm, and parsley. They'll eat aphids, beetles, squash bugs, stink bugs, and caterpillars.

Damsel bugs: Plant alfalfa, caraway, fennel, Peter Pan goldenrod, and spearmint. They'll eat aphids, leafhoppers, cabbage worms, caterpillars, mites, tobacco hornworms, and tomato hornworms.

Green lacewings: Plant angelica, cilantro (coriander), dandelions, dill, golden marguerite, yarrow, four-wing saltbush, purple poppy mallow, caraway, cosmos, Queen Anne's lace, fennel, prairie sunflowers, and tansy. They'll eat aphids, leafhoppers, mealybugs, moths, caterpillars, spider mites (especially red mites), thrips, beetle larvae as well as eggs of pest moths and whiteflies. Lacewing larvae look a bit like small alligators. They are known as "aphid lions" because they eat them.

Ground beetles: Plant evening primrose, amaranth, and clover. They'll eat ants, slugs, caterpillars, Colorado potato beetles, and cutworms.

Hover flies (also known as syrphid flies, flower flies, and drone flies): Plant common yarrow, fernleaf yarrow, carpet bugleweed, lavender globe lily, basket of gold, dill, masterwort, four-wing saltbush, purple poppy mallow, caraway, fennel, English lavender, poached egg plant, lemon balm, pennyroyal, wild bergamot, parsley, Gloriosa daisy, and statice. They'll eat aphids, caterpillars, mealybugs, thrips, and scale insects.

Ladybugs (ladybirds): Plant common yarrow, fernleaf yarrow, dill, dandelions, golden marguerite, butterfly weed, four-wing saltbush, cilantro (coriander), Queen Anne's lace, California buckwheat, fennel, prairie sunflower, Rocky Mt. penstemon, sulfur cinquefoil, alpine cinquefoil, tansies, spike speedwell, carpet bugleweed, and basket of gold. They'll eat aphids, fleas, mites, whiteflies, and Colorado potato beetles.

Mealybug destroyers: Plant angelica, dill, fennel, goldenrod, and sunflowers. They'll eat mealybugs. One mealybug destroyer can eat 250 mealybug larvae.

Minute pirate bugs: Plant alfalfa, caraway, fennel, Peter Pan goldenrod, and spearmint. They'll eat spider mites, scales, whiteflies, aphids, thrips, and caterpillars.

Praying mantises: Plant cosmos, dill, tall grasses and shrubs, and marigolds. They'll eat beetles, caterpillars, gnats, crickets, and moths.

Soldier beetles: Plant goldenrod, linden trees, marigolds, and zinnias. They'll eat grasshopper eggs, aphids, and soft-bodied insects.

Spiders: Plant tall plants so that spiders who weave webs can do this. Use mulch to attract predatory spiders. They'll eat bugs, aphids, fruit flies, roaches, grasshoppers, and mosquitoes.

Tachinid flies: Plant buckwheat, carrots, cilantro (coriander), golden marguerite, lemon balm, pennyroyal, parsley, tansy, crimson thyme, and dill. They'll eat gypsy moths, cabbage worms, cabbage loopers, stink bugs, nymphs, beetle and fly larvae, Japanese beetles, cutworms, and squash bugs.

Trichogramma wasps: plant fernleaf yarrow, common yarrow, dill, golden marguerite, masterwort, Queen Anne's lace, fennel, statice, lemon balm, parsley, marigold, tansy, and crimson thyme. These wasps lay their eggs in the eggs of moths, which will stop caterpillars from eating your plants.

If you are just starting out as a beginner and want to attract beneficial insects to your garden, then planting some marigolds, yarrow, cosmos, and dill will bring lots of beneficial insects to your garden.

If you want to know some ideas for companion flowers and herbs to attract beneficial insects at certain times of the year, you could plant sweet alyssum, rosemary, thyme, crimson clover, and bugleweed in the spring. In early to mid-summer, you could plant lavender, yarrow, mint, Queen Anne's Lace, and Roman chamomile. In late summer to fall, you could plant bee balm, mullein, goldenrod, fennel, and aster.

Other Useful Creatures

Insects are not the only creatures that can be useful in the garden. Birds, bats, frogs, and other creatures can help with pollination, pest control, fertilization, improve soil health, and support a good ecological balance in your garden.

Birds

Birds are great at getting rid of pests, and they are also great pollinators. Birds are nice to look at in the garden, and they eat a variety of insects, such as mosquitoes, aphids, grasshoppers, cutworms, and beetles. Larger birds of prey, like owls, stop rodent populations from thriving.

One of the best things you can do to attract birds is setting up nesting shelves and feeders. You buy them or make them yourself if you're good at DIY. Sunflower seeds are the most popular birdseed and will attract a lot of different birds to your feeder. You can also buy mixes, and they will usually have sunflower seeds, millet, and cracked corn—the three most popular types of birdseed. Many birds enjoy peanuts, peanut butter, cracked corn, millet, apple pieces, oranges, and even breadcrumbs. Birds also need water, so having a water source in your garden, such as a bird bath, will help attract birds. A bird bath is essentially an artificial puddle or a small shallow pond where birds may drink, bathe, and cool themselves. You can buy a bird bath or make one out of household items, like a saucer, a bowl, and so on.

If you live in an area that has hummingbirds, they adore red flowers, so you could plant some. If you were to plant sunflowers around the borders of your vegetable garden, these will attract pollinators and provide food for birds too. Having trees and bushes in your garden will provide some shelter for birds.

Birds may eat vegetables and fruits if there is limited access to other foods, like bugs or food in bird feeders. Make sure your bird feeders always have some food in them. If birds still eat your fruits and vegetables, you can place a statue of an owl or an eagle in your garden. A large decoy bird will keep birds away from your vegetables and fruit trees, but you may need a few of these if you have a large garden. You can also place a large scarecrow, and it will work just as well.

Bats

Bats eat insects, so having them come to your garden can be a good idea. They're good at eating mosquitoes, and not only do mosquitos cause painful bites, at worst they can spread diseases like malaria, Zika virus, and dengue fever. A single bat can eat 1,000 mosquitos in an hour. They will also eat flies and moths. So, if you're having a lot of mosquitoes where you live, you could try attracting bats to your garden.

If you live in an area with fruit-eating bats, they are excellent pollinators. If you have a bat house in your garden, bats will absolutely love it. You can purchase one and put it 15 to 20 feet (4.5–6 m) high using a tree or a pole. Bats are an endangered species, and therefore you'd be helping the environment by attracting bats to your garden.

Frogs and Toads

Toads and frogs will eat slugs, snails, and other insects in your garden. A toad can eat around 10,000 bugs each summer. They are efficient and far better for your garden than using pesticides.

Frogs and toads prefer damp, shady areas and need shelter to hide from predators and escape the heat from the sun. Having a pond may attract frogs. It is good to have lots of rocky areas where toads can live during the day until they come out at night. You could use upturned logs and terracotta pots to provide some daytime shelter for toads. You can create a shelter by making a small cave out of stones. You can also use a clay or ceramic flowerpot as housing for frogs and toads. Turn the pot upside down and prop it up with rocks, leaving enough room for a frog or a toad to slip inside. Locate your shelter in a quiet area that has a lot of shade.

Don't relocate adult toads into your garden—they have already chosen where they want to live. Just build an environment that is suitable for them, and they will arrive. Frogs live in water, but toads don't. Don't use pesticides near frogs or toads because they have very sensitive skin.

Lizards

Lizards are great at eating slugs and insects. If you have lizards in your garden, this is a fantastic thing, as it demonstrates that your garden is a healthy environment that is free of pollutants and heavy metals, which lizards are sensitive to. Don't use any pesticides because lizards are sensitive to them. Lizards need places to hide, like rocks, brick piles, and bushes. If you have mulched areas in your garden, lizards will appreciate this because they need some moisture due to their dry skin. They also need a source of water.

Earthworms and Centipedes

Because worms burrow into soil, this helps keep the soil aerated and allows water and oxygen to flow to the roots of plants. Worms can process organic material, and when they eat and excrete it, this makes a great compost and will give lots of nutrients to your plants. You can attract worms by adding compost or manure to your garden and watering your garden deeply. Having a compost pile will also help attract worms.

Centipedes are great at eating insects. To attract them, you can add logs or bricks to provide shelter for them during the day until they come out at night.

Snakes

Snakes will help control things like crickets and grasshoppers. They like bushes, tall grasses, piles of wood, and rocks—all these things provide good shelter for them. They like dark, shaded places, like wood piles, mulch, stones, and logs.

Hedgehogs

Hedgehogs are great at eating slugs and insects, and they look adorable. You can have a wild part of your garden for hedgehogs. You'll need to ensure they can easily get in and out of the garden—a small hole in the fence will do the job. They need a source of food and water. Hedgehogs like cat or dog food. Also, check leaf piles before moving them to ensure no hedgehogs are nesting there.

I was vaguely aware of insects in my garden until I started looking for them, and then I could see them everywhere, good and bad! We had a compost pile, and it had lots of ants. I was initially concerned about them until I researched into ants and learned that they are as good at aerating the soil as earthworms are. Our compost did look lovely even with the ants, and we used it in our garden without any issues.

While we had some beneficial insects in the garden, I was keen to attract more. So, I planted a wide range of flowers, such as marigolds, yarrow, alyssum, and cosmos, among the vegetables in my garden and let some of the herbs flower and go to seed. The flowers among the vegetables look beautiful and vibrant with their colors, and I definitely see more beneficial insects, such as ladybugs, lacewings, bees, and many others, so I'm really happy that the garden is thriving with beneficial insects.

Key takeaways from this chapter:

1. Beneficial insects eat pests, pollinate, or are parasitic and lay eggs on pests, which then kills them.
2. Try to limit the use of pesticides and insecticides because these will kill beneficial insects too.
3. Most insects in your garden are beneficial.
4. Some beneficial insects include ladybugs, lacewings, parasitic wasps, and ground beetles.
5. To attract beneficial insects, have a diverse garden with flowers, plants, mulch, shrubs, hedgerow, and small blossoms, like alyssum. Let plants go to seed, mulch your garden, put flowers among vegetables, and have a water source.
6. Companion plants that help attract beneficial insects include alyssum, dill, fernleaf yarrow, common yarrow, lemon balm, parsley, alfalfa, fennel, goldenrod, angelica, dandelion, golden marguerite, Queen Anne's lace, tansy, pennyroyal, cilantro (coriander), marigolds, verbena, poached egg plant, rosemary, thyme, and crimson clover.
7. You can attract birds, bats, frogs, and other beneficial creatures by having a water source, a bird feeder, a pond, sunflowers at the edges of the garden, bushes, trees, and bat houses on high poles or trees. Having rocky areas, logs, and pots will help attract frogs, toads, and lizards. Adding compost and watering your garden deeply will attract earthworms, which will help aerate the soil. Having tall grasses, wood piles, and rocks will attract snakes. For hedgehogs, ensure you have a hole in the fence for them to get in and out of the garden and that you provide food and water for them.

The next chapter will look at how you can attract pollinators to your garden, who will pollinate plants that need pollination, such as squash and cucumbers, and what plants can help attract them. The chapter will cover how to attract specific pollinators and how to provide homes for pollinators too.

Chapter 10: Attracting Pollinators

Plants need pollination in order to produce fruit. Pollen in plants needs moving from the anther (the male part) to the stigma (the female part) for a plant to be pollinated. Plants can be pollinated by wind, insects, or birds. Plants can be self-pollinating (tomatoes, eggplants, peppers, legumes), or they can be pollinated by wind (strawberries, corn), or they are not grown for their flowers (carrots, potatoes, onions, garlic, lettuce, broccoli, cauliflower, and herbs). Plants that need insect pollinators include fruit trees, berry bushes, cucumbers, squash, pumpkins, and watermelons.

Sometimes you may notice your plants blooming profusely, but despite lots of flowers, the harvest may be meager. This usually happens due to insufficient pollination. The use of broad-spectrum pesticides and habitat loss has led to a decline in pollinator populations. As pollinator populations decline, often the necessary insects just aren't there when you need them to pollinate your plants.

This chapter will explain what pollinators are. It will look at how you can attract pollinators in general and then focus on attracting specific types of pollinators. This chapter covers what companion plants you can plant to attract pollinators, and it concludes by looking at providing homes and habitats for pollinators.

What Are Pollinators?

Pollinators move between plants and carry pollen on their bodies, and this transfers genetic material between plants that helps them reproduce and give us vegetables, fruits, nuts, oils, fibers, and raw material. Pollen in plants needs moving from the anther (the male part) to the stigma (the female part) for a plant to be pollinated. How a plant is pollinated depends on the type of flowers they have. Self-pollinating plants have perfect or complete flowers in which both male (stamen) and female (pistil) reproductive organs are contained in the same flower. Plants with imperfect flowers have male and female flowers growing separately. When a plant is pollinated, it will produce fruit and seeds.

Many people think that only bees are pollinators, but that's not true. Pollinators include birds, bats, butterflies, moths, flies, beetles, wasps, and small mammals (but insects are generally responsible for the majority of the pollination). Nectar and pollen in flowers attract pollinators, and when they land on a flower, pollen grains stick to their bodies, and then they transfer pollen as they move from one flower to another and between plants.

Attracting Pollinators to Your Garden

Little changes can make a big difference in attracting pollinators. When farms emulate a natural habitat, they get a much better crop yield because they have more pollinators. Pollinators don't mind city life, provided they have patches of flowers. If you plant a garden that pollinators love, they will come, and you'll get a better crop yield.

Here are some ways to attract pollinators:
1. Ensure your garden has some flowers all year round.

2. Pollinators like different colored flowers, so plant a variety of different-colored flowers. Bees especially like yellow, blue, violet, white, and purple flowers. Butterflies like red, orange, yellow, pink, and blue flowers. Hummingbirds like flowers that are orange, red, violet, and pink and have a tube or funnel shape. Filling your yard with flowers in a rainbow of hues is one of the best ways to attract pollinators.

3. Pollinators like aromatic herbs, so include herbs like sage, oregano, basil, and lavender.

4. Pick flowers that are native to your area because these will appeal to pollinators more than exotic flowers, and they will be well adapted to the growing environment.

5. A bird bath with help attract birds. You can also fill shallow trays with water for other pollinators, such as butterflies and bees.

6. Try to limit the use of pesticides and insecticides because they affect pollinators too.

7. When you plant flowers, try to plant in clumps rather than just an individual plant here and there to attract more pollinators. Include flowers of different shapes to attract many different species of bees.

8. Plant flowers in the sunny part of the garden because pollinators, such as bees, prefer sunny spots to shade.

9. Have a mixture of woody and soft-stemmed plants.

10. Try not to tidy up all mess because things like dead stems and leaves are a perfect habitat for wildlife—birds need this type of thing for their nests.

11. Use a rake instead of a leaf blower. Leaf blowers are noisy and pollute the air. They can get rid of natural debris and erode and dry out soil.

12. Switch off outside lights once you've finished doing things outside because insects and birds don't like artificial light. It can hamper their navigation, reproduction, and their ability to locate food.

13. If you have a lawn, you could give up some of it to plants for pollinators. You can grow things like clover, ground ivy, black medic, vetch, and dandelions.

14. Remember to prune plants to encourage repeat bloom, and don't be too quick to deadhead plants so that bees have a chance to use the flowers.

Attracting Specific Pollinators

Bees

Bees are some of the best pollinators you can get in your garden. They pollinate over 66% of the world's crop species. There are over 20,000 species of bees in the world, and 90% of them live a solitary life, which means they don't live in hives and don't make any honey. The more bees you can attract to your garden, the better because this will help your plants produce more fruit. Bees want nectar, which has sugars and gives bees their energy, and pollen, which gives bees proteins and fats. Bees will pollinate fruit trees, vegetables, and flowers.

Honeybees and bumblebees are two of the most common kinds of bees. Honeybees pollinate fruit trees and some vegetable crops, including apples, melons, cranberries, pumpkins, squash, broccoli, and many others. Bumblebees often pollinate wildflowers, berry bushes, strawberries, and vegetable crops, including tomatoes, eggplants, peppers, melons, and many other crops, and they are the only known pollinators of potatoes worldwide.

To attract bees to your garden, try to limit the of use pesticides in your garden (which could kill the bees) and avoid monocrops. Instead, have a wide variety of plants, flowers, and herbs. Bees love flowering herbs and colorful flowers, especially ones that are blue, purple, violet, white, and yellow. They love asters, poppies, and bee balm because they can get nectar from them. Bee populations are declining, so anything you can do to help bees live and repopulate is good.

A good call is to plant native plants to attract bees, like asters, black-eyed Susans, goldenrod, joe-pye-weed, purple coneflowers, rhododendrons, sage, stonecrops, sunflowers, wild buckwheat, wild lilacs, and willows. You could combine basil, English lavender, globe thistle, marjoram, rosemary, wallflowers, and zinnias with the native plants. Other plants that can help attract bees include butterfly weed, salvia, daisies, ironweed, and anise hyssop.

Like all living creatures, bees need water. You can leave small containers with water around your garden to help attract bees and other pollinators. Bees also like some bare ground without pesticides to nest.

Beetles

While some beetles can be a nuisance, most beetles are beneficial, and they are great pollinators. Beetles are considered "dirty" pollinators, as opposed to bees or birds because they eat flower petals and also defecate on flowers. Despite that, they remain an important pollinator worldwide. Beetles visit plants, such as carrots, sunflowers, and cabbage, and flowers, like magnolias, water lilies, and buttercups. They also eat pests, work as composters, and turn plant and animal matter into fertilizer. If you live in an area that has dung beetles, they will feed upon animal feces. You can attract beetles by using mulch and creating habitats for them, such as leaf piles and stacks of deadwood. They also like compost heaps.

Birds

Birds love nectar, and they will help pollinate honeysuckle and bee balm. Hummingbirds are excellent pollinators, and they're great birds to have around your garden. Plants to specifically attract hummingbirds include lobelia, aquilegia, penstemon, bee balm, hibiscus, peony, coral bells, catmint, anise hyssop, and salvia. They like bright tubular flowers, such as cardinal flower, blue flag iris, wild columbine, spotted joe-pyeweed, jewelweed, cosmos, begonias, geraniums, petunias, zinnias, and nasturtiums.

Birds need food, water, and shelter, so you can install a bird feeder, a bird bath, and nesting shelves to attract birds to your garden. Birds love sunflower seeds, so if you plant sunflowers, this will help attract lots of birds.

Butterflies and Moths

Buddleia and lavender are two great flowers that butterflies seem to be especially drawn to. Butterflies are stunning to look at with their intricate, colorful wings. When you plant plants for butterflies, this may also attract dragonflies, spiders, and ladybugs. It's a great idea to plant native plants.

The monarch butterflies' larvae specifically need milkweed in order to thrive. They pollinate milkweed and other wildflowers. Plants that attract butterflies often have red and purple flowers. They like fresh scents and narrow, tube-like flowers. Butterflies are attracted to butterfly weed, coneflowers, asters, verbena, black-eyed Susans, daisies, ironweeds, anise hyssop, bee balm zinnias, and thistle.

Flies

There are over 85,000 different species of flies. The most important fly pollinators are hover flies and bee flies. They pollinate fruit trees and vegetables, including pear, apple, cherry, plum, mango, apricot, and peach trees as well as strawberries, rowanberries, raspberries, blackberries, roses, fennel, cilantro (coriander), caraway, kitchen onions, parsley, carrots, and many more plants. Flies love white flowers with open structure that are easy to access. Planting Queen Anne's lace, wild mustard, sweet alyssum, cilantro (coriander), dill, and other small-flowered herbs will help attract fly pollinators.

Companion Plants for Attracting Pollinators

When you're looking for companion plants to attract pollinators, look for plants that are native to the area. Your local nursery should be able to help you with this. Avoid hybrid plants because while the flowers may look pretty, they often don't have the pollen or nectar that pollinators require. Try to ensure you have flowers all year round with a variety of different heights, colors, and scents. Plant clumps of flowers rather than individual ones.

When you plant pollinator-friendly plants near your vegetables, it will give you better yields. Echinacea, rudbeckia, monarda and butterfly bushes are all great plants that can encourage pollinators.

If you plant basil next to tomatoes and lettuce, it will improve the flavor of both, and if you leave basil to flower, it will attract bees, who are excellent pollinators. Planting calendula near summer squash, sweet peas near runner beans, and cosmos near cucumbers are all great companion planting combinations that will attract pollinators. You can also plant alyssum, bachelor's button, bee balm, nasturtiums, and rosemary among your vegetables.

If you're wondering what plants you could incorporate into your vegetable garden at different times of year, here are some suggestions:

In the spring, you can plant blue wild indigo (also known as blue false indigo), native columbine, and spring crocus. In the summer, you can plant anise hyssop, beebalm, black-eyed Susans, coneflowers, joe-pyeweed, salvia, and swamp milkweed. In the fall, you can plant goldenrod and asters.

For shrubs and trees, you can plant butterfly bushes (buddleia), button bushes, pussy willow, leadplant, and fruit trees. Herbs that can help attract pollinators include basil, borage, chives, dill, lavender, oregano, and rosemary.

Bees love lavender. If you plant this among your vegetables, bees will be attracted to it, and lavender will also repel pests. You can plant lavender with lettuce, sage, tomatoes, onions, and basil. Bees, butterflies, and other pollinators also love borage because it has a strong scent and vivid flowers. It's a great companion plant for tomatoes and strawberries. You can eat borage in salad and dips, and it tastes similar to cucumber.

Marigolds and nasturtiums are great flowers to have in your garden. Both marigolds and nasturtiums are great companions to virtually any plant, and bees love them. They also have an added bonus of repelling lots of different pests. Nasturtiums can also work as a trap crop. Any caterpillars from cabbage white butterflies will eat nasturtiums and not your vegetables. I have a lot of marigolds and nasturtiums in my garden—they are a firm favorite of mine.

Providing Homes and Habitats for Pollinators

Solitary bees like to nest in soil, sand, or deadwood rather than in hives over winter. Shrubs, such as wild lilac and toyon, are good for them too. Bees use them as shelter as well as a source of pollen and nectar.

You can also buy or make a bee hotel. To make a bee hotel, you'll need a plank that is at least 4 inches (10 cm) wide, some reeds, bamboo canes, and hollow stems in a range of diameters. If you want to attach it to a wall or a fence, you will also need a mirror fixing. You will also need some basic tools and hardware, namely a saw, a drill, and nails, to put it all together.

Cut your plank of wood into 5 pieces. You'll need to assemble them in a shape of a "house" like in the picture on the right. Three pieces should be the same size—this will form the rectangle frame that will support the roof. Two of these pieces will need to be cut away at a right angle to create a sloping edge to house the roof. For the remaining two pieces, one should be slightly longer than the other as they will form the roof on top at a 90-degree angle. Drill some guide holes for the screws to fit into, and assemble the frame.

Next, cut your stems, reeds, and canes with a saw so that they fit the depth of the frame. Fill the frame with your canes, reeds, and stems, and pack them in as tightly as possible. If you have extra space, you can add circular bits of wood with holes drilled in. Attach the mirror fixing to the back of the frame if you want to attach the bee hotel to a wall or a fence. Position your bee hotel facing south, in a sunny spot that is sheltered away from any rain.

If you want to take things to the next level and attract a lot of pollinators as well as beneficial insects and other useful creatures, you can make an insect hotel (sometimes also called a bug hotel) from wooden pallets, bricks, and other scrap. They look great, and we have one in our garden, and there is another one in a nature reserve area near where we live. You can put twigs, bamboo sticks with holes, or bricks with holes in them. When using bamboo sticks, insects will often seal the hole with a plug of mud once they have put food in there and laid eggs, and when the new insects emerge, they will work their way through the mud, which will crumble easily.

If you decide to build an insect hotel, it should be level and on firm ground. The foundation needs to be strong and stable—pallets are perfect for this. You can also lay some bricks on the ground, but leave some space between them for critters to move in. Once you have a solid foundation, you can layer pallets, bricks, and planks to make "floors". You'll need to fill the gaps between the "floors". The idea is to provide all sorts of different nooks and crannies, crevices, and tunnels for different creatures. Try to include the following:

- Dead wood and loose bark for beetles, centipedes, spiders, and woodlice.
- Holes and small tubes for solitary bees made out of reeds, bamboo, and drilled logs.
- Larger holes with stones and tiles, which will provide cool and damp conditions for frogs and toads. If you put it in the center, you'll give them a frost-free place to spend the winter, and they'll help eat slugs.
- Dry leaves, sticks, or straw for ladybugs and other insects, bugs, and beetles.
- Corrugated cardboard for lacewings.
- Dry leaves, which will mimic a natural forest floor.
- You can put a hedgehog box into the base of the hotel.

Once you think you've stacked your hotel high enough, put a roof on to keep it relatively dry. Use old roof tiles or some old planks covered with roofing felt. You can also have a living green roof like in the picture on the right. A top tip is to plant some wildflowers around the hotel to give food for butterflies, bees, and other pollinating insects.[44]

Having homes for pollinators is excellent, but you do need to surround their homes with food and water too. Goldenrod is a lovely plant to place near pollinator homes, and you can put little trays with water near your insect hotel. When you plant plants for them, it will reduce the effort that pollinators need to make to search for them if you group plants together (at least 8 flowers together rather than individual flowers).

Marigolds, nasturtiums, and basil (when left to flower) tend to be my go-to plants to help attract pollinators. These are the plants I always start out with. Marigolds and nasturtiums are great companion plants for almost every other plant. I also allow herbs, such as dill, oregano, sage, and thyme, to flower too. They smell fantastic and attract lots of pollinators. I'm also a big fan of buddleia. It comes in lots of different shades, like lilac, purple, and white, and just looks fantastic, and butterflies love it. We also have an insect hotel in the corner of our garden in which we placed some wood, plant stems, bricks with holes, wooden pallets, leaves, and so on, and that has been fun to watch.

---

[44] Image from https://www.finegardening.com/article/creating-homes-for-pollinators

Key takeaways from this chapter:

1. Plants need to be pollinated in order to produce fruit and seeds.
2. Pollinators help pollinate plants by carrying pollen from one flower to another and between plants.
3. Some plants are self-pollinating, others can get pollinated by wind, and some plants need pollinators' help to get pollinated.
4. How plants are pollinated depends on the type of flowers they have. Self-pollinating plants have perfect or complete flowers in which both male (stamen) and female (pistil) reproductive organs are contained in the same flower. Plants with imperfect flowers have male and female flowers growing separately, and these plants need pollinators' help to carry the pollen from male to female flowers.
5. Contrary to popular belief, bees are not the only pollinators, although they're very important. Pollinators also include butterflies, moths, flies, wasps, beetles, birds, bats, and small mammals.
6. To attract pollinators, have flowers with bright colors all year round. Plants that are native to the area work better for attracting pollinators than exotic plants. Have a water source for pollinators—you can put small trays with water around your garden. Try to limit the use of pesticides because they affect pollinators and beneficial insects too. Plant flowers in clumps—planting at least 8 flowers together works better than having single flowers all around the place. Have flowers in a sunny area. Leave some dead leaves on the ground. Use a rake, not a leaf blower. If you have a lawn, you can give up some of it to plants that help attract pollinators.
7. Bees like asters, poppies, bee balm, black-eyed Susans, goldenrod, purple coneflowers, lavender, and salvia.
8. Beetles like mulch, leaf piles, compost, and dead wood.
9. Birds like lobelia, aquilegia, begonias, and sunflowers.
10. Butterflies and moths like buddleia, lavender, milkweed, thistles, and verbena.
11. Some examples of companion planting to attract pollinators include planting basil next to tomatoes and lettuce and letting some of the basil plants flower as well as planting calendula near squash, sweet peas near runner beans, cosmos near cucumbers, and marigolds near melons, cucumbers, and potatoes. Marigolds and nasturtiums grow well with everything and help attract pollinators, beneficial insects, and repel pests.
12. Make homes for pollinators—you can have bamboo tubes or wood with holes drilled in. You can also make an insect hotel out of bricks, pallets, and sticks.

The next chapter will give you information on how you can tell if it's the right time to harvest your vegetables, fruits, and herbs, the signs to look out for, and how to harvest them. It will also cover how you can store your harvest to get the most out of it.

Chapter 11: Time to Harvest the Bounty

So, you've started your garden by companion planting certain plants to help support other plants, protect them from pests, and give them nutrients or shade. You've ensured that your soil is as healthy as possible, and you've been watering and weeding your garden dutifully. You've done your best to control pests and attract beneficial insects and pollinators to your garden. All of these things should have given your vegetables, fruits, and herbs the optimum conditions to thrive. It's now time for the exciting part of harvesting your bounty!

So, this chapter will cover when you should harvest your crops and how you can tell they're ready to harvest. It will also cover how you should store your harvest to keep it fresh and preserved.

When and How to Harvest Your Vegetables

While seed packets provide information on how long it takes for plants to reach maturity—and this is a helpful guide—there are numerous factors that can change this, including the weather, the quality of your soil, whether your plants got enough water, and so on. But vegetables themselves give some clues as to whether they are mature, and this chapter will help you learn about these.

Some vegetables taste best when they are tender and immature. Things like peas, salad greens, zucchini, cucumbers, beans, potatoes, radishes, cabbage, broccoli, cauliflower, summer squash, and turnips fall into this category. Other plants need to ripen on the vine, such as tomatoes, melons, and winter squash. Most herbs should be harvested before they flower because when they do, they lose their flavor.

It is important to regularly check whether your vegetables are ready to be harvested because if you leave some vegetables for too long, they can become tough or overripe. For example, beans can become tough if left for too long, and zucchini can become overripe.

Before you start harvesting, there are certain tools that will come in handy. These include a clean, food-safe container that you can put your harvest in—this could be a stainless steel bowl, a plastic bowl, or a basket. You will need scissors or pruners and food-safe wipes or soap to be able to clean your tools. Ensure that you have washed your hands and tools before harvesting to avoid spreading any diseases.

For lettuce, kale, and peas, you can pinch off leaves and peas by hand. With lettuce and other leafy vegetables that sprout from the center of the plant, if you're just taking a few leaves and not harvesting the entire thing, then take the outer leaves first so that the plant can continue to grow. If something doesn't come off easily, you can use scissors or a knife. If you have root crops, like potatoes or beets, then you may need to use a fork to harvest them. With herbs and salad leaves, you can use scissors to snip off the leaves, and it's best to take the leaves from around the base of the plant first so that the plant can continue to grow.

Typically, it's best to harvest plants when the temperature is lower—in the morning or later in the evening—because plants will be less stressed. After the morning dew has dried is a good time to harvest. If you were to pick vegetables in midday heat, it can cause leafy vegetables to wilt. Don't harvest vegetables if it's wet because you could easily spread fungal diseases in wet conditions.

You can harvest daily. If you have too much produce, you can store it (this will be covered later in this chapter) or share it with friends, family, and neighbors. Storing your harvest is not the only way to preserve it, of course. You can preserve your harvest with pickling, canning, making jams, freezing, and drying, and I could write a book about it. In fact, I did, and I'd like you to have it for free as a way of saying thanks for purchasing this book. To get your free eBook about 5 easy ways to preserve your harvest, please scan the QR code on page 4 with your phone camera or send me an email to maxbarnesbooks@gmail.com and I will send you the free eBook.

Below you will find information on how to harvest different vegetables:

Arugula: Cut off leaves when they have reached 2–3 inches (5–7.5 cm). Younger leaves taste best. Older leaves can be bitter.

Asparagus: It's ready to harvest when the spears are 6–8 inches (15–20 cm) long and as thick as your pinky finger. Cut the spears with a knife at soil level. Usually, you can harvest asparagus for 4–8 weeks. If you grow asparagus from seed, it can take 3 years before the plant is productive.

Beans: They're ready to harvest when they're as thick as a pencil and you can easily snap a pod in two. You should aim to harvest every day or two.

Beets: They should be dug up when their roots are 1.5–2.5 inches (4–6.5 cm) in diameter. You can also harvest and eat the green tops and have them in salads, steamed, or stir-fried.

Bok choy: When it's 12 inches (30 cm), you can either take the whole plant and cut it with a knife at the roots, or take outer leaves with a knife, or cut all the stems to about an inch (2.5 cm) in height, and new leaves will then start to appear.

Broccoli: When it's 3–6 inches (7.5–15 cm) in diameter, cut the stalk 6 inches (15 cm) below the head. Broccoli grown at home won't get to the sizes that you find in a supermarket.

Brussels sprouts: When the sprouts are 1–1.5 inches (2.5–4 cm) in diameter, start harvesting at the bottom of the stalk where the sprouts are more mature, then move up. You can twist them off or cut them off with a knife.

Cabbage: When the head is a bit bigger than a softball, harvest the cabbage. If you leave it too long, it may split open.

Carrots: Harvest when they're 1 inch (2.5 cm) in diameter.

Cauliflower: It needs to be watched carefully, and you should harvest it before the head separates, or turns yellow, or gets brown spots. Cut with a knife below the head, ensuring you have some leaves attached to stop it from drying out.

Chard: When the leaves are 6 inches (15 cm) long, you can snip them off from the outside of the plant.

Corn: When silks go dry and brown (about 3 weeks after forming) and if the ear (the spiked part of the corn plant that contains kernels) feels rounded, it can be harvested. If it tapers and feels thin at the tip, it's not ready. If you nick a kernel with your finger, it should be succulent and have a milky substance come out. Pick corn in the morning, and place it in the fridge until cooking.

Cucumbers: Harvest them when they're 2–6 inches (5–15 cm) long. The skin should be dark, green, and glossy. If it's dull or yellow, the cucumber is past its best.

Eggplants: Harvest them when their skin is even colored and glossy. If it's dull and the eggplant is soft, it's overripe. Cut eggplants off a plant using a pruner or knife.

Garlic: If you have planted garlic in the spring, it will be ready mid-summer to early fall. If you've planted it in the fall, it will be ready in early summer. You can tell if it's the right time to harvest garlic when the leaves have turned yellow. You should carefully dig up garlic using a fork, being careful not to bruise or damage it. Then garlic needs to be dried in a single layer in the sun, ideally under a cloche, or in a greenhouse or a shed for 2–4 weeks. When the leaves are dry, you can cut off the stalks.

Kale: When the leaves are 6–8 inches (15–20 cm), they're ready to harvest. You can snap them off or use a knife. Harvest the outer leaves at the base of the plant first.

Kohlrabi: When the globes are 2 inches (5 cm) in diameter, they're ready to be harvested. Cut the globe at the root with a knife.

Leeks: Harvest when they're 1 inch (2.5 cm) in diameter. Use a garden fork to loosen the soil, then pull them up from the ground. You can leave leeks in the ground over winter and harvest when needed.

Lettuce: Harvest when it's about 6 inches (15 cm) in diameter. Use a knife to sever the head from the roots. With lettuce leaves, you can harvest them when they are 3–4 inches (7.5–10 cm) long by cutting them off with scissors from the outside. Lettuce tastes best early in the day. If you do pick it later in the day, refresh the leaves in cold water for 30 mins, dry them with paper towels, then place in a plastic bag in the fridge.

Melons: With cantaloupes, they're ready to harvest when the stem pulls easily from the melon and they smell sweet when sniffed. With honeydews, they're ready to harvest when the flower end is softer, and the rind is white or yellow. Cut melons from the vine with a knife.

Mustard greens: Use scissors or a knife to harvest the leaves when they are young, tender, and mild. Harvest leaves from the outside of the plant.

Onions: When they're about 1–2 inches (2.5–5 cm) in diameter and when more than ⅔ of the tops have dried and fallen over, they're ready to be harvested. You should be able to pull them from the ground with your hands in most cases. You can use a fork to help if they're not coming out easily. Hang them up in the sun or somewhere dry for 1–2 weeks. When the necks are dry, trim the roots and store in a cool, dry space.

Parsnips: Harvest after a few frosts for sweeter tasting parsnips. You can also leave them in the ground over winter and harvest them in the spring. Cover them with a thick layer of straw or organic mulch if you leave them over winter. To harvest, use a garden fork to loosen soil, then pull them out. Cut the foliage to ¼ of an inch (6 mm). Store in the fridge or a root cellar.

Peas: You can pull a pod from the vine and do a taste test to see if they're ready. Snip the pods off the vine with scissors or fingers. Harvest daily or every other day. If overripe peas are left on the vine, the vine will not produce anymore.

Peppers: You can harvest them ripe or unripe. Use scissors to cut them off because if you try to twist them off, you will damage the plant. You can pick green peppers, and the plant will continue to produce them. If you let peppers ripen on the vine, the peppers will be sweeter, but you won't get as many. With hot peppers, they're hotter when they're green rather than red. It can be worth wearing gloves when handling them because they can burn your hands. Also, don't rub your eyes when harvesting peppers—wash your hands first.

Potatoes: With new potatoes, they're ready to harvest once they've flowered (usually 6–8 weeks after planting). With other potatoes, leave them in the ground for 2 weeks after the plants have died back. Carefully dig them up so that you don't damage them. They can be stored in a dark and dry place for 2 weeks.

Pumpkins: When a pumpkin has a deep color, the stem has started to dry, and the rind cannot be dented when pressed with a thumbnail, it's ready to be harvested. Use a knife to sever it from the vine. Leave 3 inches (7.5 cm) of the stem attached, and don't carry pumpkins by the stem because you don't want to break it. Let them cure in a well-ventilated place for 10 days.

Radishes: Harvest radishes when they're about 1 inch (2.5 cm) in diameter. If you leave them for too long, they'll be hot, sharp, and pithy. Use a garden fork to loosen soil and pull them up.

Rhubarb: It can be harvested in mid-spring. Pull the stalk upwards and twist sideways. Don't cut the stalks. Harvest until mid-summer, at which point they start to become stringy. Don't eat rhubarb leaves because they are toxic.

Rutabagas: These are ready to harvest when their roots are 4–5 inches (10–12.5 cm) in diameter. Cool weather makes them taste better, so allow them a few frosts. Dig up the roots with a garden fork. Wash off the soil, dry the roots quickly, and store in a root cellar or a fridge.

Shallots: They are ready to harvest when they're 1–1.5 inches (2.5–4 cm) in diameter and the tops have turned brown and flopped over. Store them in a dry place for a week.

Spinach: When the leaves are 3 inches (7.5 cm) long, you can harvest them from the outside of the plant. Tender leaves are more flavorsome and easier to pinch off with fingers. When spinach flowers, stop harvesting it.

Squash: Harvest when small and tender. If the skin toughens, it will be very seedy. Cut squash from the vine with a knife. For winter squash, when the vine shrivels and dries and the rind is hard, it's ready to harvest. Let the squash cure in the sun for 10 days, don't get it wet, and bring it indoors if it looks like it's going to rain.

Sweet potatoes: When the foliage turns yellow, your sweet potatoes are ready to harvest. Lift them from the ground carefully with a garden fork. Cure them in the sun for a day, then place in the shade for 7–10 days.

Tomatoes: They are ready to harvest when fully vine ripened but still firm. You can use scissors to snip them off the plant. If you have unripe tomatoes but you're expecting a frost, then bring them indoors, and wrap the tomatoes in newspaper with space between them for air to circulate.

Turnips: Harvest when the roots are 2–3 inches (5–7.5 cm) in diameter. Harvest before the ground freezes. Turnips have edible foliage too.

Watermelons: Watermelons are ready to harvest when the rind underneath goes from greenish white to a cream or yellow color. Cut watermelons from the vine with a knife, leaving 2 inches (5 cm) of stem attached.

Storing Your Harvest

If you're planning on storing your harvested produce away for later use, you can lightly rinse greens and wrap them in a paper towel to store in the fridge. With other vegetables that you harvest, such as tomatoes, peppers, or onions, don't wash these until you need to use them. This will help prevent them from spoiling.

If you want to store vegetables and fruits to eat later, you can store some for months under the right conditions. You need to select vegetables and fruits that are unblemished and check them regularly to make sure any damaged or diseased vegetables or fruits are removed so that they won't spoil the remainder. If you have one rotten piece of fruit or a rotten vegetable, it can ruin all the rest. You can buy wooden crate storage boxes or use shallow cardboard boxes. If you stack these, ensure that there is space between them for air to circulate.

Different vegetables and fruits need different storage conditions. Temperature and humidity are the most important factors to consider. You've probably seen recommendations like "store in a cool, dry place". But exactly does "cool, dry place" mean? There are three combinations for long-term storage:

- Cool and dry (50–60°F (10–15°C) and 60% relative humidity)
- Cold and dry (32–40°F (0–4°C) and 65% relative humidity)
- Cold and moist (32-40°F (0–4°C) and 95% relative humidity)

The ideal temperature for cold conditions is 32°F (0°C). This temperature is not easy to attain in most homes, however. You can expect shortened shelf life for your vegetables the more storage conditions deviate from the ideal temperature. Shelf life shortens approximately 25% for every 10°F (5.5°C) increase in temperature.

Basements are generally cool and dry. If you decide to store vegetables in your basement, they will need some ventilation. Harvested vegetables still "breathe" and need oxygen to maintain their freshness. Also, make sure to protect your stored produce from rodents.

Refrigerators are generally cold and dry. This works well for long-term storage of garlic and onions, but not much else. If you put vegetables in plastic bags in the fridge, this will create too much humidity, which can lead to the growth of mold and bacteria. You can put vegetables in perforated plastic bags, and this will create cold and moist conditions, but only for a moderate amount of time.

Root cellars are generally cold and moist. If you store vegetables in a cellar, they'll need some ventilation and protection from rodents. You can use materials such as straw, hay, or wood shavings for insulation. If you decide to use insulation, make sure that it's clean.

You can store apples and pears—a good tip is to wrap each of them in newspaper and place these in just one layer in a container. You can store carrots, potatoes, and beets. To do so, ensure that you have removed the leafy tops off carrots and beets. Don't wrap them, and place them in a single layer. You can cover them with a layer of sand to stop them from going rubbery. You can store potatoes in hessian or paper sacks. It's good to harvest potatoes when the weather is dry and then leave them in the sun to dry. Ensure that mud is removed from potatoes to prevent mold. Make sure to store potatoes somewhere dark to stop them from going green.

Most vegetables prefer cold and moist conditions, so a root cellar is the perfect place for long-term storage of most vegetables. Storage conditions for different vegetables and fruits will be covered below.

Cool and dry conditions are suitable for some pumpkins, zucchini, winter squash, and onions.

Cold and moist conditions are suitable for root crops, such as potatoes, carrots, beets, radishes, turnips, and parsnips, as well as asparagus, beans, broccoli, cabbage, cauliflower, corn, spinach, and peas. Apples and pears can be stored in cold and moist conditions too. Produce that needs cold and moist conditions can be stored in the fridge, but it will last less because refrigerators tend to dry things out.

Some vegetables, such as cucumbers, peppers, tomatoes, and eggplants, require cool and moist storage conditions (55°F or 13°C and 90–95% relative humidity). It's difficult to maintain these conditions in a typical home, so you can expect to keep vegetables that require such storage conditions for only a short period of time.

Berries can't be stored for long. Never rinse berries before storage because it will wash off the thin protective epidermal layer. Place them on a paper towel in a tightly covered container, and store them in the fridge for 2–3 days.

If you want to store onions or shallots, these need to be dried, plaited, and stored in a dry place. You can cut the tops off and hang them in tights or netting.

Any leafy vegetables don't store well, and you should ideally eat these within a few days of harvesting them.

Below you will find a table with storage conditions for a variety of different vegetables and fruits as well as their approximate storage life:

Produce	Temperature	Relative humidity (percent)	Approximate storage life
Fruits			
Apples	30–40°F (–1 to +4°C)	90–95	1–12 months
Apricots	31–32°F (–0.5 to 0°C)	90–95	1–3 weeks
Berries			
— Blackberries	31–32°F (–0.5 to 0°C)	90–95	2–3 days

Produce	Temperature	Relative humidity (percent)	Approximate storage life
— Elderberries	31–32°F (–0.5 to 0°C)	90–95	1–2 weeks
— Gooseberries	31–32°F (–0.5 to 0°C)	90–95	3–4 weeks
— Raspberries	31–32°F (–0.5 to 0°C)	90–95	2–3 days
— Strawberries	32°F (0°C)	90–95	3–7 days
— Cherries, sour	32°F (0°C)	90–95	3–7 days
— Cherries, sweet	30–31°F (–1 to –0.5°C)	90–95	2–3 weeks
Nectarines	31–32°F (–0.5 to 0°C)	90–95	2–4 weeks
Peaches	31–32°F (–0.5 to 0°C)	90–95	2–4 weeks
Pears	29–31°F (–1.5 to –0.5°C)	90–95	2–7 months
Plums and prunes	31–32°F (–0.5 to 0°C)	90–95	2–5 weeks
Vegetables			
Asparagus	32–35°F (0–1.5°C)	95–100	2–3 weeks
Beans, green or snap	40–45°F (4–7°C)	95	7–10 days
Beets, topped	32°F (0°C)	98–100	4–6 months
Broccoli	32°F (0°C)	95–100	10–14 days
Brussels sprouts	32°F (0°C)	95–100	3–5 weeks
Cabbage, early	32°F (0°C)	98–100	3–6 weeks
Cabbage, late	32°F (0°C)	98–100	5–6 months
Carrots	32°F (0°C)	98–100	7–9 months
Cauliflower	32°F (0°C)	95–98	3–4 weeks
Celeriac	32°F (0°C)	97–99	6–8 months
Celery	32°F (0°C)	98–100	2–3 months
Chard	32°F (0°C)	95–100	10–14 days
Corn, sweet	32°F (0°C)	95–98	5–8 days
Cucumbers	50–55°F (10–13°C)	95	10–14 days
Eggplant	46–54°F (8–12°C)	90–95	1 week
Garlic	32°F (0°C)	65–70	6–7 months
Horseradish	30–32°F (–1 to 0°C)	98–100	10–12 months
Kale	32°F (0°C)	95–100	2–3 weeks
Leeks	32°F (0°C)	95–100	2–3 months
Lettuce	32°F (0°C)	98–100	2–3 weeks

Produce	Temperature	Relative humidity (percent)	Approximate storage life
Onions, green	32°F (0°C)	95–100	3–4 weeks
Onions, dry	32°F (0°C)	65–70	1–8 months
Onion sets	32°F (0°C)	65–70	6–8 months
Parsley	32°F (0°C)	95–100	2–2.5 months
Parsnips	32°F (0°C)	98–100	4–6 months
Peas, green	32°F (0°C)	95–98	1–2 weeks
Peppers, chili (dry)	32–50°F (0–10°C)	60–70	6 months
Peppers, sweet	45–55°F (7–13°C)	90–95	2–3 weeks
Potatoes, early crop	40°F (4°C)	90–95	4–5 months
Potatoes, late crop	38–40°F (3–4°C)	90–95	5–10 months
Pumpkins	50–55°F (10–13°C)	50–70	2–3 months
Radishes, spring	32°F (0°C)	95–100	3–4 weeks
Radishes, winter	32°F (0°C)	95–100	2–4 months
Rhubarb	32°F (0°C)	95–100	2–4 weeks
Rutabagas	32°F (0°C)	98–100	4–6 months
Spinach	32°F (0°C)	95–100	10–14 days
Squashes, summer	41–50°F (5–10°C)	95	1–2 weeks
Squashes, winter	50°F (10°C)	50–70	1–6 months
Sweet potatoes	55–60°F (13–16°C)	85–90	4–7 months
Tomatoes mature, green	55–70°F (13–21°C)	90–95	1–3 weeks
Tomatoes firm, ripe	55–70°F (13–21°C)	90–95	4–7 days
Turnips	32°F (0°C)	95	4–5 months

I think there is no better thing than eating vegetables and fruits you have grown yourself in the garden. It is wonderful going out into the garden with a basket and picking fresh, organic vegetables that you've grown yourself, gently rinsing them, and then cooking them for an evening meal. I still remember when we harvested produce from our garden for the first time and I roasted the vegetables and made a vegetable lasagna with rich, tangy tomato sauce between the layers and had it with a side salad. To this day, it may be one of the best meals I've ever had. The taste was phenomenal, and I felt so much pride in knowing that I've grown these tasty vegetables from seed and have nurtured them into something that fed me and my family very well. We had so much lovely produce! We shared it with family and friends and made things like pickles and chutneys. I adore gardening and getting all the lovely rewards from it, and companion planting has most definitely made my garden a prettier and a more exciting place (with gorgeous flowers among vegetables and a variety of beneficial insects and pollinators), and we definitely get more and better-quality produce from our plants.

Key takeaways from this chapter:

1. Some vegetables taste best when they are tender and immature, such as salad greens, zucchini, cucumbers, potatoes, radishes, cabbage, broccoli, cauliflower, spinach, turnips, oregano, and basil.
2. With salad or leafy greens, take leaves from the outer side of the plant so that the plant can continue to grow.
3. Harvest vegetables in the morning, ideally after the morning dew has dried.
4. Never harvest when it's wet because you could spread fungal diseases.
5. You can harvest daily.
6. Things like broccoli and cauliflower that you grow in your garden won't be as large as the ones you might find in a supermarket, but they'll be tastier.
7. When harvesting sprouts, start at the bottom of the stalk.
8. Garlic and onions need to be cured in the sun for 2 weeks.
9. You can leave parsnips and some other root vegetables in the ground over winter and dig them up when required.
10. Individually wrap apples in newspaper and store them in a root cellar.
11. Pick and cook corn when required.
12. With herbs, wrap them in a paper towel and place in a plastic bag in the fridge to reduce wilting.
13. Don't refrigerate tomatoes.

The next chapter will look at plant profiles of different vegetables and fruits. This will help you when selecting the best type of plants to grow in your garden. This chapter will give you information on how to start different plants, how much light they require, what conditions they prefer, how much water and fertilization they need, what size containers different plants need, and when they should be harvested. This will help you make better choices before selecting plants to grow. It will cover a variety of vegetables, fruits, herbs, and flowers.

Chapter 12: Plant Profiles

This chapter is here to help you make informed decisions about what plants you could grow in your garden. You will know what type of soil and what growing conditions different plants prefer, what size containers they need, how to start them, their sun requirements, how much water they need, how often they need to be fertilized, whether they need any special care, like support or pruning, and other important information regarding growing different types of plants.

All plants can be classified as annuals, biennials, or perennials—these terms are related to the life cycle of plants. Annuals complete their entire life cycle in just one year. They go from seed to plant to flower and to seed again during that one year. Only the seed survives to start the next generation, and the rest of the plant dies. Biennials take up to two years to complete their life cycle. They produce vegetation in the first year, and in the second year, they produce flowers and seeds that go on to produce the next generation. Many vegetables are biennials but are often grown as annuals. Perennials live more than two years—from three years to hundreds of years. The above-ground portion of perennial plants may die in the winter and come back from the roots the following year. Some plants may retain foliage throughout the winter. Trees and shrubs are perennials.

This chapter covers 26 vegetables, 10 fruits, 10 herbs, and 4 flowers. Clearly, this chapter won't cover every type of plant you may wish to grow in your garden, but for a beginner just starting out, it will give you some good pointers as to some of the more common plants you can grow in your garden and what to expect from them.

Vegetables

Asparagus

Asparagus prefers well-drained soils with pH levels between 6.5 to 7.0. It can grow in heavy, medium, or sandy soils, as long as the soils are well-drained. If you want to grow asparagus in containers, you'll need a container that's at least 18 inches (45 cm) deep and 12 inches (30 cm) wide.

You can start asparagus indoors 12–14 weeks before the last frost and plant it outside after the danger of frost has passed, or you can sow it directly after the last frost. Plant asparagus seeds 1 inch (2.5 cm) deep. Asparagus plants take around 3 years to reach maturity, so they are often grown from 1-year-old crowns. However, asparagus plants can be productive for 10 years and even more, so it's definitely worth the wait. Asparagus needs 3–4 feet (0.9–1.2 m) of space between plants and 12 inches (30 cm) of space between rows.

Asparagus plants need full sun with at least 8 hours of sunlight per day. Asparagus is a perennial plant, and it can be productive for 10 years or even more. The spears that we eat as a vegetable are the new shoots that emerge in spring. Asparagus is a cool-season crop, and it grows best in temperatures between 70 and 85°F (21–30°C). Asparagus needs 1–2 inches (2.5–5 cm) of water per week. You can fertilize asparagus with a balanced liquid fertilizer in early spring before the spears emerge and then again after the last harvest in June.

As mentioned previously, asparagus plants take 3 years to reach maturity. After that, you can harvest asparagus plants throughout the harvest season, which is from early May until late June. You can cut individual spears with a sharp knife 1 inch (2.5 cm) below the soil surface when they are 6–10 inches (15–25 cm) tall. In warm weather, harvest every 2–3 days for the best quality spears.

Beets (Beetroot)

Beets prefer loamy, well-drained soils with pH levels between 6.0 and 7.0. If you want to grow beets in containers, you'll need a container that's 10–12 inches (25–30 cm) deep; however, an 8-inch (20 cm) container is doable. Width is not as important as depth. The wider your container is, the more beets you can grow. You can grow 5–6 beets in a 2-gallon (7.6L) container.

Beets don't like to be transplanted, so you'll need to direct sow them 1–2 weeks before the last frost. Plant the seeds ½ inch (1.2 cm) deep. Beets need 3–4 inches (7.5–10 cm) of space between plants for smaller varieties and 6 inches (15 cm) for larger ones. Rows should be spaced 12–18 inches (30–45 cm) apart.

Beets can be grown in full or partial sun, and they will need at least 6 hours of sunlight per day. Beets are biennial plants grown as annuals. They are a cool-season crop, and they require a temperature around 50–85°F (10–30°C). Beets need 1 inch (2.5 cm) of water per week. It's a good idea to use either time-based (slow-release) fertilizer or compost to enrich the soil when they sprout and then fertilize them again with a liquid fertilizer about 5 weeks after that when they break the soil surface. Beets are a root vegetable, so they need a fertilizer that is low in nitrogen but high in phosphorus and potassium.

Beets typically take 6–9 weeks to get ready for harvest after germination. You can also harvest beet greens to use in salads—their tender leaves taste delicious. You can start harvesting greens when leaves are a few inches long by cutting the outer leaves only and leaving the small inner foliage to grow, which you can harvest later.

Broccoli

Broccoli grows best in well-drained soils with a pH between 6.0 and 6.8. To grow broccoli in containers, you'll need a container that's 12 inches (30 cm) deep at a minimum. Ideally, it needs a container that is 12–18 (30–45 cm) inches deep. Growing one plant in a single container is usually best; however, you can grow multiple plants in large containers. For example, you can grow 2–3 plants in a container that is 18 inches (45 cm) wide.

You can start broccoli from seed 7–9 weeks before the last frost. Sow the seeds ½ inch (0.6 cm) deep in individual pots filled with seed starting mix. Give them plenty of light and water them regularly. They will germinate in 1–2 weeks. You can transplant them outside around 2 weeks before the last frost once they are 3–7 inches (7.5–18 cm) tall and have 2–4 true leaves. You can also direct sow broccoli 2–3 weeks before the last frost. Broccoli needs 18 inches (45 cm) of space between plants and 18–24 inches (45–60 cm) of space between rows.

Broccoli needs full sun and at least 6 hours of sunlight per day. It's a cool-season crop, and it grows best in temperatures between 65 and 75°F (18–24°C). Broccoli is a biennial plant grown as an annual. It needs 1–2 inches (2.5–5 cm) of water per week. Fertilize broccoli 3 weeks after transplanting seedlings into the garden and then every 2–3 weeks after that. You can use a low-nitrogen fertilizer, but balanced fertilizers work well too. You may need to prune them if you notice vigorous growth. You'll need to pinch out newly developing side shoots, and you can also cut away wilting leaves from sides. But don't go too hard on it—avoid excessive pruning.

Broccoli will be ready to harvest in 60–90 days after seeding. Look out for light green buds, and cut them with 4–5 inches (10–12.5 cm) of stem, but leave the outer leaves intact because they are going to encourage new growth.

Cabbage

Cabbage prefers well-drained soil with a pH level between 6 and 7. If you want to grow cabbage in containers, your containers need to be at least 12 inches (30 cm) deep and 18 inches (45 cm) wide.

Cabbage can be direct sown or started indoors early for fall and spring crops or purchased as transplants for a fall crop. You can start cabbage indoors 6–8 weeks before transplanting. You can transplant your cabbage seedlings 1–2 weeks before the last frost after they've been hardened off outside for a week for spring harvest, or you can sow cabbage seeds directly 6–8 weeks before the first frost in the fall for fall harvest. Plant the seeds ¼ to ½ inch (0.6–1.2 cm) deep. Some cabbage varieties can require up to 24 inches (60 cm) of spacing between plants; however, most compact varieties need 1 foot (30 cm) of space, and most larger varieties need 18 inches (45 cm) of space between plants and 12–24 inches (30–60 cm) of space between rows. You can check the seed packet for spacing requirements for the specific variety you're growing.

Cabbage needs full sun with 6–8 hours of sunlight per day. Cabbage is a cool-season crop, and it grows best in temperatures between 60 and 65°F (15–18°C) and no higher than 75°F (24°C). Cabbage is a biennial plant grown as an annual. Cabbage needs 1–2 inches (2.5–5 cm) of water per week. You can fertilize cabbage with a balanced liquid fertilizer every 2–3 weeks. Compost tea works great for cabbage.

Cabbage generally takes around 70–80 days to reach maturity; however, some varieties can take up to 4–6 months to grow, depending on the type. Harvest them once they have reached the size you want and formed a firm head. To harvest, cut each cabbage head at the base with a sharp knife, remove any yellow leaves, but keep loose green leaves because they provide protection in storage, and immediately bring the head indoors, or place it in shade.

Carrots

Carrots prefer light sandy loam soils with pH levels between 6.0 and 7.0. If you want to grow carrots in containers, you'll need a container that's at least 8 inches (20 cm) deep for short or half-long varieties and 12 inches (30 cm) deep for standard length carrots. If you decide to grow really large carrots, like Imperator carrots, you'll need a container that's 16–18 inches (40–45 cm) deep because these carrots can grow up to 12 inches (30 cm) long.

Carrots don't like to be transplanted, so it's best to direct sow them. You can sow the seeds outside just after the last frost if you're growing them in the ground, or you can start them indoors 2–3 weeks before the last frost if you're growing them in containers.

Carrot seeds should be placed ¼ to ½ inch (0.6–1.2 cm) below the surface of the soil. Carrots need 2–3 inches (5–7.5 cm) of space between them and 1 foot (30 cm) of space between rows.

Carrots like full sun. They need at least 6 hours of sunlight per day. They are biennial plants grown as annuals. Carrots are a cool-season crop, and the ideal temperature for them is 60–72°F (15–22°C). If you live in a warm area, you can grow them in the fall or maybe even in the winter. Carrots need 1 inch (2.5 cm) of water per week when young, but as the roots mature, you can increase the water to 2 inches (5 cm) per week. You can fertilize carrots 5–6 weeks after sowing with a liquid fertilizer that is low in nitrogen and high in phosphorus and potassium. Keep the soil moist because if the soil dries out, the roots may crack, and you will get a poor harvest.

You can usually harvest carrots 60–75 days after sowing. Pull one up and see how it is when you think the time is right.

Cauliflower

Cauliflower grows best in well-drained soils with pH levels between 6.0 and 7.0. If you want to grow them in containers, you'll need a container that's 12 inches (30 cm) deep and 10–12 inches (25–30 cm) wide. You can grow one plant in a pot this size, and it's best to grow cauliflower plants in individual pots. However, you can grow 2–3 plants in large pots, barrels, or grow bags.

Cauliflower is best started indoors. You can start cauliflower seeds indoors about a month before the last frost. Sow the seeds in seed starting mix ½ inch (1.2 cm) deep. Once the seedlings have germinated and plants have 3 or 4 leaves, you can transplant them outside. This should be done about 2 weeks before the last frost.

Cauliflower grows best in full sun, and it needs 6–8 hours of sunlight per day. It's a cool-season crop, and it does best in moderate temperatures (60–75°F or 15–24°C). Cauliflower is a biennial plant grown as an annual. Cauliflower needs 1–2 inches (2.5–5 cm) of water per week. It needs to be fertilized a lot. You can add compost or well-rotted manure to the soil when you plant them. You'll need to add compost in mid-season as well. Alternatively, you can use a balanced liquid fertilizer once a month or according to the product's instructions.

Cauliflower is typically ready to harvest 3–4 months after planting. It's ready to be harvested when the head is fully developed. It should be 6–12 inches (15–30 cm) in diameter and still compact.

Celery

Celery prefers well-drained soils with pH levels between 5.8 and 6.8. If you want to grow it in containers, you'll need a container that's at least 8 inches (20 cm) deep. You can grow several plants in one container if it's wide enough—they need to be spaced 8–10 inches (20–25 cm) apart.

Celery has a long growing season, so it's best to start it from seed indoors and transplant it outside when it is ready. You can sow the seeds 10–12 weeks before the last frost. It's a good idea to soak celery seeds in water overnight before sowing. When the seedlings are 2 inches (5 cm) tall, transplant them into individual pots. Introduce them to the outdoors gradually because they don't like cold weather. Seedlings should be transplanted outside 8 to 10 inches (20–25 cm) apart with 12–24 inches (30–60 cm) of space between rows.

Celery grows best in full sun, but it can grow in partial sun too. It needs 5–7 hours of sunlight per day. Celery is a cool-season crop that prefers temperatures between 60 and 70°F (15–21°C). Celery is a biennial plant grown as an annual. Celery needs 1–2 inches (2.5–5 cm) of water per week. You can add compost at the time of planting, and then you can fertilize it with a potassium-rich liquid fertilizer every month.

When celery starts to grow, you can tie the stalks together to keep them together and stop them from sprawling. You can harvest whole plants or just a stalk or two as you need them to keep the plants growing longer. The darker the stalks are, the more nutrients they contain, but darker green stalks are tougher. You can store celery in the fridge in a plastic bag for a few weeks. When celery is ready to harvest, the stalks will typically be around 12–18 inches (30–45 cm). It usually takes 130–140 days to grow before harvesting. Harvest stalks from the outside in. You can harvest the plants whole, but cutting individual stalks will keep plants producing for a longer period of time.

Collard Greens

Collard greens prefer well-drained soil with a pH level between 6.0 and 7.5. They grow big, so if you want to grow them in containers, you'll need big ones that are a least 3 gallons in volume (14.4L), but 5-gallon (19L) containers would be ideal.

I would suggest direct sowing collard greens after the last frost for spring harvest or 3 months before the first frost for fall harvest; however, you can start them indoors 4–6 weeks before the last frost and transplant them outside when the seedlings are 4–6 inches (10–15 cm tall) and daytime temperatures reach 50°F (10°C). Plant the seeds ¼ to ½ inch (0.6–1.2 cm) deep. Collard greens need 12–18 inches (30–45 cm) of space between plants and 18–36 (45–90 cm) inches of space between rows.

Collard greens prefer growing in full sun, but they will tolerate some shade as long as they get at least 5 hours of sunlight per day. They are a cool-season crop, and they prefer temperatures between 55 and 75°F (13–24°C). Collard greens are a biennial crop grown as an annual. They are quite thirsty and need 2 inches (5 cm) of water per week. Collard greens don't need a lot of fertilizing—you can fertilize them every 4–6 weeks with a high-nitrogen liquid fertilizer, although a balanced fertilizer would work fine too.

Collard greens usually take 80 days to grow from seed to harvest. You can harvest the leaves as needed or harvest whole plants. Collard leaves are ready for harvest as soon as they reach usable size. You can pick a couple of outer leaves at a time—use scissors or a sharp kitchen knife to cut the leaves about an inch (2.5 cm) from where they jut out of the soil. They will be most tasty when picked young—less than 10 inches (25 cm) long and dark green. If you want to harvest the whole plant, you can cut it off above the crown if there's still some time for it to produce a few more leaves before the growing season ends. Or if the growing season is ending soon, you can pull the whole plant up and cut the roots off once it's out of the ground.

Corn

Corn grows best in loamy, well-drained soils with pH levels between 6.0 and 6.8. Corn can be grown in containers. You can choose dwarf varieties that won't exceed 4–5 feet (1.2-1.5 m) in height to grow in containers. You'll need a container that is at least 12 inches (30 cm) wide and deep to grow corn. Each container of this size can hold 4 corn plants.

Corn does not transplant well, so it's best to direct sow it 2–3 weeks after the last frost. If you grow corn in containers, you can start it indoors earlier and then move the containers outside 2–3 weeks after the last frost. Corn needs 8–10 inches (20–25 cm) of space between plants and 2.5–3 feet (75–90 cm) of space between rows.

Corn grows best in full sun with at least 8 hours of sunlight per day, but 10 hours is ideal. It's a warm-season crop, and it grows best in temperatures between 85 and 95°F (30–35°C). Corn is an annual. It needs 1 inch (2.5 cm) of water per week. Corn needs to be fertilized with a balanced liquid fertilizer once the plants are 4 weeks old and then again when the plants are 8–10 weeks old. Corn plants are sturdy and shouldn't need support.

Corn usually takes 90–120 days to grow from seed to harvest, depending on the variety and the weather. Corn is ready for harvest about 20 days after the silk first appears. Corn silk is the long, thread-like strands of plant material that grow underneath the husk of a fresh ear of corn. At harvest time, the silk turns brown, but the husks are still green. When you go to harvest corn, simply take an ear of corn, and bend it downwards and away from the stalk, and it should snap right off. Be careful not to damage the stalk because there might be a few more ears ready to pick in a week or so.

Cucamelons

Cucamelons prefer well-drained soils with pH levels between 6.0 and 7.0. To grow them in containers, you'll need a container that's at least 5 gallons (19L) in volume, and you can grow 1 plant in a container this size. You can grow 3–4 plants in large 20–25-gallon (76–95L) containers. Cucamelons are wonderful in salads, with a taste that is between a cucumber and a lime.

You can start cucamelons indoors 4–6 weeks before the last frost. The seeds should be sown 3/8 inch (1 cm) deep with the blunt end downwards. When the seedlings have grown, put them into individual 4-inch (10 cm) pots to grow further. When the threat of frost has passed, you can transplant them outside. You can also direct sow them after the last frost. Cucamelons need 12–16 inches (30–40 cm) of space between plants and should be planted only in a single row per garden bed. They'll need canes to support them.

Cucamelons grow best in full sun. They need 6–8 hours of sunlight per day. They are a warm-season crop, and they grow best in temperatures between 65 and 75°F (18–24°C). Cucamelon is a perennial crop in tropical climates, but it's most commonly grown as an annual in other climates, where it is planted in the spring. Cucamelons need 1 inch (2.5 cm) of water per week. You should fertilize them once or twice during the growing season with a high-potassium liquid fertilizer. They can grow up to 1 foot (30 cm) tall and 7–10 feet (2.1–3 m) wide, so they'll need a stable support to thrive, such as a trellis. If the main shoot reaches 8 feet (2.4 m), you can pinch out the growing tip, and you can pinch out the side shoots when they've grown to 16 inches (40 cm).

They will fruit between July and September. When they are the size of olives or grapes, they are ready to eat. Cucamelons usually take 60–70 days to grow after transplanting. Fruits start to appear 2–3 weeks after flowering. Pick them when they're nice and firm. If you leave them on the plant for too long, then they can become bitter and soggy.

Cucumbers

Cucumbers prefer well-drained soils with pH levels between 6.0 and 7.0. To grow cucumbers in containers, you will need large pots that ideally hold 5 gallons (19L) of soil or more and are at least 8 inches (20 cm) deep. The containers need to be 10–12 inches (25–30 cm) wide. You can grow 2–3 plants in a 10-inch (25 cm) container and 4–6 plants in a 20-inch (50 cm) container.

Cucumbers are best started in the ground 1–2 weeks after the last frost. Seeds should be planted 1 inch (2.5 cm) deep. You can start them indoors 3 weeks before planting, and they will transplant OK. Place the cucumber plants outside 2 weeks after the last frost. Cucumbers don't like frost or cold, so don't plant them out too soon. Cucumbers need 3–5 feet (0.9–1.5 m) of space between plants if grown at ground level; however, trellised cucumbers need only 1 foot (30 cm) of space. Rows should be spaced 4–5 feet (1.2–1.5 m) for ground level plants and 1.5–2 feet (45–60 cm) for trellised plants.

Cucumbers like to grow in full sun and need 6–8 hours of sunlight per day. They are a warm-season crop that grows best in temperatures between 75 and 85°F (24–30°C). Cucumbers are annual plants. They need 1–2 inches (2.5–5 cm) of water per week. You can fertilize cucumbers every 3 weeks with a phosphorus- and potassium-rich liquid fertilizer. The main thing cucumbers need to grow well is lots of water. If you think of how much of the inside of a cucumber is water, it's no wonder that they need to be watered regularly. Don't grow cucumbers too large because they can start to taste bitter. Cucumbers can grow on a vine or on a bush. Vines tend to be more common. They have large leaves and will produce an abundant crop. You will need to have a trellis or a fence to support them. Vine varieties can grow 6–8 feet (1.8–2.4 m) tall, and bush varieties can grow 24–36 inches (60–90 cm) tall and wide.

Cucumbers typically take 55–70 days to grow from germination to harvesting. Cucumbers are ready to harvest when they are bright, medium to dark green, and firm. You should avoid harvesting them when they are yellow, puffy, have sunken areas, or wrinkled tips.

Eggplants

Eggplants prefer sandy loam or loam soils with pH levels between 6.0 and 7.0. To grow them in containers, you'll need a container that's at least 12 inches (30 cm) deep. It's best to grow them in individual containers.

Eggplants are best started indoors 4–6 weeks before the last frost. Seeds should be planted ¼ to ½ inch (0.6–1.2 cm) deep. You can plant up to two seeds in each cell of a seed starting tray or sow two seeds in each container directly. Seedlings will be ready to transplant in about 6–8 weeks. They can be transplanted outside 2–3 weeks after the last frost. Eggplants need 18 inches (45 cm) of space between plants and 30–36 inches (75–90 cm) of space between rows.

Eggplants grow best in full sun and need 6–8 hours of sunlight per day. They are a warm-season crop that grows best in temperatures between 70 and 85°F (21–30°C). They are biennial plants grown as annuals. Eggplants need 1 inch (2.5 cm) of water per week. Eggplants need to be fertilized every 2 weeks with a liquid fertilizer that is high in phosphorus. You can use a balanced fertilizer too. Growing eggplants is similar to growing tomatoes. You don't need to prune eggplants, but doing so will help improve the productivity of your plants. You'll need to remove suckers when the plants are mature. You can also remove yellowing or diseased leaves and branches growing tall and lanky. Eggplant bushes can grow quite tall, so you'll need to tie your plants to a stake.

Eggplants usually take 2–3 months to grow to harvest after transplanting. Harvest eggplants with skin that is glossy and thin. Simply cut a short piece of stem above the cap attached to the top of the fruit with a sharp knife or pruners to harvest them.

Garlic

Garlic prefers well-drained soils with pH levels between 6.0 and 7.0. To grow it in containers, you'll need a container that's 8 inches (20 cm) deep. You can plant 3 cloves in a 6-inch (15 cm) pot, 6 cloves in an 8-inch (20 cm) pot, and 8–10 cloves in a 12-inch (25 cm) pot.

Garlic is grown from cloves. Gently separate cloves, and plant them at a depth of 1 inch (2.5 cm) fat end downwards, pointy end up directly in the soil or desired containers. You would typically plant garlic in March, but it depends on the climate you live in. Garlic should be spaced 6 inches (15 cm) between plants and 10–12 inches (25–30 cm) between rows.

Garlic grows best in full sun, and it needs 6–8 hours of sunlight per day. It's a perennial crop grown as an annual. Garlic is a cool-season crop, and it requires cool air temperatures of 32 to 50°F (0–10°C) during its first two months of growth when roots are established and bulbs begin to form. It needs 1 inch (2.5 cm) of water per week during the growing season. You can fertilize garlic in early spring with a liquid fertilizer that is high in nitrogen—blood meal is perfect for garlic. You can fertilize it again when bulbs begin to form, usually in early May.

If you plant garlic in March, you'll need to water it throughout April to June, and you should be able to harvest it in July or August. Garlic is easy to grow, and it has a long growing season. If you have purchased a hardneck (rather than softneck) variety, this will produce a flower that you should remove when it appears so that the energy can go into growing the bulb instead. If you intend to store garlic, leave it to dry for a few days in the sun before storing.

Green Beans

Green beans prefer clay or silt loam soils with pH levels between 6.0 and 7.0. You can grow beans in containers—they need to be at least 6–7 inches (15–18 cm) deep for bush beans and 8–9 inches (20–23 cm) deep for pole beans. If you want to grow several bean plants in one container, it should be wide enough so that the plants don't touch each other. If you want to make use of vertical space, then pole beans are a good option. They can grow up fences, stakes, and other support systems. Pole beans will take longer to grow before you're able to harvest them, though. You can also get bush beans which tend to grow 18–24 inches (45–60 cm) in height, and you can usually harvest these within 2 months.

Green beans don't like being transplanted, so it's best to direct sow them. Sow the seeds 1 inch (2.5 cm) deep just after the last frost. It is best to plant beans in the spring, and they will start to flower 8 weeks later.

Bush green beans will grow 2 feet (60 cm) tall and wide, while pole beans can grow anywhere between 6 and 15 feet tall (1.8–5 m) and 2–3 feet (60–90 cm) wide.

Green beans require full sun—they need 6–8 hours of sunlight per day. Ensure that there isn't too much shade where you plant them. Green beans are a warm-season crop that grows best when temperatures range from 65 to 85°F (18–30°C). They are annual plants. Green beans need 1–1.5 inches (2.5–3.8 cm) of water per week. They don't need to be fertilized much. Beans enrich the soil with nitrogen themselves, so you can fertilize them with a low-nitrogen liquid fertilizer once a month during the growing season. Pole beans will need a support that is 6–8 feet (1.8–2.4 m) tall, and it's best to have the support in place before planting. Supports should be placed 3–4 feet (0.9–1.2 m) apart.

When beans are the size of a small pencil, they can be harvested, which is typically 50–55 days after planting. They are ready to harvest when the pods are 4–6 inches (10–15 cm) long and slightly firm and before the beans protrude through the skin.

Kale

Kale prefers loamy, well-drained soils with pH levels between 6.0 and 7.5. Kale grows quickly, and just 3–4 plants would be enough for a family of four each week. To grow kale in containers, you'll need a container that's 12 inches (30 cm) wide and 8 inches (20 cm) deep.

You can start kale indoors 4–6 weeks before the last frost for spring harvest or 3 months before the first frost for fall harvest. Seeds should be planted ½ inch (1.2 cm) deep and 1 inch (2.5 cm) apart. You can plant kale in the spring or fall. If you're planting in the spring, you can transplant the seedlings 1–2 weeks before the last frost, and if you're planting in the fall, you should transplant them 6–8 weeks before the first frost. You can also direct sow kale 1–2 weeks before the last frost for spring harvest or 3 months before the first frost for fall harvest. Kale needs 12–18 inches (30–45 cm) of space between plants and 18–30 inches (45–75 cm) of space between rows.

Kale is a vegetable that likes to be grown in full or partial sun. It needs at least 6 hours of sunlight per day, but it grows best in full sun with 6–8 hours of sunlight per day. Kale is a cool-season crop that grows best in temperatures between 65 and 75°F (18–24°C). Kale is a biennial plant grown as an annual. Kale needs 1–1.5 inches (2.5–3.8 cm) of water per week. You can fertilize kale once a month. Fish emulsion works great for kale in my experience.

Kale usually takes about 3 months to grow from seed to harvest. When kale leaves are approximately the size of your hand, they're ready to be harvested. Harvest lower outer leaves, leaving inner leaves to grow. You can harvest a good fistful of leaves each time you harvest, but don't take more than a third of a plant at a time. If any leaves are yellow, compost them.

Leeks

Leeks grow best in well-drained soil with pH levels between 6.0 and 7.0. If you want to grow leeks in containers, you'll need a container that's 10 inches (25 cm) wide and 2–3 gallons (7.6–11.4L) in volume. You can grow 5 leeks in a container this size.

Leeks are best started indoors. You can start leeks indoors 10–12 weeks before the last frost and transplant them outside 1 week after the last frost. Sow the seeds ¼ to ½ inch (0.6–1.2 cm) deep. When you go to transplant them, plant them 6 inches (15 cm) apart with 12–16 inches (30–40 cm) of space between rows.

Leeks grow best in full sun with 6–8 hours of sunlight per day. Leeks are a cool-season crop, and they grow best in temperatures between 55 and 75°F (13–24°C). Leeks are technically perennials, although many gardeners treat them as annuals. Leeks need 1 inch (2.5 cm) of water per week. Leeks need a lot of nitrogen. You can fertilize them with fish emulsion or any other nitrogen-rich liquid fertilizer about 3 weeks after planting and then continue to fertilize every 3–4 weeks during the growing season.

Leeks have a long growing season and take 120–150 days to grow to maturity. Leeks are ready for harvest when their white stem or shaft is 3 inches (7.5 cm) long. You should harvest leeks before they start to widen too much at the base. Also, don't allow leeks to form bulbs. You can harvest leeks from loose soil by gently twisting and pulling them up. Leeks have large root systems, so you can use a hand fork or a garden fork to loosen the soil before lifting them.

Lettuce

Lettuce prefers well-drained, sandy loam soils with pH levels between 6.0 and 7.0. Lettuce is very easy to grow in containers, and the containers don't have to be too deep—6 inches (15 cm) deep is sufficient. You can grow lettuce leaf, which means you can grow this closer together than a whole head of lettuce—you can put them approximately 4 inches (10 cm) apart.

Lettuce seeds are small and should be planted ¼ inch (6 mm) deep. I would recommend direct sowing lettuce 2–4 weeks before the last frost. You can also start lettuce indoors 1 month before the last frost and transplant the seedlings outside when they are 2–3 inches (5–7.5 cm) tall. Introduce lettuce seedlings to the outdoors gradually, increasing their time spent outdoors over a week. Spacing will depend on the type of lettuce you're growing. Loose leaf lettuce needs 4 inches (10 cm) of space between plants and 12 inches (30 cm) of space between rows. Romaine lettuce needs 8 inches (20 cm) of space between plants and 12–18 inches (30–45 cm) of space between rows. Iceberg lettuce needs 16 inches (40 cm) of space between plants and 12–18 inches (30–45 cm) of space between rows.

Lettuce needs full or partial sun to grow and at least 5–6 hours of sunlight per day. It grows best in full sun with 8 hours of sunlight per day, though. Lettuce is a cool-season crop that prefers temperatures between 60 and 70°F (15–21°C). Lettuce is an annual plant. It's quite thirsty and will need 1.5–2 inches (3.8–5 cm) of water per week. You can fertilize lettuce every 2 weeks with a balanced liquid fertilizer. Lettuce can keep growing for quite some time—the key requirement is that it gets plenty of water. If the weather is really hot, then lettuce may want some shade in the afternoon.

Lettuce grows fairly quickly. Leaf varieties reach maturity in 30 days, but they can be harvested as soon as they reach the desired size. Other types of lettuce require 6–8 weeks to reach full harvest size. It's best to harvest lettuce in the morning and take young and tender leaves. Always take the outer leaves, and let the inner leaves grow.

Onions

Onions grow best in well-drained soils with pH levels between 6.0 and 7.0. To grow them in containers, you'll need a container that is 10 inches (25 cm) deep. It also needs to be as wide as possible to make it worth your while. Onions need at least 3 inches (7.5 cm) of soil around them to grow properly.

You can grow onions from seed or sets. Sets are essentially baby onions. Growing from sets is easier and quicker than growing from seed; however, growing from seed is not difficult. Growing from seed also allows for more choice of variety. You can start seeds indoors 8–10 weeks before the last frost. Sets should be started 6 weeks before the last frost. Plant the seeds about ½ inch (1.2 cm) deep, and water them regularly. Sets should be planted 1–2 inches (2.5–5 cm) deep. You can transplant the seedlings outside 2–4 weeks before the last frost. You can also direct sow seeds 1–2 weeks before the last frost or plant sets 2–4 weeks before the last frost. Onions should be spaced 2–4 inches (5–10 cm) apart with 12–18 inches (30–45 cm) of space between rows.

Onions need full sun. Onions begin to form bulbs when a certain day length is reached. Short-day onion varieties begin to form bulbs when they receive 11 or 12 hours of daylight; intermediate-day (or day-neutral) onions need 12 to 14 hours of daylight, and long-day varieties require 14 or more hours of daylight. Onions are a cool-season crop that grows best in temperatures between 55 and 75°F (13–24°C). They are biennial plants grown as annuals. Onions need 1 inch (2.5 cm) of water per week. You'll need to fertilize your onions with a liquid fertilizer that's high in nitrogen every 2–3 weeks.

Onions need 90–100 days to grow from seed to harvest. You'll know they're ready to harvest when the leaves droop and turn yellow or brown. Gently loosen the soil around them, and then lift the onions out to harvest them. All varieties of onions will grow green stalks, and you can harvest them 3–4 weeks after planting once they reach 6–8 inches (15–20 cm) in height. Simply cut the largest outer ones, leaving at least an inch (2.5 cm) above the soil. Harvest about a third of the stalks each time.

Peas

Peas prefer well-drained soils with pH levels between 6.0 and 7.0. Peas grow well in containers, and you can grow dwarf or bush varieties of peas. You don't need to have a massive container, and it's more important for the container to be wide rather than deep. An 8–12-inch (20–30 cm) deep container is fine, and it should be as wide as possible. You can grow multiple plants in one container—they need to be spaced 2 to 3 inches (5–7.5 cm).

I would recommend direct sowing peas 4–6 weeks before the last frost. Seeds should be planted 1–2 inches (2.5–5 cm) deep. You can soak your seeds in water for 24 hours before planting to speed up the germination process. You can also start peas indoors 6–8 weeks before the last frost, and you can transplant the seedlings 4–6 weeks before the last frost. Peas need 2–3 inches (5–7.5 cm) of space between plants and 18 inches (45 cm) of space between rows.

Peas can grow in partial sun, but they grow best in full sun. They need 6–8 hours of sunlight per day. Peas are a cool-season crop that grows best in temperatures between 55 and 65°F (13–18°C). They don't like temperatures over 70°F (21°C). Peas are annual plants. They need 1 inch (2.5 cm) of water per week. Peas don't need lots of fertilizing. Feeding them with a balanced liquid fertilizer every 2–3 weeks is enough. Peas are natural climbers, and they need support to grow in most cases. Bush or dwarf varieties can do without support, but they won't produce a bountiful crop. Vining peas definitely need a trellis—they can grow up to 8 feet (2.4 m) tall. Bush peas can grow 18–30 (45–75 cm) tall and can also benefit from support, especially when they grow over 2 feet (60 cm) tall.

Most varieties of peas need 60–70 days to grow from planting to harvest. Harvest pea pods when they are bright green and noticeably full. They should be plump and swollen.

Peppers

Peppers prefer loam or sandy loam soils with pH levels between 6.0 and 7.0. You can grow any variety of peppers in containers, including bell preppers and chili peppers, and their requirements are quite similar. The correct pot to grow peppers needs to be at least 12 inches (30 cm) deep and have good drainage.

Peppers need a lot of warmth and are best started indoors in most climates. You should start them indoors 6–10 weeks before the last frost. For bell peppers, plant the seeds about an inch (2.5 cm) deep, and for chili peppers about ¼ inch (0.6 cm) deep. Seeds will germinate in 1–3 weeks. Transplant the seedlings outside at least 2 weeks after the last frost when they have at least 2 sets of true leaves. Pepper plants need to be spaced 18 inches (45 cm) apart with 30–36 inches (75–90 cm) of space between rows.

Peppers require full sun, and they need at least 6–8 hours of sunlight per day, but they will grow best with up to 12 hours of sunlight per day. Peppers are a warm-season crop that grows best in temperatures between 70 and 80°F (21–27°C). Peppers are perennial plants grown as annuals. They can grow 3–6 feet (0.9–1.8 m) tall and 18–24 inches (45–60 cm) wide. They need 1–2 inches (2.5–5 cm) of water per week. Peppers need to be fertilized regularly, just like tomatoes. A liquid fertilizer with a lower nitrogen number is perfect, but a balanced fertilizer works well too, and you should use it every 2 weeks. Pepper plants can benefit from having support—stakes and cages are popular options for that. Pinching pepper plants in early stage of their growth will help them become bushier and promote growth. You can pinch pepper plants when they are at least 6 inches (15 cm) tall—simply clip the growing tip. You can also deadhead the flowers if they start appearing too early—this will help direct the plant's energy into growth.

Bell peppers take 2–3 months to be ready for harvesting after transplanting, and chili peppers can take 2–4 months to grow. You can harvest bell peppers when they're green once they reach full size and remain firm. Or you can leave them to ripen, and their color will change into red, yellow, or orange. As for chili peppers, you can harvest them once they reach their mature size and color, but the longer you leave them to ripen, the hotter they will become.

Potatoes

Potatoes prefer well-drained, sandy, slightly acidic soils with pH levels between 6 and 6.5, although they can tolerate soils with pH levels as low as 5. To grow them in containers, you will need a large container that has good drainage. It should be at least 16 inches (40 cm) deep and 16 inches (40 cm) wide, and you can plant 4–6 seed potatoes in a container this size.

Potatoes are grown from seed potatoes. A seed potato is a potato that is replanted and used to grow more potatoes. You can get them at a garden center or a nursery. Make sure to get ones that are certified and disease-free. You can cut larger seed potatoes (larger than a chicken egg) that have multiple eye buds in half to grow more potatoes. When you're cutting, make sure that each side has at least 2 sprouts. Leave them for a few days after cutting so that the wound can heal, or they will rot otherwise. You can pre-sprout seed potatoes—this will help them develop sprouts, but it's not necessary. It's only required if you live in a climate that has short summers. To pre-sprout your seed potatoes, leave them in a cool, dark place for 2–3 weeks prior to planting.

Plant your seed potatoes 2 weeks after the last frost. They should be planted 6–8 inches (15–20 cm) deep with the majority of the eyes facing upwards and spaced 1 foot (30 cm) apart. After placing the seed potatoes, cover them with soil.

Potatoes grow best in full sun. They ideally need 8 hours of sunlight per day, but they can grow in partial sun too. Potatoes are a cool-season crop, and they grow best in temperatures between 60 and 70°F (15–21°C). Potatoes are perennial plants grown as annuals. They need 1–2 inches of water per week. You can fertilize them with a balanced liquid fertilizer once a month.

Potatoes usually take about 3 months to grow from planting to harvest. Wait until the tops of the vines have yellowed and started to die back before harvesting potatoes.

Pumpkins

Pumpkins prefer well-drained soils with pH levels between 6.0 and 6.8. Did you know that you can grow large pumpkins in containers? You will need a very larger container that can hold 20–25 gallons (76–95L) of soil, though. You can grow smaller varieties in a 10-gallon (38L) container.

I would suggest direct sowing pumpkins 2 weeks after the last frost. Plant the seeds 1 inch (2.5 cm) deep. You can start pumpkin seeds indoors 3–4 weeks before the last frost and transplant them outside 2–3 weeks after the last frost. Pumpkins need to be spaced 2 feet (60 cm) apart with 6–10 feet (1.8–3 m) of space between rows.

Pumpkins need full sun, ideally 8 hours of sunlight per day. Pumpkins are a warm-season crop that grows best in temperatures between 65 and 95°F (18–35°C). Pumpkins are annual plants. They can grow 10–30 inches (25–75 cm) tall and 4–16 feet (1.2–4.8 m) wide, so they will take a lot of space. Pumpkins need 1–2 inches (2.5–5 cm) of water per week. Pumpkins need to be fertilized every 2–3 weeks with a balanced or low-nitrogen liquid fertilizer. Bone meal and compost tea are great for that. Smaller pumpkin varieties will need a strong support, such as an A-shaped trellis.

Pumpkins usually take 3–4 months to grow from planting to harvesting. You can harvest them when they harden and take a uniform and intense color. You can press a pumpkin with your thumb to see if it's ready to be harvested. If the bark is hard and it sounds hollow—it's ready.

Radishes

Radishes prefer well-drained soil with pH level between 6.0 and 7.0. To grow them in containers, you'll need a container that is at least 6 inches (15 cm) deep, but if you have bought larger radishes, they may need an 8–10-inch (20–25 cm) deep container. Most radishes need 2 inches (5 cm) of spacing, so you'll need a wide container if you want to grow lots of radishes in one pot.

Like with all root crops, it's best to direct sow radishes. You can direct sow them 4–6 weeks before the last frost. Plant the seeds ¼ to ½ an inch (0.6–1.2 cm) deep. Radishes need to be spaced 2–3 inches (5–7.5 cm) apart with 8–12 inches (20–30 cm) of space between rows.

Radishes can grow in full or partial sun. They need at least 6 hours of sunlight per day. Radishes are a cool-season crop that grows best in temperatures between 55 and 65°F (13–18°C). Radishes can be either annual or biennial plants depending on the variety, but they are grown as annuals. They need 1 inch (2.5 cm) of water per week. Radishes don't need a lot of fertilizing, but you can use a phosphorus-rich liquid fertilizer, such as bone meal, a couple of times during the growing season.

Radishes take 20–70 days to grow from planting to harvesting depending on the variety. Early maturing varieties can be harvested in 20–40 days, while Asian radish varieties take 40–70 days to grow until harvest. A good way to tell if your radishes are ready to be harvested is to simply pull one from the soil. You can harvest them when they're about 1 inch (2.5 cm) in diameter. You can also harvest radish tops. Harvest young and green leaves, and use them in salads and soups.

Spinach

Spinach grows best in well-drained soil with pH level between 6.5 and 7. Spinach has a deep taproot, so if you want to grow it in containers, you'll need a container that is at least 10 inches (25 cm) wide and deep.

You can start spinach indoors 6 weeks before the last frost and transplant it outside right after the last frost. You can also direct sow spinach 4 weeks before the last frost. Plant the seeds ½ inch (1.2 cm) deep. Spinach plants need 2–4 inches (5–10 cm) of space between plants, although some larger varieties may need 3–6 inches (7.5–15 cm) of space. Your seed packet should have information on how much space your particular variety needs. Rows need to be spaced 1 foot (30 cm) apart.

Spinach prefers full sun but can tolerate some shade. It needs at least 4 hours of sunlight per day; however, 4–6 hours is ideal. It's a cool-season crop, and it grows best in temperatures between 50 and 60°F (10–15°C). Spinach is an annual crop. Spinach needs 1–1.5 inches (2.5–3.8 cm) of water per week. You should fertilize spinach every 2–3 weeks during the growing season with a balanced liquid fertilizer.

Spinach is usually ready for harvest in 6–10 weeks. You can harvest leaves as needed or harvest an entire plant. When the outer leaves are about 6 inches (15 cm) long, they're ready to be harvested. Simply hold each leaf with one hand, and cut the stem with the other one. Harvest no more than a third of a plant at once. If plants are near the end of the season, you can pull up or cut the entire plant.

Tomatoes

Tomatoes prefer well-drained soil with pH level between 6.0 and 6.8. To grow them in containers, you will need a large container that is 24 inches (60 cm) deep and 20 inches (50 cm) in diameter. Some tomatoes will grow up to 6 feet (1.8 m) tall, so you will need stakes and maybe a trellis to help grow these up. Another thing to be aware of is how many tomatoes you actually want because all the tomatoes will need to be harvested at the same time, and you'll need to be ready to use them and preserve what you don't want to use immediately. So, it's worth having plenty of mason jars if you plan to grow lots of tomatoes.

Many people start with seedlings rather than seeds because they take a while to grow. If you decide to purchase seedlings, always get them from a reputable nursery. Plants should be dark green, short, stocky, and have stems the size of a pencil or thicker. They should not have yellow leaves or spots.

If you decide to grow tomatoes from seed, they are almost always started indoors. I would suggest that you start them indoors 6 weeks before the last frost and put the seeds ½ inch (1.2 cm) deep in trays. You can transplant them outside 2 weeks after the last frost. The key warning, though, is not to put them outside too soon because tomatoes love warmth and will not withstand cold weather. Tomato plants need to be spaced 2–3 feet (60–90 cm) apart with 4 feet (1.2 m) of space between rows.

Tomatoes need full sun, ideally at least 8 hours of sunlight per day. Tomatoes are a warm-season crop, and they love warmth. They grow best in temperatures between 70 and 85°F (21–30°C). Tomatoes can be grown as perennials in their native tropical climate of South and Central America, but they are grown as annuals in other climates. Before tomatoes start to grow, you will see little yellow flowers. Tomatoes need 1–2 inches (2.5–5 cm) of water per week. They should be first fertilized when you plant them in the garden and then again when they set fruit. After tomato plants start growing fruit, you can fertilize them every 2–3 weeks until harvest. You can get a fertilizer especially formulated for tomatoes, usually with a ratio like 3-4-6 or 4-7-10. You can pinch off small stems and leaves between branches and the main stem. You can stake tomato plants, and I'd recommend doing that, as tomato plants can grow 3–10 feet (0.9–3 m) tall. You can also remove leaves from the bottom 12 inches (30 cm) of the stem.

Tomatoes can be harvested 60–100 days after planting. You can harvest them anytime they've begun to show a bit of color. Bring them indoors, and they'll ripen within a few days.

Zucchini

Zucchini prefer well-drained, loamy soils with pH levels between 6.0 and 7.5. You can grow them in containers. The perfect pot to grow zucchini in needs to be 14–18 inches (35–45 cm) wide and deep.

Zucchini can be started either indoors or directly in the soil. Zucchini plants have delicate roots and can be difficult to transplant, so I would suggest direct sowing them. You can direct sow them just after the last frost. Plant the seeds 1 inch (2.5 cm) deep. A top tip is to plant zucchini seeds on their sides to reduce the chance of them rotting. You can start them indoors, but you'll have to be careful when transplanting the seedlings so as not to damage their delicate roots. You can start zucchini indoors 4–6 weeks before the last frost and transplant the seedlings outside 1–2 weeks after the last frost. Zucchini plants should be spaced 18–24 inches (45-60 cm) apart with 4 feet (1.2 m) of space between rows.

Zucchini grow best in full sun—they need 6–8 hours of sunlight per day. They are a warm-season crop that grows best in temperatures above 70°F (21°C). Zucchini are annual plants. They need 1–2 inches (2.5–5 cm) of water per week. Zucchini don't need a lot of fertilizing. You can fertilize them once in the spring and once in the summer with a balanced liquid fertilizer. Zucchini plants can grow up to 2 feet (60 cm) tall and 2–3 feet (60–90 cm) wide. They do not necessarily need support, but they will definitely appreciate it. You can either stake them or get an A-shaped trellis.

Zucchini usually take 45–55 days to grow from seed to harvest. When you come to harvest them, remember that you can eat male zucchini flowers. You can fill and lightly batter them, but remember to leave some of these in order to pollinate the female flowers. Male flowers have a long, thin stem. Female flowers have a swollen base behind the flower—this is the ovary that later develops into a zucchini after germination. When you harvest zucchini, you can cut or twist them off. Smaller zucchini are denser and have a nutty taste. Bigger zucchini are more watery, so don't be tempted to grow your zucchini to a massive size before harvesting them. They taste better when they're smaller.

Fruits

Apples

Apple trees prefer loamy, well-drained soils with pH levels between 5.8 and 7.0. You can grow dwarf varieties in containers. You'll need a container that is 18–22 inches (45–55 cm) in diameter and 10–15 gallons (38–57L) in volume for a dwarf apple tree.

Standard apple trees can grow 25–35 feet (7.5–10 m) tall, so they are too large for containers in most cases. You can get semi-dwarf and dwarf apple trees—they grow 6–20 feet (1.8–6 m) tall. They will bloom and produce apples in the summer or fall. Apple trees need good air circulation so that their leaves can dry and not attract fungus after it has rained. Dwarf varieties of apple trees need to be spaced 8 feet (2.4 m) apart, while full-sized trees need to be spaced 15 feet (4.5 m) apart.

If you want to grow apple trees from seed, you will have a really long wait, up to 8 years before the trees can bear fruit. Dwarf varieties mature quicker and can bear fruit 2–3 years after planting. You can buy apple trees from a nursery. If you do so, then it's best to buy more than one because most apple trees require another apple tree of a different variety nearby for cross-pollination to produce fruit. You can get self-pollinating apple trees, including dwarf varieties, but they will produce more fruit if another tree is nearby for cross-pollination. It's also important to attract bees to your garden to help with pollination.

Apple trees like to be grown in full sun. They need 1 inch (2.5 cm) of water per week. They need to be fertilized 3 times a year. First, in early spring before flowering, which is around mid-April in most temperate areas. Then you'll need to fertilize them again about a month later after flowering is completed around the end of May. And then, you should fertilize them again about a month after that, around the end of June. You can prune your trees once a year to let in more light and air.

Blueberries

Blueberries like acidic soil with a pH level between 4 and 5.5 pH, and it's best to water them with rainwater rather than tap water (which contains lime and can make soil more alkaline). You'll need a container that is at least 12 inches (30 cm) in diameter for blueberry bushes. As the plants grow, you may need to repot them into 20-inch (50 cm) containers. Blueberry bushes grow up to 4 feet (1.2 m) tall, and they spread to around 3 feet (90 cm). When you plant them, you should ensure they are spaced 5 feet (1.5 m) apart with 10–12 feet (3–3.6 m) of space between rows. If you want to grow them in containers, you can buy potting mixes with lower pH levels, but they can a bit more difficult to find. You can use potting mixes for azaleas and rhododendrons to grow blueberry bushes in.

They prefer full sun, but they can grow in partial sun too. They need 6–8 hours of sunlight per day. Blueberries need to be watered regularly. If you plant two or more of these, they will do better than just a single plant. Blueberry bushes should be fertilized 3 times a year—first in the spring when buds break, then 6 weeks after that, and then again after harvest. Blueberries respond well to any nitrogen-rich fertilizer, but they require fertilizers with an ammonium form of nitrogen, such as cottonseed meal. Any fertilizer sold for azaleas or rhododendrons also works well for blueberries.

For the first couple of years, you shouldn't need to prune blueberries. After this time, you can prune them in February or March and get rid of a quarter of the older branches, keeping the newer ones. When you harvest blueberries, gently pick off the deepest blueberries. If any are green, allow them to fully ripen before picking them off. The more years go by, the greater the harvest you will get from them.

Cherries

Cherry trees prefer well-drained soils with pH levels between 6.0 and 7.0. They can be grown in containers. Like with other fruit trees, you will need a large container. A 15-gallon (57L) container is enough for a tree that is 5 feet (1.5 m) tall. Standard cherry trees can grow up to 35 feet (10 m) tall, so naturally they'll be too large for containers, but you can get dwarf varieties that grow 6.5–8 feet (2–2.5 m) tall but still produce full-sized fruit.

You can grow cherry trees from cuttings, seeds, or pits, but it will take years until they mature. They can start producing fruit after 2 years but will reach full cropping between 4 and 5 years, so I would suggest buying a tree from a nursery. There are two main varieties of cherry trees—sweet and sour. Sweet cherries are usually eaten, and sour cherries are typically used for cooking or baking. Sweet cherry trees need to be spaced 35–40 feet (10.7–12.2 m) apart, and their dwarf varieties need 5–10 feet (1.5–3 m) of space. Sour cherry trees need to be spaced 20–25 feet (6–7.6 m) apart, and their dwarf varieties need 8–10 feet (2.4–3 m) of space.

Cherry trees need full sun, ideally 6–8 hours of sunlight per day. Young cherry trees need 2–3 inches (5–7.5 cm) of water every 1–2 weeks, while mature trees only need 1 inch (2.5 cm) of water every 1–2 weeks. Cherry trees don't need a lot of fertilizing—you can use a low-nitrogen fertilizer in the spring 2–3 weeks before the trees blossom. You should prune cherry trees once a year, but try to do it in the warmer months because pruning in the winter makes trees more vulnerable to diseases.

Figs

Fig trees prefer well-drained soil with pH level between 6.0 and 7.5. They can be grown in containers. Fig trees require a 15–20-gallon (57–76L) container. They take 3–5 years to mature, so like with other fruit trees, I'd suggest buying a tree from a nursery. They grow 10–30 feet (3–10 m), but you can get dwarf trees that grow 4–6 feet (1.2–1.8 m) tall. Full-sized trees need to be spaced 12–25 feet (3.6–7.6 m) apart, and dwarf trees need to be spaced 8 feet (2.4 m) apart.

Fig trees need full sun, ideally 7–8 hours of sunlight per day. They need 1–1.5 inches (2.5–3.8 cm) of water per week. Fig trees are more tolerant to dry soil than wet soil. Yellow foliage and dropping leaves are signs of underwatering. You can fertilize them with a balanced fertilizer once a month, beginning when the trees start to put on new leaves and stopping before the end of July.

If you're growing fig trees in containers, I would suggest moving your fig trees indoors for the winter. You can place them in an unheated garage or a basement. Once they're indoors, reduce watering significantly. Only water them when the top 2 inches (5 cm) of the soil are dry. You can move them back outside in the spring after the last frost, gradually introducing them to outdoor conditions over the course of a few weeks.

Gooseberries

Gooseberries prefer well-drained soils with pH levels between 5.5 and 7.0. You can grow them in containers. You will need a 10-gallon (38L) container to grow a gooseberry bush. Gooseberry bushes tend to grow to a height of 5 feet (1.5 m) and are about 5 feet (1.5 m) wide. They need to be spaced 4–5 feet (1.2–1.5 m) apart with 6–8 feet (1.8 m–2.4 m) of space between rows. They will give you berries for 15 years, and you can expect a yield of 7–8 lb (3–3.6 kg) from each bush.

You can grow gooseberry bushes from seed; however, they are commonly sold as dormant bare root or live potted plants, and I'd suggest going that route. It's best to plant gooseberry bushes in the spring. You can grow gooseberry bushes up trellises, walls, or fences.

Gooseberries prefer full sun but can grow in partial sun too. Ideally, they need 8 hours of sunlight per day. They need 1 inch (2.5 cm) of water per week. Gooseberries typically need to be fertilized twice a year with a balanced fertilizer—once in early spring just as the buds begin to swell and again in midsummer after the fruit has set. You may decide to put nets over the bushes when the berries are starting to ripen to prevent birds from eating them. It's worth thinning out the bushes in June and getting rid of some gooseberries the size of a pea at this point. You can prune them once a year, and it's best to do it in the winter or early spring before new growth starts to sprout. Gooseberry bushes tolerate temperatures below freezing well, so you can leave them outside over winter if you're growing them in containers.

Lemons

Lemon trees prefer well-drained, sandy loam soils with pH levels between 6.0 and 7.5. You can grow smaller lemon trees in a 5-gallon (19L) container, but for larger trees you'll need at least a 10-gallon (38L) container. Lemon trees grow 10–20 feet (3–6 m) tall, but you can get dwarf varieties that stay under 10 feet (3 m) tall, usually 3–5 feet (0.9–1.5 m) tall.

I'd suggest buying lemon trees from a nursery, as it takes 3–6 years to grow a lemon tree from seed to maturity, but you can grow them from cuttings or from seed. If you decide to grow from seed, you could let the seeds dry out for a couple of weeks. Then when they are dry, plant them 1 inch (2.5 cm) deep in a seed starting tray or a container and cover with plastic wrap. Let the seedling get to 10 inches (25 cm) before transplanting it outside. Lemon trees should be spaced 12–25 feet (3.6–7.6 m) apart, while dwarf varieties need to be spaced 6–10 feet (1.8–3 m) apart.

Lemon trees need full sun. They need 8 hours of sunlight to grow. They need 1 inch (2.5 cm) of water per week. Lemon trees should be fertilized with a balanced fertilizer no more than 4 times per year and only when there is active growth, so you can fertilize them from spring right before glowering and until the start of fall. Lemon trees are quite sensitive to the cold, and freezing temperatures can damage or even kill them. If you're growing them in containers, you could bring them indoors over winter.

Melons

Melons grow best in well-drained, sandy loam soils, with pH levels between 6.0 and 6.5. You can grow full-sized melons in containers, although they will often outgrow the containers they are in. You'll get the best results with dwarf cultivars that produce smaller fruit and shorter vines. You'll need a container that is at least 16 inches (40 cm) deep and 14 inches (35 cm) wide or 5 gallons (19L) in volume.

Melons are best started indoors 4 weeks before the last frost. You can transplant them outside 1 week after the last frost. In warmer climates, you can direct sow melons 1–2 weeks after the last frost. Plant the seeds ½ to 1 inch (1.2–2.5 cm) deep. Melons need 24–36 inches (60–90 cm) of space between plants and 5–6 feet (1.5–1.8 m) of space between rows.

Melons need full sun—at least 8 hours of sunlight per day. They are a warm-season crop, and they grow best in temperatures between 65 and 95°F (18–35°C). Melons are annual plants. Melons need 1–2 inches (2.5–5 cm) of water per week. Melons do best when treated with fertilizer in 2 or 3 applications during the growing season. Phosphorus- and potassium-rich fertilizers are best, but a balanced fertilizer will work fine too.

Melons usually take 80–90 days to grow to maturity after transplanting. Harvest when fruits produce their characteristic melon fragrance and start to crack near the stem. A fully ripe melon will separate from the vine with light pressure. You can also cut melons from the vine with a sharp knife. Leave an inch (2.5 cm) of stem attached to the fruit to keep it from rotting if you don't plan to use the harvested melon immediately.

Peaches and Nectarines

Peach trees prefer well-drained, loamy soils with pH levels between 6.0 and 7.0. You can grow smaller trees in a 5-gallon (19L) container, but you'll need a 10–15-gallon (38–57L) container for larger trees. Unlike apple trees, peach trees have no dwarf rootstock to keep the trees small. Instead, some varieties naturally grow smaller. They are called natural dwarfs; however, they produce full-sized fruit. They grow 6–10 feet (1.8–3 m) tall. There are also small nectarine trees. Full-sized peach trees should be spaced 15–20 feet (4.5–6 m) apart, and dwarf trees should be spaced 10–12 feet (3–3.6 m) apart.

Like with other fruit trees, I'd suggest getting a tree from a nursery because peach trees can take 3–4 years to mature. They need full sun, ideally 8 hours of sunlight per day. Peach trees need 1–1.5 inches (2.5–3.8 cm) of water per week. You only need to start fertilizing them when they begin bearing fruit, which usually takes 3–4 years. Mature trees should be fertilized twice a year with a balanced fertilizer once in early spring (usually around March) and once in late spring (usually around May). Most peach trees grow compact and don't require pruning. You can prune them if they start getting a bit too large.

Raspberries

Raspberries prefer well-drained loam or sandy loam soils with pH levels between 5.5 and 6.5. You can grow them in containers. You'll need a container that's 16–20 inches (40–50 cm) wide and deep for a raspberry bush.

You can purchase one-year-old raspberry canes from a nursery to plant them. One bush alone can provide you with hundreds of berries in a season. Ideally, you should plant them in the spring, and they will bloom in the summer or fall. It's best to soak the roots of plants for a couple of hours before planting. Raspberry canes should be spaced 18 inches (45 cm) apart with 8–10 feet (2.4–3 m) of space between rows so that you can move freely between them. Rows should be no less than 5 feet (1.5 m) apart because otherwise they'll tend to grow together and create a giant, impenetrable, hard to maintain hedgerow. You can cut the canes down to 9 inches (23 cm) tall after planting, which will encourage new growth. Generally, raspberry bushes will produce fruit a year after you have planted them. You will need to prune the bushes once a year.

Raspberries like to grow in full sun. They need 6–8 hours of sunlight per day. The more sun the bush gets, the more raspberries it will produce. They need 1 inch (2.5 cm) of water per week. You should fertilize them once a year in the spring with a balanced fertilizer. You can also give your raspberry bushes some compost or aged manure every year. They grow 4–8 feet (1.2–2.4 m) tall and 3–5 feet (0.9–1.5 m) wide. You may need supports to keep the canes in place. You could use a trellis or a fence.

After you have harvested your berries, cut the canes that produced them back to the ground. Prune only the old canes (the brown stems that produced berries), and leave the younger green ones. You can tie canes to supports with strings. When it comes to harvesting berries, you'll need to pick them every few days. Try to collect them when it's dry, and you shouldn't need to pull too hard. When they're ripe, it shouldn't be difficult to remove them from the vine.

Strawberries

Strawberries prefer well-drained, sandy loam soils with pH levels between 5.5 and 6.5. You can grow individual strawberry plants in containers that are 6–8 inches (15–20 cm) deep and wide. Or you can grow multiple plants in one container if you space them 10–12 inches (25–30 cm) apart.

Strawberries are best started from seed indoors. You can start them indoors 8 weeks before the last frost. Sow the seeds thinly, and press them into the growing medium. They can take anywhere between 1 and 6 weeks to germinate. You can transplant the seedlings outside after the last frost when they have 3 sets of true leaves. Don't bury the crown when you plant them. The crown should be at the surface of the soil so that it doesn't rot. Strawberries need to be spaced 12–18 inches (30–45 cm) apart with 30 inches (75 cm) of space between rows.

Strawberries like to be grown in full sun. They need 6–8 hours of sunlight per day. Strawberries are short-term perennials that continuously replicate and renew themselves, and they can be productive for 4–5 years, but they can also be grown as annuals that you replant each year. They need 1–1.5 inches (2.5–3.8 cm) of water per week. You can fertilize them with a balanced fertilizer once in the spring about a month after you plant them and then again in late summer to early fall. Established strawberries should be fertilized once a year after the final harvest.

When your strawberries bloom depends on what type of strawberry plants you've purchased. If you have got June-bearing strawberries, then you will need to harvest all the fruit in one go over 3 weeks. Ever-bearing strawberries will produce most of the crop in the spring and some throughout the summer and then another crop in late summer or early fall. Day-neutral varieties will produce fruit all throughout the season until the first frost. I personally like June-bearing strawberries, and while you'll need to wait a year until your first harvest, they taste incredibly delicious, and it's worth the wait.

It is advisable that in the first year you pick off the flowers—this will discourage the plants from fruiting and will help focus their energy on building strong roots instead. This will help you have a bigger yield of berries the following year. If you live in a very cold area, once the strawberries have finished, you can cut the plants down to about an inch (2.5 cm) and place 4 inches (10 cm) of mulch on them. You can remove the mulch in early spring after the last frost.

Herbs

Basil

Basil likes well-drained soils with pH levels between 6.0 and 7.0. To grow basil in containers, you'll need a container that's 10–12 inches (20–25 cm) deep.

Basil is my favorite herb, and I absolutely adore it. I love the smell, and it's so versatile—it can add such a boost of flavor to many dishes. You can get a variety of flavors of basil: sweet, purple, lemon, and Thai. Basil is best started indoors 6–8 weeks before the last frost. The plant does like warmth, and it won't grow well without it. When you sow basil seeds, put them ¼ inch (0.6 cm) deep. You can transplant the seedlings outside 1–2 weeks after the last frost when they've grown 3 pairs of true leaves. You can also direct sow basil 1–2 weeks after the last frost. Basil plants should be spaced 12 inches (30 cm) apart with at least 18 inches (45 cm) of space between rows.

Basil prefers to grow in full sun with 6–8 hours of sunlight per day, but it can grow in partial shade too. Basil is a warm-season crop that prefers temperatures between 50 and 85°F (10–30°C). It is an annual herb. It needs 1–1.5 inches (2.5–3.8 cm) of water per week. You can fertilize basil every 3–4 weeks with a balanced liquid fertilizer. If you know there will be a bad frost, harvest basil before this because the cold will destroy basil plants.

Basil usually takes 3–4 weeks to grow from planting to harvest. When the plants are 8 inches (20 cm) tall, they are ready to harvest. It's best to harvest basil in the morning. Picking the leaves will encourage more growth. If you don't need them immediately, you can store them to use when required by freezing or drying the leaves.

Cilantro (Coriander)

Cilantro (coriander) prefers well-drained soils with pH levels between 6.5 and 7.5. Like dill, cilantro (coriander) has a long taproot, so if you want to grow it in containers, you'll need a container that is 12 inches (30 cm) deep and 18 inches (45 cm) wide.

Cilantro (coriander) doesn't like to be transplanted, so it's best to direct sow it. You can direct sow it outside after the last frost, or if you're growing in containers, you can start it indoors directly in the desired containers 2 weeks before the last frost and move them outdoors after the last frost. Plant the seeds ¼ to ½ inch (0.6–1.2 cm) deep. Cilantro (coriander) plants need to be spaced 6–8 inches (15–20 cm) apart with 12 inches (30 cm) between rows.

Cilantro (coriander) grows best in full sun with 6–8 hours of sunlight per day. It's a cool-season crop, and it grows best in temperatures between 60 and 70°F (15–21°C). Cilantro (coriander) is an annual herb, although it may survive winter in mild climates. It needs 1 inch (2.5 cm) of water per week, and you can fertilize it a couple of times during the growing season with a nitrogen-rich or a balanced liquid fertilizer.

You can harvest the leaves when the plants are at least 6 inches (15 cm) tall, which typically occurs about a month after sowing seeds. Don't harvest more than a third of the leaves at a time. If you want to harvest seeds, you'll need to let your plants flower, which can take around 100 days from sowing seeds. To harvest seeds, leaves seed heads on your plants to dry out, and then shake them into a paper bag to release the seeds, or you can snip the entire seedhead, place it into a paper bag, put the bag in a cool, dark, well-ventilated place, and allow the seeds to finish drying in the bag for easier harvest.

Chives

Chives prefer well-drained soils with pH levels between 6.0 and 7.0. To grow them in containers, you'll need a container that is 6–8 inches (15–20 cm) deep, and you can grow multiple plants in one container if you space them 6 inches (15 cm) apart.

Chives look very pretty when they're growing because of their lovely purple flowers. They also smell and taste fantastic and can really enhance the taste of many dishes, giving them that wonderful onion taste but without the need to cut up an onion.

Growing chives from seed is quite easy. You can direct sow them 4–6 weeks before the last frost. Plant the seeds ¼ inch (0.6 cm) deep. You can also start them indoors 6–8 weeks before the last frost. They germinate best on a heat pad or a warm windowsill. You can transplant the seedlings outside 1–2 weeks after the last frost. Chives need 6–12 inches (15–30 cm) of space between plants and 12 inches (30 cm) of space between rows.

Chives grow best in full sun with 6–8 hours of sunlight per day, but they can grow in partial shade too. They are a cool-season crop, and they grow best in temperatures between 60 and 70°F (15–21°C). Chives are a perennial herb, and I've always found them incredibly resilient—they spring back up year after year. They need 1 inch (2.5 cm) of water per week. You can fertilize them every 4–6 weeks with a balanced liquid fertilizer.

Chives take 60 days to grow from seed to harvest. When you harvest chives, it's best to cut leaves from the base of the plant with a pair of scissors. Don't eat the stems of flowering shoots.

Dill

Dill prefers well-drained soils with pH levels between 5.5 and 6.5. Dill has a long taproot, so to grow it in containers, you'll need one that is at least 12 inches (30 cm) deep and wide.

Dill doesn't transplant well, so it's best to direct sow it. You can sow the seeds ¼ inch (0.6 cm) deep after the last frost. If you're growing it in containers, you can plant the seeds directly into the desired pots a month before the last frost. You can move them outdoors once the plants are 4–6 inches (10–15 cm) tall and the danger of frost has passed. Dill plants should be spaced 10–12 inches (25–30 cm) apart with 2–3 feet (60–90 cm) of space between rows.

Dill grows best in full sun with 6–8 hours of sunlight per day. Dill is a cool-season crop, and it grows best in temperatures between 60 and 70°F (15–21°C). It is an annual herb. Dill needs 1 inch (2.5 cm) of water per week. It doesn't need a lot of fertilizing. A light feeding of a phosphorus-rich or a balanced liquid fertilizer applied once in late spring should be enough.

Dill is usually ready for harvest 90 days after planting. To harvest, snip the stems of the leaves right where they meet the growth point on the main stem with a pair of scissors.

Mint

Mint prefers well-drained soils with pH levels between 6.0 and 7.5. To grow it in containers, you'll need one that's 10–12 inches (25–30 cm) deep and wide.

You can grow mint from seed; however, germination is undependable. I'd suggest getting a mint plant from a nursery, and then you can propagate it via cuttings. If you decide to grow mint from seed, you can start seeds indoors 8–10 weeks before the last frost. Plant them ¼ inch (0.6 cm) deep. You can transplant the seedlings outside after the last frost. You can also sow it directly after the last frost. Mint plants need to be spaced 12–18 inches (30–45 cm) apart with 18 inches (45 cm) of space between rows.

Mint can grow in either full or partial sun, but it grows best in full sun with 6–8 hours of sunlight per day. Mint is a hardy perennial herb, and it generally prefers cooler temperatures. It grows best in temperatures between 60 and 75°F (15–24°C). Mint needs 1–2 inches (2.5–5 cm) of water per week. Mint doesn't need a lot of fertilizing. You can fertilize mint in early spring with a balanced liquid fertilizer and then every 4–6 weeks after that during the growing season.

Mint takes 90 days to grow from planting to harvest. It's best to harvest mint leaves right before flowers appear. You can start harvesting individual leaves as needed when the plants reach at least 4 inches (10 cm) in height.

Oregano

Oregano prefers well-drained, sandy loam soils with pH levels between 6.0 and 8.0. To grow it in containers, you'll need a container that's 10–12 inches (25–30 cm) deep and wide.

You can start oregano indoors 4 weeks before the last frost. Plant the seeds ¼ inch (0.6 cm) deep. For some varieties, you don't need to cover the seeds with soil—you can simply sprinkle them on the surface of the soil. Your seed packet should have information on how deep the seeds should be planted. You can transplant the seedlings outside 1–2 weeks after the last frost. You can also sow it directly after the last frost.

Oregano plants need to be spaced 12 inches (30 cm) apart with 18 inches (45 cm) of space between rows.

Oregano prefers to grow in full sun with 6–8 hours of sunlight per day. The more sun it gets, the stronger the flavor will be. Oregano is a hardy perennial herb, but it prefers warmer climates. It grows best in temperatures between 60 and 80°F (15–27°C). Oregano needs 1 inch (2.5 cm) of water per week. Oregano typically doesn't need a lot of fertilizing. If you added compost to your garden beds, you won't need to do much else in terms of fertilizing. If you have a bushier plant, you can prune it once it's at least 4 inches (10 cm) tall. Pinch the top part along with the first set of leaves just above the leaf node. This will make your plant grow thick and lush.

Oregano usually takes 45 days to grow from planting to harvesting. You can start harvesting leaves as needed once the plant is at least 6 inches (15 cm) tall. Never harvest more than ⅔ of all leaves. Oregano loses flavor after flowering, so it's best to harvest it before that.

Parsley

Parsley prefers well-drained soils with pH levels between 6.0 and 7.0. To grow it in containers, you'll need a container that's 10 inches (25 cm) wide and deep.

You can start parsley indoors or direct sow it. You can start it indoors 6–10 weeks before the last frost. Soaking the seeds in water for 12–24 hours before planting can help with germination. Plant the seeds ¼ inch (0.6 cm) deep. They can be a bit finicky, so you can plant 2–3 seeds in each seed starting tray cell or container. Parsley is frost hardy, so you can move it outside 2–4 weeks before the last frost, or you can wait until after the last frost, just in case. You can also direct sow it 3–4 weeks before the last frost. Parsley plants need to be spaced 6–8 inches (15–20 cm) apart with rows 12–18 inches (30–45 cm) apart.

Parsley grows well in full or partial sun. It needs at least 6 hours of sunlight per day. Parsley is a biennial herb grown as an annual. It's a hardy herb, and it grows best in temperatures between 50 and 70°F (10–21°C). Parsley needs 1–2 inches (2.5–5 cm) of water per week. It doesn't need a lot of fertilizing. You can fertilize it every 4–6 weeks during the growing season with a balanced or phosphorus-rich liquid fertilizer. You can remove the flower stalks, and this should help the plant focus on foliage growth instead. You can also pick dead, faded, and yellowed leaves from time to time.

Parsley typically takes 70–90 days to grow from planting to harvest. You can start harvesting parsley leaves as needed 2–3 months after planting. Wait until the stems are divided into three sections before harvesting. Instead of only picking the leaves from the top, cut the entire stem carefully from the base—parsley stems are also edible and tasty.

Rosemary

Rosemary prefers sandy soils with pH levels between 6.0 and 7.0. Rosemary needs some space for its roots to expand, so to grow it in containers, you'll need a container that's 12 inches (30 cm) wide and deep.

Rosemary is rather difficult to grow from seed. The germination rate is quite low, and it will take months until the plant can produce usable leaves. It's much easier to grow rosemary from cuttings, so I'd suggest getting a plant from a nursery and then propagating it via cuttings.

If you decide to grow it from seed, I would recommend that you start them indoors. You can start them indoors 10 weeks before the last frost. Plant the seeds ¼ inch (0.6 cm) deep. You can transplant the seedlings outside 1–2 weeks after the last frost. Rosemary plants need to be spaced 1.5–3 feet (45–90 cm) apart with 1.5–2 feet (45–60 cm) of space between rows.

Rosemary likes to grow in full sun with 6–8 hours of sunlight per day. Rosemary is a perennial shrub, but it prefers warmer climates. It grows best in temperatures between 60 and 80°F (15–27°C). Rosemary can grow quite big, so if you put it in a container, it could be that in a few years it will need to be transplanted into a bigger container. It needs 1 inch (2.5 cm) of water every 1–2 weeks. Rosemary doesn't like sitting in moist or wet soil, so water it only when the top 2 inches (5 cm) of the soil are dry. Rosemary doesn't need a lot of fertilizing. You can fertilize it with a balanced liquid fertilizer once a month during the growing season. You can cut the plants back if they start to become woody.

Rosemary takes 80–100 days to grow from planting to harvest if you grow it from cuttings. If you grow it from seed, it can take a year to grow to maturity. You can harvest rosemary by pulling sprigs off the main stem. If you need large branches to roast, then you could use secateurs to remove these. You can dry rosemary, but you can't freeze it.

Sage

Sage prefers well-drained sandy or loamy soils with pH levels between 6.0 and 7.0. To grow it in containers, you'll need one that's 10 inches (25 cm) wide and deep.

You can grow sage from seed, but just like rosemary, sage is rather difficult to grow from seed. I'd suggest getting a plant from a nursery and then propagating it via cuttings.

If you decide to grow it from seed, I would recommend starting them indoors 6–8 weeks before the last frost. Plant the seeds ⅛ inch (3 mm) deep. You can transplant the seedlings outside 1–2 weeks after the last frost. Sage plants need to be spaced 12–18 inches (30–45 cm) apart with 18 inches (45 cm) of space between rows.

Sage is an herb that likes to be grown in full sun with 6–8 hours of sunlight per day. Sage can be an annual or a perennial herb depending on your climate. It can be grown as a perennial in colder to moderate climates and as an annual in hotter climates. It grows best in temperatures between 60 and 70°F (15–21°C). Sage needs 1 inch (2.5 cm) of water per week. Sage doesn't need a lot of fertilizing. In fact, overfertilizing it can result in weaker flavor. You can use a balanced liquid fertilizer every 4–6 weeks during the growing season. If the plants become woody, you can prune them. You need to give sage plants a good pruning every year. It's best to do it when new growth starts to appear, young leaves unfurl, and new buds form in the spring. Sage plants need to be replaced every couple of years to remain productive.

Sage typically takes 75 days to grow from cuttings to harvest. To harvest sage, you can pinch off some leaves or sprigs from it. Try not to harvest too much from the plants in the first year. When the plants are fully established, you can harvest them 3 times in a growing season. Don't harvest them in the fall so that the plants can prepare for winter. Fresh sage tastes best, but you can freeze or dry it. If you're drying it, hang sprigs in a warm area and allow to air dry.

Thyme

Thyme prefers well-drained soils with pH levels between 6.0 and 8.0. If you want to grow it in containers, it doesn't need to be large. A container that's 6–8 inches (15–20 cm) deep and wide is more than enough.

You can grow thyme from seed or cuttings. You can start it indoors 6–10 weeks before the last frost. Plant the seeds ¼ inch (0.6 cm) deep. You can transplant the seedlings outside after the last frost. You can also direct sow it after the last frost. Or you can save yourself the hassle of growing from seed and get a plant from a nursery and then propagate it via cuttings. Thyme plants need to be spaced 12–24 inches (30–60 cm) apart with 18–24 inches (45–60 cm) of space between rows.

Thyme prefers to grow in full sun with 6–8 hours of sunlight per day. Thyme is a perennial herb. It grows best in temperatures between 65 and 85°F (18–30°C). It's an herb that doesn't need too much water. It only needs 1 inch (2.5 cm) of water every 10–15 days. Thyme doesn't need a lot of fertilizing. You can fertilize it with a balanced liquid fertilizer every 6–8 weeks during the growing season. Just like rosemary, thyme likes dry conditions, so you can grow them together. You can prune thyme back in the spring and summer. If you've had the plants for 3–4 years, you may want to replace them, as they may not taste as flavorful.

You can harvest thyme all year round, but to get the most flavor, harvest it just before it starts flowering. Cut only a few stems in the first year. Many gardeners don't harvest thyme in the first year at all. It's best to cut off the top 5–6 inches (12.5–15 cm) when you harvest this and do it in the morning. Don't wash it because doing so will remove the essential oils. You can freeze it or dry the leaves in the oven or by hanging them.

Flowers

Marigolds

Marigolds prefer well-drained, loamy soils with pH levels between 6.0 and 7.5. If you want to grow them in containers, their size will depend on the variety you're growing. Smaller varieties, such as French or Signet, need a 6–8-inch (15–20 cm) container, while larger one, like African or Mexican, need a 12-inch (30 cm) container.

Marigold seeds are easy to germinate, so there is really no advantage to starting them indoors. You can direct sow them 1–2 weeks after the last frost, and they will bloom in 8 weeks. Plant the seeds ⅛ inch (3 mm) deep. French marigolds need to be spaced 8–10 inches (20–25 cm) apart, and African marigolds need 10–12 inches (25–30 cm) of space between plants.

Marigolds are a beautiful, vibrant orange color, and they are an asset to any garden. They've been mentioned a lot in this book, and for a good reason. They are a perfect companion plant for pretty much any crop because they grow well with everything, and they help repel pests and attract pollinators and beneficial insects, such as butterflies, bees, and ladybugs.

Marigolds can grow in full or partial sun. They need 5–6 hours of sunlight per day. They need around 1.5 inches (3.8 cm) of water per week. They typically don't need fertilizing, especially if your soil has been enriched with compost. Most marigolds are annuals, but some varieties are perennials. Most varieties of marigolds are self-seeding, so they may appear to be perennials, but in reality, they are just coming back from seed. They typically grow 6–18 inches (15–45 cm) tall. They will bloom from late spring and until fall. You can deadhead marigolds flowers, which will make the plant look better and encourage further growth.

There is a wide variety of marigolds available all in warm, sunny colors. They can be from 6 inches (15 cm) to 4 feet (15 cm–1.2 m) tall and from 6 inches (15 cm) to 2 feet (15–60 cm) wide. French marigolds are the most common type. There are also tall African marigolds and Signet marigolds, which are edible and can be used in salads and pastas. If you're growing the taller African marigolds, you should plant them in early spring after the last frost because they take longer to grow and mature. But other types can be planted any time in the spring or summer. The taller varieties need to be protected from strong winds and may need a support stake.

Nasturtiums

Nasturtiums prefer well-drained soils with pH levels between 6.0 and 8.0. To grow them in containers, you'll need ones that are 10–12 inches (25–30 cm) in diameter.

Nasturtiums are best sown directly in the garden because they have delicate roots and don't transplant well. You can sow them directly 1–2 weeks after the last frost. Plant the seeds ¼ to ½ inch (0.6–1.2 cm) deep. Nasturtiums need to be spaced 10–12 inches (25–30 cm) apart with at least 12 inches (30 cm) of space between rows.

Nasturtiums do best in full sun. They need 6–8 hours of sunlight per day. They are an annual plant. Nasturtiums need 1 inch (2.5 cm) of water per week. They don't need to be fertilized. If you fertilize them, it will increase foliage growth but won't help increase flower growth. They are fast growing and easy to look after. There are many different types of nasturtiums, including bushy plants, trailing plants, and climbers, so if you like these, you can add a variety of different types to your garden. The leaves and flowers are edible, and they have a peppery taste. Depending on the type you buy, they can be 1–10 feet (30 cm–3 m) tall, and 1–3 feet (30–90 cm) wide. They bloom from May to September.

Geraniums

Geraniums prefer well-drained soils with pH levels between 6.0 and 6.5. To grow them in containers, you'll need them to be 12 inches (30 cm) in diameter. These flowers thrive in terracotta pots. You can grow geraniums in hanging baskets too.

You can get edible scented-leaf geraniums. Geraniums come in pink, red, purple, bronze, and white. They are best started indoors. They take 12–16 weeks to grow from planting to blooming. You can start them indoors 8–10 weeks before the last frost. Plant the seeds ¼ inch (0.6 cm) deep. You can transplant the seedlings outside after the last frost. Geraniums need to be spaced 8–12 inches (20–30 cm) apart.

Geraniums need full or partial sun depending on the variety. Annual geraniums need the most sun. Geraniums are usually grown as annuals, but they can be grown as perennials in warmer climates. They need 1 inch (2.5 cm) of water per week. You can fertilize them every 4–6 weeks with a balanced liquid during spring and summer. Cut the plants back late summer, and it's worth taking cuttings in case you have any losses. If you're growing them in containers, it's best to move containers with geraniums indoors over winter and bring them out again in May. If you deadhead flowers, then more will grow.

Petunias

Petunias prefer well-drained soils with pH levels between 6.0 and 7.0. You can grow 3 petunia plants in a 12-inch (30 cm) container, or you can grow individual plants in 6–8-inch (15–20 cm) containers.

Petunias are best started indoors. You can start petunias indoors for 8–10 weeks before the last frost. Plant the seeds ¼ inch (0.6 cm) deep. You can transplant the seedlings outside after the last frost. Spacing depends on the variety. Larger ones, like grandifloras and multifloras, need to be spaced 12 inches (30 cm) apart. Medium-sized ones, like floribundas, need 8–10 inches (20–25 cm) of space between plants. And smaller ones, like millifloras, need to be spaced 4–6 inches (10–15 cm) apart.

Petunias prefer full sun. They need at least 6 hours of sunlight per day. Petunias can be grown as perennials in frost-free climates, but they are typically grown as annuals. They need 1–2 inches (2.5–5 cm) of water per week. Petunias should be fertilized once a month with a balanced liquid fertilizer to help encourage them to grow and bloom. If you prune them, it's advisable to fertilize them afterwards. If they look scruffy, they will soon grow more flowers and look better. You can deadhead old flowers, and this will make them look more attractive.

They will bloom in the spring, summer, and fall. Petunias come in a wide range of colors. They flower for a long time, which means they are plants that give you good value for money and make your garden look great. Midway through the summer they may get leggy, and you'll need to prune them back to half their height.

My personal favorite plants to grow are tomatoes; I just think they're incredibly versatile. They're tangy, sweet, and have a rich taste. You can use them in salads, eat them as a snack, make soups out of them, and make delicious sauces for pizzas, pastas, and other dishes. But I also love the great variety of vegetables, fruits, herbs, and flowers that we grow. They all bring something to our table in terms of flavor, great nutrition, vitamins, and help us live a healthy, organic, and sustainable lifestyle.

Key takeaways from this chapter:

1. Whether buying seeds or seedlings, be certain to check all plant information thoroughly to see how big the plants grow, what sun requirements they have, what soil type they prefer, when to plant them, how deep to plant the seeds, how far apart you should space them, and when to prune them.
2. You may need to thin seedlings out to give the strongest ones room to grow.
3. Some plants, such as carrots, don't like to be transplanted, so it's best to sow them directly. Other plants may need to be grown indoors and then transplanted outside when ready—check this before purchasing.
4. You may need to provide support for climbing plants or plants that grow tall. You can use stakes, canes, fences, or trellises to provide support for plants that need it.
5. Many vegetables and fruits taste better when they're smaller, so there's no need to grow them to a huge size.
6. Remember that dwarf varieties of plants and trees are a great option if you don't have a lot of space.
7. Some plants, like sage, will need to be replaced after a few years because they won't be as flavorful with time.

Conclusion

Companion planting has numerous benefits that make it so worthwhile, from helping your plants to be healthier to protecting them naturally from pests. Companion planting helps plants get the nutrients they need and will make the soil richer and more sustainable in the long term. By using companion planting techniques, you can grow vegetables organically without the need for damaging chemical pesticides. Your garden will have a more varied beautiful appearance being interspersed with vibrant, colorful, and amazing smelling flowers and herbs. Your garden will thrive with beneficial insects and pollinators, which will give you healthier plants and generally be much better for the environment. It's a beautiful thing to see bees gathering pollen and butterflies fluttering around lilac buddleia bushes and lavender. It's wonderful to know you have toads, birds, bats, and hedgehogs visiting your garden. There's nothing not to love about companion planting. I truly hope that you get as much pleasure from it as I do.

This book has outlined the many benefits of companion planting and organic gardening in Chapter 1. Chapter 2 covered how you can pick the perfect location for your garden and when to plant it. Chapter 3 gave detailed information about which plants you can companion plant together and which you should avoid. Chapter 4 focused on looking at soil and how to create the perfect growing medium, using cover crops, and making compost and organic fertilizers. As any good gardener knows, the soil is the life and health of the garden, so it's crucial to get this right. In Chapter 5, information was given on how you could start a garden, whether you decide to do this in the ground, in raised beds, or in containers, and it looked at starting plants from seed and growing seedlings. Chapter 6 covered the necessary maintenance of a garden, including watering, fertilizing, weeding, pruning plants, and providing support for plants that need it. Chapter 7 focused on pest control and dealing with diseases using organic options, using polyculture, trap crops, crop rotation, attracting beneficial insects, and it emphasized the important of preventing diseases from the outset. Chapter 8 looked at how you can manage weeds with mulch and companion planting. Chapter 9 looked at how you can attract beneficial insects and other creatures, such as birds, bats, and frogs, to your garden. Chapter 10 looked at attracting pollinators, such as bees, wasps, beetles, and birds, and the types of plants that would attract them and also homes you could provide for them. Chapter 11 covered harvesting your bounty from your vegetable garden, looking at how you know when to harvest, how to do this safely to not damage plants, and how to store your produce to keep it fresh. Finally, Chapter 12 covered plant profiles to provide you information about the plants you might want to grow so that you have a good indication as to their sun requirements, whether they're better started indoors or sown directly, how much water they require, how often they should be fertilized, and more.

This concludes the end of this book. I think it's a really exciting topic that you can constantly work upon to improve your soil quality and your garden to make it a better environment for beneficial insects, pollinators, and wildlife so that you can grow delicious produce to make a sustainable life for you and your family for generations to come.

I'm sure there are lots of things you can be doing, whether that's planning out your garden, ordering seeds, potting up seeds or planting out seedlings, working out what combinations of plants you want to put together, weeding, watering, making an insect hotel, observing your garden to see what type of insects you currently have in there, or gathering your harvest. Have a wonderful time, and most importantly, enjoy it!

Resources

Companion Planting

Almanac. 2022. Companion Planting Guide for Vegetables. *Almanac*. 26th May 2022.

https://www.almanac.com/companion-planting-guide-vegetables

Burpee. 2021. Companion Planting Guide. *Burpee*. Online 13th May 2021.

https://www.burpee.com/blog/companion-planting-guide_article10888.html

Charbonneau, Jordan. 2017. 7 Benefits of Companion Planting. Online. *Southern Exposure Seed Exchange*. 13th April 2017.

https://blog.southernexposure.com/2017/04/7-benefits-of-companion-planting/

Clapp, Leigh. 2021. Companion planting – your ultimate guide. Online. *Homes & Gardens*. 12th March 2021. https://www.homesandgardens.com/advice/companion-planting

Hassani, Nadia. 2021. What is Companion Planting? A Guide to Companion Planting in Your Vegetable Garden. *The Spruce*. Online. 29th November 2021. https://www.thespruce.com/companion-planting-with-chart-5025124

Hicks-Hamblin, Kristina. 2021. The Scientifically-Backed Benefits of Companion Planting. *Gardener's Path*. 29th September 2021. Online.

https://gardenerspath.com/how-to/organic/benefits-companion-planting/

Meza, Naomi. 2019. Get the Most from Your Garden with Companion Planting. 19th April 2019. Online. *Greenway Biotech*.

https://www.greenwaybiotech.com/blogs/gardening-articles/get-the-most-from-your-garden-with-companion-planting

Tonoli, Minette. 2017. Companion Planting Principles. *Meadowsweet*. Online. 26th September 2017.

https://meadowsweet.co.nz/2017/09/26/companion-planting-principles/

Organic Gardening

Matthew Thorpe, MD, PhD and Rachael Link, MS, RD. 2021. Are Pesticides in Foods Harming Your Health? *Healthline*. May 26, 2021. Online.

https://www.healthline.com/nutrition/pesticides-and-health

N.C. Cooperative Extension. 2016. What is Organic Gardening? *N.C. Cooperative Extension*. Online. 26th September 2016.

https://pender.ces.ncsu.edu/2014/04/what-is-organic-gardening-2/

Rinkesh. 2022. What is Organic Gardening? *Conserve Energy Future*. Online.

https://www.conserve-energy-future.com/start-an-organic-garden.php

SaferBrand. 2022. Why Choose Organic Gardening? *Safer Brand*. Online.

https://www.saferbrand.com/advice/organic-gardening/why-organic

Yares, Kat. 2021. Five Benefits of Growing an Organic Garden. *Gardening Know How*. Online. 14th June 2021.

https://www.gardeningknowhow.com/special/organic/five-benefits-of-growing-an-organic-garden.htm

No-Dig Gardening

Dowding, Charles. 2022. A Beginner's Guide. Why Use No Dig and How to Start. *Charles Dowding*. Online. https://charlesdowding.co.uk/start-here/

Garden Organic. N.d. The No-Dig Method. *Garden Organic*. Online.

https://www.gardenorganic.org.uk/no-dig-method

Mitchel-Pollock, Margarita. 2021. No dig gardening: The 7 layers of a no dig garden explained. *CountryLiving*. Online. 28th August 2021.

https://www.countryliving.com/uk/homes-interiors/gardens/a37393447/no-dig-gardening-method/

Wolfe, Mark. 2021. What is the No-Dig Gardening method, and Why You Should Try It This Spring. 3rd February 2021. Online.

https://www.bobvila.com/articles/no-dig-gardening-method/

Compost

Beck, Andrea. 2022. Your Step-by-Step Guide on How to Make Compost to Enrich Your Garden. *Better Homes and Gardens*. Online. 13th May 2022.

https://www.bhg.com/gardening/yard/compost/how-to-compost/

Ellis, Mary Ellen. 2021. What to do With Compost – Learn About Compost Uses in the Garden. *Gardening Know How*. Online. 27th December 2021.

https://www.gardeningknowhow.com/composting/basics/what-to-do-with-compost.htm

Jeanroy, Amy. 2022. How to Make Your Own Compost. *The Spruce*. Online 23rd March 2022.

https://www.thespruce.com/how-to-make-compost-p2-1761841

Soil

DPI. N.d. Check Your Soil Structure. *Department of Primary Industries*. Online.

https://www.dpi.nsw.gov.au/agriculture/soils/guides/soil-structure-and-sodicity/check

Green, Jenny. 2018. How to Loosen Hard Soils. *SF Gate*, Online, 14th December 2018.

https://homeguides.sfgate.com/loosen-hard-soils-23930.html

Pleasant, Barbara. 2020. Use Cover Crops to Improve Soil. *MotherEarthNews*. Online. 7th July 2020.

https://www.motherearthnews.com/organic-gardening/cover-crops-improve-soil-zmaz09onzraw/

Rhoades, Heather. 2022. Improving Compacted Soil – What to Do When Soil is Too Compact. *Gardening Know How*. Online.

https://www.gardeningknowhow.com/garden-how-to/soil-fertilizers/improving-compacted-soil.htm

Rowlawn. 2022. Soil Structure. *Rowlawn*. Online.

https://www.rolawn.co.uk/soil-structure

Shanstrom, Nathalie. 2021. What is Soil Structure and Why is it Important? *Deeproot*. Online. 23rd June, 2021. https://www.deeproot.com/blog/blog-entries/what-is-soil-structure-and-why-is-it-important-2/

Fertilizing

All That Grows. 2022. Organic Fertilizers: Everything You Need to Know. *All That Grows*. Online. https://www.allthatgrows.in/blogs/posts/organic-fertilizers

Cary, Bill. 2022. When and how to add organic fertilizers to your soil. *Lohud*. Online.

https://eu.lohud.com/story/life/home-garden/in-the-garden/2014/05/01/add-organic-fertilizers/8578063/

Pennington. 2022. All You Need to Know About Organic Fertilizer. *Pennington*. Online.

https://www.pennington.com/all-products/fertilizer/resources/what-is-organic-fertilizer

Choosing the Perfect Location for Your Garden

Almanac. 2021. Where to Put a Vegetable Garden. Online. *Almanac*. 21st December 2021.

https://www.almanac.com/where-put-vegetable-garden#

Andrychowicz, Amy. 2022. How Much Sunlight Does my Garden Get – The Ultimate Sun Exposure Guide. *Get Busy Gardening*. Online.

https://getbusygardening.com/how-to-determine-sun-exposure/

MLGG. 2022. How to Determine the Best Sun Exposure for Your Garden. *My Little Green Garden*. Online. 28th May 2022.

https://mylittlegreengarden.com/sun-exposure-for-your-garden/

Neveln, Viveka. 2020. How to Understand Your Yard's Sunlight so you Know What to Plant Where. Online. 1st June 2020. https://www.bhg.com/gardening/how-to-garden/understanding-your-yard-s-sunlight/

Poindexter, Jennifer. 2022. 12 Steps to Choosing the Best Location for Your Vegetable Garden. *Morning Chores*. Online.

https://morningchores.com/vegetable-garden-location/

Starting a Garden

Anderson, Tanya. 2022. How to Start a Vegetable Garden from Scratch. Online. *Lovely Greens*. 8th March 2022. https://lovelygreens.com/tips-for-starting-a-new-vegetable-garden/

Borchert, Mikayla. 2021. When is the Best Time to Start Growing a Garden? *Family Handyman*. Online. 13th September 2021.

https://www.familyhandyman.com/article/when-to-start-a-garden/

Collier, Sommer. 2014. Selecting Your Seeds. *A Spicy Perspective*. Online. 13th March 2014.

https://www.aspicyperspective.com/select-seeds/

Gardener's Supply Company. 2022. How to Start Seeds. *Gardener's Supply Company*. 15th February 2022. Online. https://www.gardeners.com/how-to/how-to-start-seeds/5062.html

Harlow, Ivory. 2015. How to Transplant Vegetable Seedlings. *Farm and Dairy*. Online. 15th May 2015. https://www.farmanddairy.com/top-stories/how-to-transplant-vegetable-seedlings/258509.html

Iannotti, Marie. 2022. How to Start Seeds Indoors. *The Spruce*. Online. 14th June 2022.

https://www.thespruce.com/successful-start-seed-indoors-1402478

Minnesota State Horticultural Society. 2020. Three Ways to Determine When to Plant. Online. 19th April 2020. https://northerngardener.org/three-ways-to-determine-when-to-plant/

Sparks, Madaline. 2022. When to Start Planting Vegetables in Your Garden, a Month-by-Month Guide. *RealSimple*. Online. 28th April 2022.

https://www.realsimple.com/home-organizing/gardening/outdoor/month-by-month-vegetable-gardening-guide

Welch, Sara. 2019. How to Select Seeds for Your Garden. *Farm and Dairy*. Online. 18th February 2019. https://www.farmanddairy.com/top-stories/how-to-select-seeds-for-your-garden/537928.html

Maintaining Your Garden

Harrington, Jenny. N.d. Steps to Take Care of a Vegetable Garden. *SFGate*. Online.

https://homeguides.sfgate.com/steps-care-vegetable-garden-68300.html

Ianotti, Marie. 2021. How to Take Care of a Vegetable Garden. *The Spruce*. Online 14th November 2021. https://www.thespruce.com/vegetable-garden-maintenance-1403170

MacKenzi, Jill. 2018. Watering the Vegetable Garden. *University of Minnesota Extension*. Online.

https://extension.umn.edu/water-wisely-start-your-own-backyard/watering-vegetable-garden

Tilley, Nikki. 2021. Watering the Garden – Tips on How and When to Water the Garden. *Gardening Know How*. Online. 25th June 2021.

https://www.gardeningknowhow.com/garden-how-to/watering/watering-garden.htm

Raised Beds

Almanac. 2022. A Step-by-Step Guide to Building an Easy DIY Raised Garden Bed. *Almanac*. Online.

26th May 2022. https://www.almanac.com/content/how-build-raised-garden-bed

Burke, Nicole. 2021. The Best Way to Water a Raised Bed. *Gardenary*. Online. 28th May 2021. https://www.gardenary.com/blog/the-best-way-to-water-a-raised-bed

Gardener's Supply Company. 2022. The Basics: Gardening in Raised Beds. *Gardener's Supply Company*. 3rd March 2022. Online. https://www.gardeners.com/how-to/raised-bed-basics/8565.html

Margaret. 2021. How to Water Raised Beds: The Complete Guide. Online. *Crate & Basket*. https://crateandbasket.com/how-to-water-raised-beds/

Container Gardening

Enjoy Container Gardening. N.d. Container Garden Maintenance. *Enjoy Container Gardening*. Online. https://www.enjoycontainergardening.com/blog/container-garden-maintenance/

Gardenuity. 2020. How to Get Your Container Garden the Sunlight it Needs. 5th March 2020. Online. *The Sage*. https://blog.gardenuity.com/how-to-get-your-container-garden-the-sunlight-it-needs/

Kevin. 2022. Best Location for Container Gardening: 4 Clear-Cut Steps. *Gardening Mentor*. Online. https://gardeningmentor.com/best-location-for-container-gardening/

Michaels, Kerry. 2022. How to Start a Container Garden. *The Spruce*. Online. 5th May 2022. https://www.thespruce.com/before-you-make-your-first-container-garden-847850

Pest Control

Dekker, Sylvia. 2022. How to Use Trap Crops as Decoys to Control Insect Pests. *Gardener's Path*. Online. 26th February 2022. https://gardenerspath.com/how-to/disease-and-pests/trap-crop-decoys/

Dore, Jeremy. 2010. Trap Cropping to Control Pests. *GrowVeg*. Online. 4th June 2010. https://www.growveg.com/guides/trap-cropping-to-control-pests/

Herring, Barbara, 2018. 10 Common Garden Pests – and Natural Pesticides to Keep Them Away. *Eco Warrior Princess*. Online. 29th January 2018. https://ecowarriorprincess.net/2018/01/10-common-garden-pests-and-natural-pesticides-to-keep-them-away/

Ianotti, Marie. 2020. Companion Planting to Control the Insects in Your Garden. *The Spruce*. Online. 21st October 2020. https://www.thespruce.com/companion-planting-1402735

Johnson, Scott. 2022. Organic Pest Control for Your Garden That Really Works. *Lawn Starter*. Online. 4th January 2022. https://www.lawnstarter.com/blog/gardening-2/organic-pest-control-that-works/

Miller, Carley. 2022. 21 Companion Plants for Pest Control. *Bustling Nest*. Online. https://bustlingnest.com/companion-plants-for-pest-control/

Organic Lesson. 2018. 14 Beneficial Insects for Natural Garden Pest Control. *Organic Lesson*. 26th February 2018. Online. https://www.organiclesson.com/beneficial-insects-garden-pest-control/

Sim, Adriana. 2022. Organic Pest Control Methods for Your Vegetable Garden. *Tiny Garden Habit*. Online. https://www.tinygardenhabit.com/organic-pest-control-methods-for-your-vegetable-garden/

Tooker, John. 2020. Using Polycultures to Improve Productivity and Pest Control. *Penn State Extension*. Online. 17th March 2020. https://extension.psu.edu/using-polycultures-to-improve-productivity-and-pest-control

Walliser, Jessica. 2017. Guide to Vegetable Garden Pests: Identification and Organic Controls. *Savvy Gardening*. Online. https://savvygardening.com/guide-to-vegetable-garden-pests/

Ziton, Tyler. 2022. 7 Companion Plants that Prevent Pests and Diseases. *Couch to Homestead*. Online. https://couchtohomestead.com/companion-plants-for-pests-and-diseases/

Disease Management

Poindexter, Jennifer. 2022. Most Common Vegetable Garden Diseases and Solutions. *Clean Air Gardening*. Online. https://www.cleanairgardening.com/most-common-vegetable-garden-diseases-and-solutions/

Salisbury. 2021. Crop Rotation is the Key to Breaking Disease Cycles. Online. https://salisburygreenhouse.com/crop-rotation-is-the-key-to-breaking-disease-cycles/

Smith, Cheryl. 2022. 10 Easy Steps to Prevent Common Garden Diseases, *University of New Hampshire*. Online. https://extension.unh.edu/resource/10-easy-steps-prevent-common-garden-diseases-fact-sheet

The Big Greenk. 2022. 5 Common Garden Vegetable Diseases. *The Big Greenk*. Online. 1st February 2022. https://thebiggreenk.com/blog/5-common-garden-vegetable-diseases/

University of Georgia Extension. 2020. Disease Management in the Home Vegetable Garden. *University of Georgia Extension*. Online. https://extension.uga.edu/publications/detail.html?number=C862&title=Disease%20Management%20in%20the%20Home%20Vegetable%20Garden

Vanderlinden, Colleen. 2022. Preventing Plant Diseases With Good Gardening Practices. *The Spruce*. Online. 16th May 2022. https://www.thespruce.com/prevent-plant-diseases-in-your-garden-2539511

Weed Control

Burke, Kelly. 2022. Organic Methods for Killing Weeds Safely. *The Spruce*. Online. 16th March 2022. https://www.thespruce.com/green-weed-killers-2152938

Muntean, Laura. 2021. How to manage garden weeds with mulch. *Agrilife Today*. 26th March 2021. Online. https://agrilifetoday.tamu.edu/2021/03/26/how-to-manage-garden-weeds-with-mulch/

Smith-Heavenrich. 2001. Weeds as Companion Plants. *Maine Organic Farmers and Gardeners*. Online. https://www.mofga.org/resources/weeds/weeds-as-companion-plants/

Vanderlinden, Colleen. 2020. Mulch for Weed Control and Soil Health. *The Spruce*. Online. 7th Feb. 2020. https://www.thespruce.com/mulch-for-weed-control-soil-health-2539779

Walliser, Jessica. 2017. Organic weed control tips for gardeners. *Savvy Gardening*. Online. https://savvygardening.com/organic-weed-control-tips/

Attracting Beneficial Garden Insects and Pollinators

American Pest Professionals. 2019. 6 Beneficial Garden Animals That Seem Like Pests. *American Pest Professionals*. 18th March 2019. Online. https://www.americanpestpros.com/6-beneficial-garden-animals-that-seem-like-pests

Barth, Brian. 2015. How to attract beneficial bugs. *Modern Farmer*. 25th June 2015. Online. https://modernfarmer.com/2015/06/how-to-attract-beneficial-bugs/

Hadley, Debbie. 2019. Four Tips for Attracting Beneficial Insects to Your Garden. *Thoughtco*. 5th June, 2019. Online. https://www.thoughtco.com/attract-beneficial-insects-to-control-garden-pests-4054078

Hoffman, Fred. 2014. Plants that attract beneficial insects. *Permaculture News*. Online. 4th October 2014.

https://www.permaculturenews.org/2014/10/04/plants-attract-beneficial-insects/

Ianotti, Marie. 2022. How to Attract Bees and Other Pollinators to Your Garden. *The Spruce*. Online. 18th March 2022. https://www.thespruce.com/bee-plants-1401948

Oder, Tom. 2021. Beneficial Insects: How to Attract Good Bugs to Your Garden. *Treehugger*. Online. 19th August 2021.

https://www.treehugger.com/beneficial-insects-how-to-attract-good-bugs-to-your-4863469

Penn State Extension. 2015. Attracting Beneficial Insects. *Penn State Extension*. Online. 30th July 2015. https://extension.psu.edu/attracting-beneficial-insects

Pollination Guelph. 2022. Making Homes for Pollinators. *Pollination Guelph*. Online.

https://www.pollinationguelph.ca/making-homes-for-pollinators

Stauffers. 2021. Hummingbirds, Butterflies, and Bees: Attracting Pollinators to Your Garden. *Stauffers of Kissel Hill*. Online. 12th April 2021.

https://www.skh.com/thedirt/attracting-pollinators-to-your-garden/

Suzuki, David. 2022. How to Attract Pollinators. *David Suzuki Foundation*. Online.

https://davidsuzuki.org/living-green/how-to-attract-pollinators/

Sweetser, Robin. 2022. Attract the Bugs That Are Good for Plants! *Almanac*. 24th January 2022. Online. https://www.almanac.com/beneficial-insects-garden

Walliser, Jessica. 2016. The best plants for beneficial insects. *Savvy Gardening*. Online.

https://savvygardening.com/plants-beneficial-insects/

White, Jason. 2021. 11 Animals That Can Actually Help Your Garden Grow. *All About Gardening*. Online. 3rd November 2021.

https://www.allaboutgardening.com/animals-help-garden/

Xerces Society. 2021. Who are the pollinators? *Xerces Society*. Online. https://www.xerces.org/pollinator-conservation/about-pollinators

Harvesting and Storing Your Produce

Chadwick, Pat. 2020. Guidelines for Harvesting Vegetables. *Piedmont Master Gardeners*. Online.

https://piedmontmastergardeners.org/article/guidelines-for-harvesting-vegetables/

Ianotti, Marie. 2020. When and How to Harvest Garden Vegetables. *The Spruce*. Online. 17th September 2020. https://www.thespruce.com/when-to-harvest-vegetables-1403402

Poindexter, Jennifer. 2022. How to Store Your Garden Harvest Properly to Keep It Fresh Longer. *Morning Chores*. Online.

https://morningchores.com/how-to-store-your-harvest/

Tong, Cindy. 2021. Harvesting and storing home garden vegetables. *University of Minnesota Extension*. Online. https://extension.umn.edu/planting-and-growing-guides/harvesting-and-storing-home-garden-vegetables

Plant Profiles

Almanac. 2022. Growing Guides. *Almanac*. Online. https://www.almanac.com/gardening/growing-guides

Garden Design. 2022. 21 Easy Flowers for Beginners to Grow *Garden Design*. Online.

https://www.gardendesign.com/flowers/easy.html

Noyes, Amber. 2021. The 15 Best Vegetables to Grow in Pots and Containers. *Gardening Chores*. Online. 28th April 2021.

https://www.gardeningchores.com/best-vegetables-to-grow-in-pots/

Index

A

alyssum, 125, 126
angelica, 102, 126
anise hyssop, 134
anthracnose, 107
ants, 92
aphid midges, 127
aphids, 91
apple trees, 162
asparagus, 147
asparagus beetles, 92
attracting beneficial insects, 125
attracting pollinators, 131

B

Bacillus thuringiensis (Bt), 102
Bacillus thuringiensis kurstaki (Btk), 102
Bacillus thuringiensis var. san diego (Bt var. san diego), 102
bacterial diseases, 112
bacterial leaf spot, 112
bacterial soft rot, 113
basil, 103, 134, 167
bats, 129
bee flies, 134
bee hotel, 135
bees, 132
beetles, 133
beets (beetroot), 148

beneficial insects, 124
birds (pests), 92
birds (pollinators), 133
birds (useful creatures), 128
black rot, 113
black spot, 108
blight, 108
blossom-end rot, 114
blue Hubbard squash, 105
blueberries, 162
borage, 103, 134
braconid wasps, 127
broccoli, 148
buckwheat, 54
building raised beds, 63
bumblebees, 132
butterflies, 133

C

cabbage, 149
cabbage worms, 93
caraway, 102
caring for potted plants over winter, 88
carrot rust flies, 93
carrots, 149
caterpillars, 93
catnip, 103
cauliflower, 150
celery, 150
centipedes, 129

cereal rye, 54
chamomile, 116
changing pH level of soil, 50
cherry trees, 163
chives, 103, 134, 168
choosing the perfect location for your garden, 19
cilantro (coriander), 102, 103, 126, 167
clubroot, 109
codling moths, 93
cold and dry storage conditions, 142
cold and moist storage conditions, 142
collard greens, 151
Colorado potato beetles, 93
common garden diseases, 106
common garden pests, 91
companion planting and organic gardening, 14
companion planting basics, 11
companion planting benefits, 12
companion planting for weed control, 122
companion planting principles, 14
companion plants for attracting beneficial insects, 126
companion plants for attracting pollinators, 134

companion plants for disease management, 116
companion plants for pest control, 103
companion plants list, 35
compost, 54
contact weed killers, 83, 119
cool and dry storage conditions, 142
cool and moist storage conditions, 143
corn, 151
cosmos, 102
cotyledons, 69
cover crops, 53
crimson clover, 54
crop rotation, 116
cucamelons, 152
cucumber beetles, 94
cucumbers, 153
cutworms, 94

D

damping off, 71, 109
damsel bugs, 127
dappled sun/shade, 23
deadheading plants, 85
dealing with diseases, 106
determining when to plant your garden, 24
determining your soil structure and texture, 48
diatomaceous earth, 101

dill, 102, 103, 126, 134, 168
direct sowing, 68
disease prevention, 115
downy mildew, 109
drip irrigation for containers, 82
drip irrigation for in-ground gardens, 80
drip irrigation for raised beds, 80

E

earthworms, 129
eggplants, 153
evaluating sun requirements and exposure, 22

F

fennel, 34, 102, 126
fertilizing, 56, 83
fig trees, 163
filling containers, 66
filling raised beds, 64
flea beetles, 94
flies, 134
frogs, 129
full shade, 23
full sun, 22
fungal diseases, 107

G

gardening tools, 28
garlic, 103, 154
geraniums, 174

gooseberries, 164
gray mold, 110
green beans, 154
green lacewings, 127
ground beetles, 127
grow lights for starting seeds, 70
growing seedlings, 71

H

half-hardy crops, 27
hand weeding, 83, 119
hardy crops, 26
harvesting, 138
hedgehogs, 130
homemade organic fertilizers, 57
homemade organic fungicides, 107
homemade organic herbicide, 119
homemade organic pesticides, 99
honeybees, 132
horseradish, 103
hover flies, 127, 134

I

insect hotel (bug hotel), 135
insecticidal soap, 99
intercropping, 105
issues with seeds, 70

K

kale, 155

L

ladybugs (ladybirds), 127
last frost date, 24
lavender, 104, 134
leaf miners, 94
leeks, 155
lemon trees, 164
lettuce, 156
lizards, 129

M

maintaining your garden, 82
making compost, 55
marigolds, 104, 134, 172
mealybug destroyers, 127
mealybugs, 95
melons, 165
Mexican bean beetles, 95
mint, 104, 169
minute pirate bugs, 127
mixing potting soil, 66
mosaic virus, 113
moths, 133
mulching, 120
mustard, 54

N

nasturtiums, 104, 134, 173
nectarine trees, 165

neem oil, 99
no-dig gardening, 50

O

oilseed radish, 54
onions, 156
oregano, 104, 134, 169
organic fertilizers, 56
organic fungicides, 107
organic gardening basics, 14
organic gardening benefits, 16
organic herbicides, 119
organic pesticides, 99
organic seeds, 67
other diseases, 114
other useful creatures in the garden, 128

P

parsley, 170
partial shade (or part shade), 22
peach trees, 165
peas, 157
pennyroyal, 104
peppers, 158
pest control, 99
petunias, 174
pH level of soil, 50
phenology, 25
pill bugs, 96
pinching plants, 86
planning your garden, 19
plant families, 33

plant growth stages, 84
plant profiles, 147
pollinators, 131
polyculture for pest control, 106
potatoes, 158
powdery mildew, 110
praying mantises, 127
preventing animals from eating plants, 87
propagating plants from cuttings, 74
providing homes and habitats for pollinators, 135
pruning plants, 86
pumpkins, 159

R

radishes, 159
raspberries, 166
rejuvenating hard or compacted soil, 52
repotting plants, 88
root-knot nematodes, 96
rosemary, 104, 134, 170
rue, 104, 126
rust, 111

S

sage, 104, 171
seed starting mix, 68
shallow hoeing, 83, 119
slugs, 96

snails, 96
snakes, 129
soil structure and texture, 47
soldier beetles, 127
spider mites, 96
spiders, 127
spinach, 160
springtails, 97
squash bugs, 97
staking plants, 87
starting a container garden, 64
starting a no-dig garden bed, 51
starting a raised bed garden, 61
starting an in-ground garden, 60
starting seeds, 67
starting seeds indoors, 68
storing your harvest, 142
strawberries, 166
succession planting, 26
sun exposure, 22
sun requirements for plants, 22

support for tall or vining plants, 86

T

tachinid flies, 127
tansy, 102, 104
tender crops, 27
thrips, 97
thyme, 104, 172
toads, 129
tobacco hornworms, 98
tobacco mosaic virus, 114
tomato hornworms, 98
tomato spotted wilt virus, 114
tomatoes, 105, 160
transplanting seedlings, 73
trap crops for pest control, 105
trellises, 86
Trichogramma wasps, 128
true leaves, 69
types of fertilizers, 57

V

verticillium wilt, 112
vine weevils, 98
viral diseases, 113

W

watering containers, 81
watering in-ground gardens, 78
watering raised beds, 80
weed control, 119
weeding, 83
whiteflies, 98

Y

yarrow, 102, 126

Z

zinnias, 126
zucchini, 161

Printed in Great Britain
by Amazon